CHEF PAUL PRUDHOMME'S LOUISIANA KITCHEN

CHEF PAUL PRUDHOMME'S LOUISIANA KITCHEN

Paul Prudhomme

PHOTOGRAPHY BY TOM JIMISON

WILLIAM MORROW AND COMPANY, INC., NEW YORK

Portions of this book have appeared in *Bon Appétit* and *The Ladies' Home Journal.*

Library of Congress Catalog Card Number: 83-63236

ISBN: 0-688-02847-0

Printed in the United States of America

45 46 47 48 49 50

BOOK DESIGN BY JAMES UDELL

To my wife, K. Hinrichs Prudhomme,
who made this book possible,
and to the memory of my mother, Hazel Reed Prudhomme,
who taught me so much

Acknowledgments

Special thanks to Paulette Rittenberg for allowing me to teach her about Cajun and Creole cooking, for her invaluable assistance in testing, retesting and writing all the recipes, and for pulling the book together. I'm also very grateful to Myra Peak for her extraordinary writing and editorial ability—and to Paulette and Myra for being fantastic typists to boot! Sincere appreciation to Tom Jimison for the genius of his photography, to Sandra Day for additional editorial assistance, and to Steve and Lori Taylor for their constant help and friendship over the years. I also want to remember Sylvia Auerbach, a good friend who will be missed.

I couldn't have written this cookbook and at the same time have run my restaurant without a great deal of dedication and support from my wonderful staff at K-Paul's Louisiana Kitchen. My sincere thanks to my cooking staff: William Barlow, Jan Birnbaum, Frank Brigtsen, Jerry Fitzpatrick, William W. Goodson III, Cheryl Hollingshed, Kathryn Hurst, Paul Miller, George Rhode IV and Raymond Sutton; and to my front-of-the-house staff: Marcia Anglem, Sherry Bando, Tammey J. Brisco, John Brooke, Deborah Damico, Wilbert Doridain, Diane Hagen, Rhonda Madách, Sandra Hanson, Clay Hinrichs, Robert Holmes, Sally Lincks, Kathleen Molloy, Frederick Ogletree, Carrie Pierson, Mary Anna Savois, Joanne Sealy, John Strand, Jr., Anne-Marie Sweeny, Michael Thompson and Sandra Torres.

Contents

List of Color Pictures

Introduction

When the taste changes with every bite and the last bite is as good as the first, that's Cajun! I'm a Cajun and that's Louisiana cooking.

Cajuns originated in Southern France, emigrated to Nova Scotia in the early 1600's and settled a colony that came to be called Acadia. In the mid-1700's the British drove them out of Nova Scotia and many of them migrated to Louisiana, where they were well received by the large population of French. They usually settled along waterways and turned to their traditional country practice of fishing, trapping and farming for a living. Two of my ancestors were among those Acadians who migrated from Nova Scotia to Louisiana. Some of their descendants settled around the area of Opelousas, where I was born.

I grew up the youngest of thirteen children—ten boys and three girls. My family worked the land as sharecroppers, farming on borrowed land and paying the landlord a third of the profits from the cotton and sweet-potato crops. (My father spent forty-two years farming, following a pair of mules.) We also raised our own vegetables and animals for eating.

Fabulous food is a part of Cajun pride. It's our tradition to always celebrate with food and to welcome guests with food and coffee. I was seven years old when I began cooking with my mother, when my youngest sister got married. The most important thing to my mother was the health of her family and the joy of setting a good table, and she was an awesome cook. Everybody thinks his mother is the best cook—but mine really was! She had to be, to prepare interesting meals day in and day out for such a large family. Cooking with her was like working for a small restaurant. It was incredible what she could do, especially considering that the best food we raised was sold. My mother also was a great storyteller, and she talked to me a lot about food—its lore, the different kinds of food and how they're prepared. All of this is still an inspiration to me.

At the time I worked with my mother, I thought that it was just my job and that it was hard work. I know now that those years were a unique opportunity. The time I spent with her next to the stove, in the fields digging up roots and vegetables, and in the barnyards feeding and slaughtering animals provided me with an exceptional experience. As I've gotten older, I've realized how important living close to the land was and how real it was—not only for me and my family, but for all the people who live close to the land.

When I was seventeen, not fully knowing what was happening, not realizing why, I set out to become a cook. (The only thing I knew for sure was that I enjoyed eating!) I traveled around the country for twelve years, working full time at restaurants with chefs of every professional and ethnic background. In addition to learning new techniques and methods and the cuisines of various parts of the country, I shared my own heritage of cooking by fixing Cajun and Creole dishes. I was struck by the reactions to my food, from people all over the country. I began to understand how unique the traditional foods of my family were. I came to realize that the joy of cooking Cajun and Creole food was not just that *I* appreciated its goodness so much, but that there was this great pleasure I got from watching other people eat it and seeing the joy in their eyes. At the same time, I would notice when I returned home for visits that my Cajun family and friends didn't seem to recognize the uniqueness of their cooking. I felt it was one of those situations where if you see something every day, you *don't* see it; if you taste something every day, you don't realize that it's unique.

That's one of the things that led me back to Louisiana. And I decided that Louisiana was *the* place to cook, not only because it was important to me to keep the Cajun culture alive, but because the most creative cooking in the nation was going on in Louisiana. Cooks and cooking as an art were most appreciated here.

Louisiana is a terrific setting for a cook because of its bountiful natural resources, including a variety of wildlife and a wealth of fresh seafood that is extraordinary because of the state's diverse water resources: the brackish waters in the coastal wetlands and in many of the southernmost lakes, the salt water of the Gulf, and the freshwater lakes and streams throughout the state. Also, our subtropical climate produces a taste in fruits and vegetables that is unmatched—when the taste is there, it's just really staggering!

It took me many years to understand that it was the use of local fresh products that was the single most important factor in good eating. One of my strongest memories of my mother's cooking is her use of only fresh ingredients. We had no refrigeration, so we'd go out in the fields to get what we needed. When we dug up potatoes, within two hours they'd be in the pot, cooked and eaten. *I* couldn't seem to get a potato to taste like my mother's until I realized that it wasn't anything that was done in the kitchen—it was just the freshness of the potato that made it completely different. This principle carries over to all foods.

The ingredients in Cajun food have always depended on what you could get, so it changed depending on where you were. If you lived near New Orleans or the coast, you used seafood. But where we lived, there was no salt water and no transportation to reach it, so we had crawfish, which live in sweet water; and we had an endless supply of game, and there was chicken, pork, beef and all kinds of vegetables.

Cajuns still make use of the plentiful crawfish, as well as chicken and pork (which is frequently smoked) and seasonal game. Filé powder, parsley, bay leaves, cayenne and black peppers and a variety of other hot peppers are the primary seasonings. Rice, an abundant Louisiana crop, is a staple of Cajun cooking.

People often ask me what's the difference between Cajun and Creole cooking. Cajun and Creole cuisines share many similarities. Both are Louisiana born, with French roots. But Cajun is very old, French country cooking—a simple, hearty fare. Cajun food began in Southern France, moved on to Nova Scotia and then came to Louisiana. The Acadians adapted their dishes to use ingredients that grew wild in the area—bay leaves from the laurel tree, filé powder from the sassafras tree and an abundance of different peppers such as cayenne, Tabasco peppers, banana peppers and bird's-eye peppers that grow wild in South Louisiana—learning their uses from the native Indians.

The evolution of Creole cooking, just like the Cajun, has depended heavily on whatever foods have been available. But Creole food, unlike Cajun, began in New Orleans and is a mixture of the traditions of French, Spanish, Italian, American Indian, African and other ethnic groups. Seven flags flew over New Orleans in the early days, and each time a new nation took over, many members of the deposed government would leave the city; most of their cooks and other servants stayed behind. The position of cook was highly esteemed and the best paid position in the household. Those cooks, most of whom were black, would be hired by other families, often of a different nationality. Of course, the cooks would have to change their style of cooking. Over a period of time, they learned how to cook for a variety of nationalities, and they incorporated their own spicy, home-style way of cooking into the different cuisines of their employers. This is the way Creole food was created. Creole cooking is more sophisticated and complex than Cajun cooking—it's city cooking.

Today, in homes, there is still a distinction between Cajun and Creole cooking; in restaurants, little distinction remains. That's why I've begun referring to the two together as one—Louisiana cooking.

I feel that food is a celebration of life; it's a universal thing: shared needs and shared experiences. It keeps us alive, it affects our attitudes, it's a social experience. But, there's more to it: Watching people eat something that they've never tasted quite so good, or eat something that they didn't believe could *be* that good, watching their eyes and their whole expressions change, and even their attitudes toward the cook change—*that's* what keeps me cooking! And I think that's what cooking food is about, whether you're cooking in the commercial market or at home.

I think cooking is a very personal thing. You have to draw on the past, on what you've read, what you've tasted and what you've seen prepared. But I think that anyone can show imagination with food. First, you need to build your confidence. Start by reading cookbooks to see the different ways people combine foods. Keep in mind that there is only a limited number of foods available in this world to work with—which is fascinating, because people all over the world take these basics and make them taste completely different. People in your own neighborhood, the people next door, have the same products to work with, and yet each person ends up with a distinctive dish.

With all this in mind, use your imagination when approaching a single ingredient, like pepper, for example. If you put pepper in a dish, you don't want to taste the pepper first; you want it there as an accent—but you don't want it to take over. And think about this one: I've found a lot of magic in working with a single ingredient to produce a "redundancy" of flavor. For example, if you're stuffing an eggplant, don't just stuff it! Hollow out a slice of the eggplant to put the stuffing in, then use the pulp in the stuffing and in the sauce. That's exciting!

If I could get across just one idea, it would be for you to treat each ingredient so that you bring out its best quality. If that's done, you can't fail to have a terrific dish. (And don't be timid about it—just jump right in the skillet!)

I try to make my food "round" in taste. We have a variety of taste buds in our mouths and when food is "round," it touches all of them in turn. One way I make food "round" is to use red, white and black peppers in the same recipe, which you'll see I do frequently (as a matter of fact, not just frequently, but in nearly every recipe except desserts!). Different peppers excite taste buds in different parts of the mouth, and this makes you feel that you want another bite—that you just have to have another bite. The peppers also cleanse the palate and keep the food interesting by making it change with each bite. This keeps your taste buds happy!

You'll notice in the cookbook that I often call for the same combinations of vegetables, such as onions, celery and bell peppers, or onions, celery, bell peppers and garlic. The secret of getting different tastes from these same combinations is in the amount of each you use. For example, in one recipe you might see one cup of onions and one-half cup of celery, and then in another you'll see the reverse of that. That's typical of my Cajun cooking.

Something else I like to do with these particular vegetables is to add a portion of them in the early stages of cooking and then add the rest later; when you do this, you achieve levels of taste and texture. You'll notice this, for example, in some of the recipes that call for a portion of the vegetables to be "caramelized" (bringing out the sweetness and giving you a deep color) and the remainder to be added later (leaving this portion colorful and somewhat crunchy).

You may also notice the long cooking time in many of the recipes. This method stems from a tradition in old Cajun and Creole cooking—long, *long* cooking times. In the old recipes for such things as stuffed eggplant, stuffed mirliton and other stuffed vegetables—even in foods like red beans and black-eyed peas and sometimes seafood—it's that long cooking time that establishes a taste you can't get any other way, a uniquely Cajun and Creole quality. I still use a variation of that method in some of the recipes in this book. (*Footnote:* Looks like hell, but tastes wonderful!)

In almost every recipe in the book, I use a combination of seasonings or "seasoning mixes." I've found this is the best way to use dry herbs and spices. The mixes are a direct result of my experience as a young man working in restaurants that didn't season their food; I would yearn to season the food and so would mix up little packets of different herbs and spices, sneak them into the restaurants and use them as I cooked. (Of course, not only did I get the packets confused, but I got into trouble with more than one chef!)

In putting this book together, what I wanted foremost was for each recipe to work for you. I wanted the recipes not only to have a genuine Louisiana taste, but to be simple, direct, and useful for you in your home. It seemed especially important to me that the home cook, using a noncommercial stove and familiar cookware, be able to take grocery store ingredients and reproduce perfectly the recipes in the book. That's why I did not test the recipes for the manuscript in my restaurant kitchen. Instead, I built a small test kitchen with a regular home range and reworked the recipes for more than a year.

When a recipe is long, this does not indicate that it is difficult. The book is a teaching tool as well as a recipe book; therefore, in addition to specific instructions in the text of recipes, there is also information about cooking methods and the reasons for using them. The same instructions are often repeated almost word for word in different recipes so they will be right there in front of you when you need them. Of course some recipes are harder to do than others. If you want to start out with the simpler ones first, the chapters are organized with the easiest at the beginning.

And we made a lot of general notes about ingredients and procedures and things that are special to Louisiana and Cajun cooking—such as the seasoning mixes, why I use powdered garlic and margarine (which otherwise you might find surprising), my own method for making roux, and explanations of Cajun words like "mirliton," "pirogue," "panéed," and "etouffée." I hope you'll read them all in Notes from Our Test Kitchen before you start to cook from this book.

CHEF PAUL PRUDHOMME'S LOUISIANA KITCHEN contains what I know about pleasing people with food. I hope you and I will continue to grow as cooks and to create new and exciting dishes. Please let me hear of and learn from your successes and failures. The important thing is to have fun, to experiment and to trust yourself. When you do this and use only the freshest ingredients possible, you'll find that new excitement comes to your dinner table. Remember, the measure of a good dish is that "it makes you want to take another bite." So—good cooking! Good eating!

Paul Prudhomme

NOTES FROM OUR TEST KITCHEN

Louisiana Language and Ingredients

Andouille: The most popular Cajun smoked pure-pork sausage. Pronounced ahn-*doo*-i.

Creole Tomatoes: The traditional growing area for Creole tomatoes is the reclaimed Mississippi River delta. The soil here has a higher salt content than most other places in the world, and the level of other minerals in the soil is ideal. I think tomatoes are influenced tremendously by the moisture content of the land and air, and Louisiana (much of which is below sea level) is a perfect place for growing them. Creole tomatoes are always vine-ripened, they have a lower acid content than ordinary tomatoes, a better texture—and much more flavor! I always recommend that cooks use the best products possible; if there is a local vine-ripened tomato that's especially good in your area, by all means try to use that one whenever you can.

Etouffée: "Etouffée" literally means "smothered"; in Louisiana cooking it signifies covered with a liquid. In my family it refers to a dish with a cooked roux in the etouffée sauce. (In French Louisiana we don't put the accent on the first "e." That would mean to smother a *person*!)

Gumbo: Gumbo is a Cajun soup almost always containing a cooked roux (see page 26) and sometimes thickened with okra or gumbo filé (see page 22); it usually contains a variety of vegetables and meats or seafood and is served over rice. Many people top their gumbo with gumbo filé. Gumbo recipes start on page 195.

Ham, Cure 81: This is the most consistent, best-tasting ham distributed nationally and readily available.

Jambalaya: Jambalaya, pronounced djum-buh-*lie*-ya, is a rice dish highly seasoned and strongly flavored with any combination of beef, pork, fowl, smoked sausage, ham (or tasso) or seafood, and often containing tomatoes. According to the *Acadian Dictionary* (Rita and Gabrielle Claudet, Houma, Louisiana, 1981), the word "jambalaya" ". . . comes from the French 'jambon' meaning ham, the African 'ya' meaning rice, and the Acadian [language] where everything is 'à la.'" Jambalaya recipes start on page 215.

Lagniappe: A popular term in south Louisiana, "lagniappe" means "a little something extra"—as a gift or a show of appreciation. There are lagniappes of information at the end of a number of the recipes in this book.

Mirliton: A mirliton is a green pear-shaped vegetable from a West Indian vine of the cucumber family, available in many parts of the United States. In Latin grocery stores mirlitons are known as chayotes and in other locations may be referred to as vegetable pears or christophines. The seed is edible and delicious in salads.

Pirogue: A pirogue is a dugout canoe used in bayou country as a means of transportation and for fishing, hunting and trapping. Typically, pirogues have flat bottoms and are just wide enough to kneel in; they can be paddled or poled through the swamps. We make "pirogues" out of hollowed vegetables such as mirlitons, zucchini and eggplants and fill them with various stuffings and sauces. After hollowing out vegetables to make pirogues, see page 34 for ways to use up what you have left over.

Praline: The Louisiana praline is a candy patty popular in the South, made with brown sugar, nuts (especially pecans) or seeds, and sometimes butter and/or cream.

Tasso: A very highly seasoned Cajun smoked ham. Pronounced *tah-so.*

Seasonings

Seasoning Mixes: I explain in the Introduction that I started to use mixes like these when I was working in *other* people's restaurants! Many of the recipes in this book have ingredients listed under the separate heading of **Seasoning mix**. In these mixes, the proportions of herbs and spices vary greatly from one type of recipe to another, and the amounts of some of these ingredients are often small. When all the seasonings are well mixed together ahead of time in a small bowl, they are convenient to handle and to distribute evenly in a dish as you cook it. You just measure out portions of the mix with measuring spoons (measure *level*), rather than having to measure different amounts of each seasoning for different steps in the recipe—and the final amount of each seasoning is controlled. It's not unusual for a recipe to have eight or more seasonings, so you can see that measuring them needs to be convenient if it's going to be right.

The seasoning mixes in this book are specially calibrated for every recipe. In my restaurant I use Louisiana Cajun Magic ™, the brand name of seven different blends of herbs, spices and salt, which I created for different kinds of foods to teach my cooks to produce a *consistent* taste each time in dishes cooked to order. Cajun Magic is on the market, and very soon there will be national distribution. Then it will be possible for any home or professional cook to season Louisiana dishes even more conveniently with authentic Louisiana flavor.

Peppers: Black (ground), white (ground), red (ground and preferably cayenne), jalapeños (fresh), Tabasco (fresh), cayenne (fresh), finger (fresh), banana (fresh) and bird's-eye (fresh)—these are staples of my Cajun and Creole seasonings. My method for controlling dried ground as they are measured into a dish is the seasoning mix described just above. When a lot of pepper is used, one needs to know how it works.

There are many results to be had from peppers, and of course "heat" is one of them. But the ultimate purpose of peppers is to achieve flavors, and these flavors are sensations in the palate that come at different times—when you first put a bite of food in your mouth, when you're chewing it, after you've swallowed it. Each kind of pepper works differently, and when they are balanced correctly they achieve an "after-you-swallow" glow. They are also played off against the other ingredients in a dish. For example, in many recipes such as stuffings, we use the methods of caramelization and long cooking times of vegetables to bring out their natural sugars, which contrast so well with the peppers. A special example is the Lamb Curry on page 135. There, what we've done is to use fresh fruits and nuts that have various amounts of natural sugars in combination with various (and large) amounts of peppers. The stages of tasting are particularly obvious in the makeup of this dish, but the same "play-off" principle is used in all our peppery dishes.

Creole Mustard: A brown mustard with mustard seeds in it. It is better than prepared yellow mustard, being comparable in quality to the finest brown mustards—mellow, full-bodied and slightly tart.

Garlic and Onions: I sometimes call for both fresh garlic and onions *and* garlic and onion powders. I've experimented with this dual system and found that the combination of the powdered ingredients in the seasoning mixes and the fresh in other steps of the recipes makes the final effect more balanced and interesting. Herb and spice companies label these garlic and onion products sometimes as powder and sometimes as granulated. There no longer seems to be much difference, so we just say powder in our recipes.

Gumbo Filé (Filé Powder): An herb of ground young sassafras leaves often used as a flavoring and/or thickener in gumbos and other Cajun dishes.

Sage: There are two types available—rubbed and ground. For rubbed sage, the sage leaf is scraped; for ground sage, the leaf is ground up. Rubbed sage has a stronger flavor than the ground. Our recipes specify which to use.

SEAFOOD

Crabmeat: Fresh lump crabmeat is available commercially in packages of various sizes, usually one pound. It is packed on ice. The meat has been cooked (actually, only blanched). Cooking raw crab, even briefly, makes removing the meat from the shells much easier. Lump crabmeat and peeled crawfish tails (see next) are the only seafoods that I use precooked.

Crawfish: In Louisiana, crawfish may be purchased readily (there is a lot of demand) in three forms: Live; fresh tails, blanched and "picked" (peeled) in 1-pound bags packed in ice; and frozen peeled tails in 1-pound bags. These same forms are shipped from Louisiana to markets throughout the country, but there's no doubt that where there isn't the demand, there aren't going to be crawfish. Make friends with a good fish market and create the demand!

If you purchase live crawfish and blanch and peel them yourself, be sure to save the fat—the orange substance in the head also attached to the upper part of the tail. It adds incredible richness to crawfish dishes; it can often be substituted for some or all of the butter in a recipe. It is wonderful!

A note of caution: Crawfish don't freeze well, and especially not the fat. The oils in the fat, since they freeze poorly, turn rancid quickly and will give your crawfish dishes a fishy taste.

Peeled crawfish tails and lump crabmeat are the only seafoods I use that are precooked, and then I mean blanched, not fully cooked. This means that if you or your source of supply does it right, the crawfish are plunged into boiling water and left only for a few seconds, just until they turn red.

Do not substitute shrimp for crawfish unless the recipe indicates that either may be used.

"Crayfish" is a spelling that won't do in Louisiana, though it's probably all right elsewhere.

Shrimp: Shrimp with their heads as well as shells are easy to get in Louisiana, but not in many parts of the country. Buy shrimp with their heads, to make seafood stock, if you can; if not, at least buy them with shells, which is possible almost anywhere. Shrimp fat, the orange substance in the heads, makes shrimp dishes rich, full, sweet tasting and wonderful.

Shrimp are *not* a substitute for crawfish, but many Louisiana recipes work well for either shellfish. All recipes assume fresh, *un*cooked shrimp. Never use frozen shrimp if you can help it.

Oysters: Louisiana or Gulf oysters are wonderful. For those people who are oyster connoisseurs or who truly believe the motto "Eat oysters and love longer," our local preferences are Bayou Cook, Four Bayou, Bay Adam or Bay Baptiste oysters. But it's more important for oysters to be fresh than that they come from Louisiana. If there are good native oysters where you live, those are the ones you want. From a fish market you can trust on freshness, you might as well buy oysters conveniently shucked and packed in their liquor in containers. Our recipes specify shucked oysters by weight, with a rough estimate of how many medium-size oysters the weight is likely to amount to.

Louisianians love oysters served freshly opened and raw on the half-shell and also sauced and broiled, sautéed, fried . . . any way you can think of. If a recipe containing oysters does not call for the oyster liquor to be used, be sure to reserve it when you drain it off and use it promptly in a seafood stock, in a sauce, in a pasta dish. You can't allow such a great flavor to go to waste!

Butter and Oil, Pan Frying and Frying

Butter: Unless otherwise indicated, I recommend using unsalted butter because it's generally a superior product. And, because salted butter has an unpredictable amount of salt, it's easier to control the overall salt level in a dish by using unsalted butter.

Margarine: Margarine is not a substitute for butter. I use it, often with butter, instead of oil (see next).

Oil: Peanut oil is best for deep frying, especially when you're using a batter on the food. It gives a "nutty" taste more quickly than other oils. Recipes in which foods are deep fried merely specify vegetable oil, because any fresh (unused) cooking oil is certainly acceptable, but put peanut oil on your market list! Vegetable oil is best for pan frying (see Panéed foods farther on).

At times, I call for both butter and oil in the same recipe. I want the taste of butter, but butter alone doesn't have enough oil in it to produce the action needed in some dishes—for example, to caramelize vegetables. I usually prefer the taste of margarine to olive or vegetable oil for frying when butter is also being used, and margarine does have enough oil in it to do what I want.

How to Test Temperatures of Oil for Frying and Pan Frying: When oil is as shallow as ¼ inch, you can use several methods to test the oil's temperature. First, use a deep-fry thermometer as a guide; but, just to be sure the oil's at the proper heat, take a little flour, sprinkle it on the oil, and if it runs around and says "buzz, buzz," it's ready! You can also tilt the pan so the thermometer bubble is completely submerged in the oil.

With oil any deeper than ¼ inch, a deep-fry thermometer always does the trick, except that some recipe directions indicate how to get the proper heat by telling you to heat the oil until it begins to smoke.

It's helpful to use a thermometer with a clip so you can leave the thermometer in the oil throughout the frying process.

Panéed Foods: "Panéed" is New Orleans terminology for pan frying. For the best pan-fried crust on meat or fish, the oil for frying should be just deep enough to come up the sides of the food but not to cover the top. In this way, the food is in contact with the pan bottom, which creates different levels of texture in the crust and adds to the interest of each bite.

It is important that the oil be hot enough (at least 300° for chicken, for instance) to seal the meat in the bread-crumb or other coating without the oil penetrating the coating, which leads to a greasy crust. And it is essential that the food always be in contact with the pan bottom, so never crowd pieces of food together; fry the pieces in batches if necessary. Always drain on paper towels unless otherwise directed.

Fried Foods: There are four keys to frying foods well.

1) Use only fresh (unused) oil. The molecules in fresh oil are close together and relatively inactive. Food dropped into fresh hot oil acts like an irritant to the oil, which responds very quickly by immediately sealing the batter, and the oil then cannot get to the food inside. All crumbs, drops of batter, salt or water that fall or are released into the oil during frying separate the molecules and therefore weaken the oil's ability to seal the breading or batter. That's why you should shake off excess breading or batter before frying.

Even frying unbattered foods (such as French fries) affects the oil's ability to seal off the outer surface of food so the inside won't be greasy. As a matter of fact, simply heating oil in the first place *begins* to break it down, and the more you reheat it, the less like the original oil it is. That's why you should change oil frequently, instead of putting oil aside to be used again.

2) Use enough oil to completely submerge whatever you're frying; generally this is from ½ inch to 4 inches deep.

3) Heat the oil to the proper temperature—350° unless otherwise stipulated. One of the wonderful things about deep frying is that if the temperature is right, when a cube of food is browned, that will be precisely when it is cooked through—whether you have a 1-inch cube or a 5-inch cube. If the oil is not hot enough, it will start to enter the batter instead of sealing off the food inside. The result will be a hard and greasy crust. Also, if the oil is *too* hot, the crust will not adhere properly, it will brown too fast (leaving the inside of the crust gummy) and the food itself won't cook through properly. If necessary, cook the pieces in batches so as not to lower the oil's temperature below the correct level. But whether you fry in batches or not, keep adjusting the heat as needed to maintain the temperature throughout the frying process.

4) Don't bread or batter food until just before placing each piece in the hot oil. Breading and batter are basically a type of glue used to form a tight barrier around the food. But remember what happens when you let homemade glue (flour and water) sit for any length of time—it gets gummier and gummier, then finally hardens. Likewise, the longer breaded or battered food sits before being cooked, the gummier (and finally harder) the "glue" becomes, resulting in a hard crust. And also, oil penetrates hardened breading or batter, which not only leads to a greasy crust but also causes the food inside to cook before the crust has browned properly; by the time the crust *is* browned, the food inside is overcooked. If you fry each piece at the right temperature immediately after breading or battering it, you have all the ingredients working together to produce correctly cooked food within a very light and delicate crust.

Roux

A roux is a mixture of flour and oil. The cooking of flour and fat together to make roux is a process that seems to go back as far as my ancestors of four hundred years ago. Traditionally, the fat used was animal fat, though today various oils are used, and the roux was, and often still is, made by very slow cooking. For example, when I was a boy, my mother used to start with a paste of animal fat and flour and cook it for several hours. Over the years I've developed a way to cook roux so it can be made in a matter of minutes, over very high heat, and with very few exceptions this is the method used in this book's recipes.

The basic reason for making a roux is for the distinctive taste and texture it lends to food. This roux taste and texture is characteristic of many dishes that Louisiana Cajuns make.

The first few times, making a roux may seem difficult, and, certainly, using oil heated to over 500° has an element of danger to it. However, once you've made roux several times and become more accustomed to handling the high temperature, you will find it to be extremely rewarding because of the uniqueness of the finished product—and, as lagniappe, you're sure to get praise from everyone who tastes your cooking!

How to Make a Roux

Color pictures 2a–2d

A few overall points may be helpful:

The usual proportion of oil to flour is fifty-fifty.

Roux can be made in advance, cooled and then stored in an air-tight jar for several days, in the refrigerator or at room temperature. If roux is made ahead, pour off excess oil from the surface and reheat (preferred), or let it return to room temperature before using.

In general, light and medium-brown roux are used in sauces or gravies for dark, heavy meats such as beef, with game such as elk and venison, and with dark-meat fowl such as duck, geese and blackbirds. They give a wonderful, toasted nutty flavor—just the right enhancement—to these sauces and gravies. Dark red-brown and black roux are used in sauces and gravies for sweet, light, white meats such as pork, rabbit, veal, and all kinds of freshwater and saltwater fish and shellfish. In addition, black roux are best to use in gumbos because the darkest roux result in the thinnest, best-tasting gumbos of all; but it takes practice to make black roux without burning them, and dark red-brown roux are certainly acceptable for any gumbo. (See color pictures 2a–2d.)

You'll notice that I make exceptions to these general guidelines in some recipes. These exceptions simply reflect my preference for the flavor of a particular roux with the combined flavors of the other ingredients in certain dishes. (For example, I prefer the flavor of a medium-brown roux in Grillades and Grits—a veal dish—and in Sticky Chicken, rather than a darker roux.)

My approach to roux derives from the tradition of Cajun cooks, who view roux as being essentially of two types—medium brown and black; and who also classify meats as basically of two types—heavy, dark, somewhat bitter ones, and light, white, sweet ones. Traditionally, Cajun cooks use light roux with dark meats and dark roux with light meats. This is because they know intuitively, whether they can verbalize it or not, that these particular combinations lead to wonderful-tasting food. Working within this tradition, I've developed variations and given you in this book the roux-meat combinations which I think are best. You'll find that as you gain more experience and skill in making roux, you'll want to experiment with the endless combinations of roux colors and the flavors of other ingredients you're using—especially meats—to find those combinations that excite your taste buds the most!

Several words of advice are essential:

1) Cooked roux is called Cajun napalm in my restaurant's kitchen because it is extremely hot and sticks to your skin; so *be very careful* to avoid splashing it on you; it's best to use a *long*-handled metal whisk or wooden spoon.

2) Always begin with a very clean skillet or pot—preferably one that is heavy, such as cast iron (and never a nonstick type). If possible, use a skillet with flared sides because this makes stirring easier and thus makes it less likely the roux will burn. In addition, use a large enough skillet so that the oil does not fill it by more than one-fourth of its capacity.

3) The oil should be smoking hot before the flour is added.

4) Once the oil is heated, stir in the flour gradually (about a third at a time) and stir or whisk quickly and *constantly* to avoid burning the mixture. (Flour has moisture in it, and adding it to hot oil often creates steam—another good reason for using long-handled whisks or spoons.)

5) If black specks appear in the roux as it cooks, it has burned; discard it (place it in a heatproof container to cool before discarding), then start the roux over again—*c'est la vie*!

6) As soon as the roux reaches the desired color, remove it from the heat; stir in the vegetables, which stop the browning process and enhance the taste of the finished dish, and continue stirring until the roux stops getting darker (at least 3 to 5 minutes).

7) While cooking roux (bringing it to the desired color), if you feel it is darkening too fast, immediately remove it from the heat and continue whisking constantly until you have control of it.

8) Care and concentration are essential for you to be successful with this fast method of making roux. Especially the first few times you make a roux, be certain that any possible distractions—including children—are under control. In addition, have all cooking utensils and required vegetables or seasoning mixtures prepared ahead of time and near at hand before you start cooking.

Some Other Ingredients

Flour: All flour in our recipes is *un*sifted unless specified sifted.

Green Onions: Many people call these scallions, and just as many call them green onions. Our recipes say green onions, because that's what we call them in Louisiana. They are common everywhere. The white bulb at the bottom is slender, not round. The shape of the bulb isn't important; what matters is that there should be plenty of fresh and tender, edible green tops—which some rather scarce small round onions called green onions also have.

Pecans: Pecans are usually specified in the recipes as "dry roasted." This is important for flavor. Place shelled pecans—halves or pieces—in a large *un*greased roasting pan and roast in a 425° oven for 10 minutes, stirring occasionally. The roasted pecans may be added either hot or cold to the other ingredients in a recipe, and they can be stored in a covered container in the refrigerator.

Roasting gives pecans extra flavor by bringing the sugar and oil in them to the surface. When you roast chopped pieces rather than whole halves, much more of the surface is in contact with the heat of the pan. So, if a recipe calls for roasted pieces, chop up pecan halves *before* roasting. Recipes call sometimes for pieces, sometimes for halves, but it's worth remembering that shelled pecans packaged in pieces cost less then halves.

Rabbit: I strongly recommend that you use fresh rabbit if possible. However, I realize that in many parts of the country it is difficult to find, and I know that families in rural areas hunt for rabbit in season and freeze the meat for use throughout the year. The popularity of the rabbit dishes at K-Paul's and their growing popularity in other restaurants in the United States should result in more fresh rabbit being available. Meanwhile, frozen cut-up rabbit is already quite widely distributed.

Rabbit is inexpensive, as easy to handle as chicken, and if it is young can be substituted for chicken in many recipes. But to those who are not familiar with it, it can seem like a problem. A butcher who takes the trouble to carry fresh rabbit should know that service to customers has to be provided, too. Have the rabbit cut up, and boned, as recipes require. Watch how it's done; you can learn to do it yourself. The basic parts of a rabbit are the front legs, hind legs, the whole loin section (there are two loins, one on either side of the backbone) and the breast (rib section).

Cooking rabbit is interesting, and economical, because the parts can all be used in different ways. The back legs can be boned and pounded (as you would veal) to flatten them; you will have one serving per leg that is excellent for pan frying. The front legs and breast can be smothered, fried or stewed; or they can be boned, cut into bite-size pieces and cooked in sauces to serve over pasta. The small tender loins can be cut from the bone, pan fried and served with a sauce to make a delicious appetizer.

Stocks: Cooking with stocks definitely gives depth to the taste of dishes and makes them more exciting. And especially when the time is taken to make a *rich* stock, it can actually make the difference between a good dish and a fantastic one.

Making stock is simple. Use the ingredients you commonly have in your kitchen. Whenever possible, use the meat or poultry bones and drippings, seafood shells or carcasses, and vegetable trimmings that are provided by the ingredients in the recipe you are making. But it's also easy to purchase at a very reasonable price such stock-making items as chicken backs and necks, beef marrow or soup bones, pork neck bones, and, if you have a fish market available, you should easily be able to obtain fresh fish carcasses.

When you can, use shrimp stock in shrimp dishes, rabbit stock in rabbit dishes, beef in beef dishes . . . ; but you *can* make substitutions such as a general seafood stock for shrimp stock, beef stock for turtle, and chicken stock for rabbit or goose stock.

There are a very few no-no's when making stocks: *Don't* use bell peppers, spices or livers. There's no set rule regarding amounts of ingredients to use in making stock, but we've provided proportions that we think are ideal. Because stock really is simple to make, you can multiply at will the ingredients for the basic 1-quart recipe to make larger quantities.

To Make 1 Quart of Basic Stock

About 2 quarts cold water

Vegetable trimmings from the recipe(s) you are serving, *or*
- 1 medium onion, unpeeled and quartered
- 1 large clove garlic, unpeeled and quartered
- 1 rib celery

Bones and any excess meat (excluding livers) from meat or poultry, or shells or carcasses from seafood, used in the recipe(s) you're cooking, *or*

For Fowl and Game Stocks: 1½ to 2 pounds backs, necks and/or bones from chickens, guinea hens, ducks, geese, rabbits, etc.

For Beef or Turtle Stocks: 1½ to 2 pounds beef shank (preferred) or other beef or turtle bones

For Pork Stock: 1½ to 2 pounds pork neck bones (preferred) or other pork bones

For Seafood Stock: 1½ to 2 pounds rinsed shrimp heads and/or shells, or crawfish heads and/or shells, or crab shells (2½ to 3 quarts), or rinsed fish carcasses (heads and gills removed), or any combination of these. (You can also substitute oyster liquor for all or part of seafood stock called for in a recipe.)

Note: If desired, you can first roast meat bones and vegetables at 350° until thoroughly browned. Then use them to make your basic stock. (When you brown the bones and vegetables, the natural sugar in both caramelizes on the surface, which gives the stock a fuller taste and adds color when it dissolves in the stock water.)

Always start with *cold* water—enough to cover the other stock ingredients. Place all ingredients in a stock pot or a large saucepan. Bring to a boil over high heat, then gently simmer at least 4 hours, preferably 8 (unless directed otherwise in a recipe), replenishing the water as needed to keep about 1 quart of liquid in the pan. The pot may be uncovered or set a lid on it askew. Strain, cool and refrigerate until ready to use. (**Note:** Remember that if you are short on time, using a stock simmered 20 to 30 minutes is far better than using just water in any recipe.)

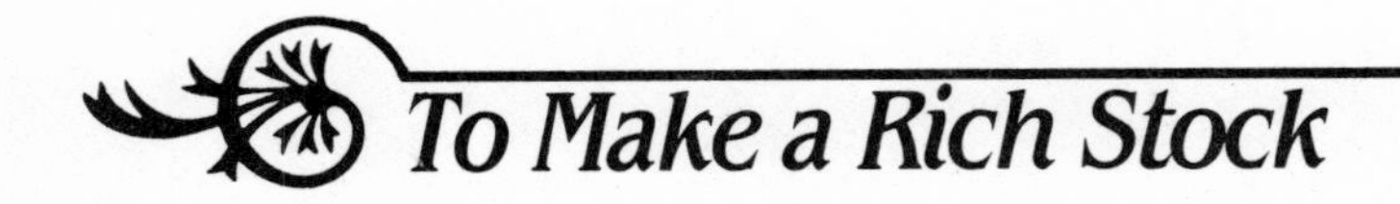

To Make a Rich Stock

Strain the *basic* stock, then continue simmering it until evaporation reduces the liquid by half or more. For example, if your recipe calls for 1 cup of *rich* stock, start it with at least 2 cups of strained *basic* stock. (*Rich* stocks are needed when a sauce requires lots of taste but only a limited amount of liquid, for example, **Oyster Sauce for Beef**, page 246. They are also excellent for general use.)

1. Opposite: *Crawfish Etouffée*

a

b

2a. *Light-brown Roux: Used most often in sauces and gravies for heavier dark meats such as beef, venison and other game; also for dark-meat fowl such as wild duck and goose. This is the one roux that is not made over very high heat.*

2b. *Medium-brown Roux: Used instead of light-brown roux when a somewhat stronger, deeper and nuttier roux flavor is desired.*

c

d

2c. *Dark Red-brown Roux: Used for light, sweet meats such as domesticated fowl and rabbit, pork, veal and seafoods. You may also use it for gumbos.*

2d. *Black Roux: Used when you want a stronger flavor than dark red-brown roux gives. It takes practice to make a black roux without burning it, but it's really the right color roux for a gumbo.*

4. Mama's Yeast Bread

3. Clockwise from upper right: *Southern Biscuit Muffins; Mama's Yeast Rolls; Bran Muffins; Banana Muffins; Jalapeño and Cheese Rolls*

a

b

5. *Blackened Redfish*

This just may be the most popular single dish we make at K-Paul's. If you don't have a commercial hood vent over your stove, making blackened redfish may smoke you out of the kitchen. It's worth it! But it's also a great dish to cook outdoors on a gas grill. (A charcoal fire doesn't get hot enough to "blacken" the fish properly.)

For this demonstration, my wife K. is assistant chef. The complete recipe is the first one in the Fish & Seafoods chapter.

c

a. *Draw the fish fillets through melted butter in a skillet, coating both sides.*

b. *Sprinkle seasoning mix generously on the fish, also on both sides.*

c. *Transfer the buttered and seasoned fish to a very hot skillet. (It can't be too hot.)*

d

e

f

g

d. *Add a teaspoon of melted butter on top of the fish. Chances are it will flare up.*

e. *After about 2 minutes, turn the fish over.*

f. *There will be plenty of smoke as the fish blackens.*

g. *K. transfers the finished fillet to a serving dish. It's served piping hot with more melted butter.*

6. *Seafood Crêpe*

To Make a Light Stock

Light stocks are called for in sauces in which you need to be careful that the stock flavor does not overpower other ingredients. In this case, simply simmer the *basic* stock ingredients for ½ to 1 hour instead of the usual 4 to 8 hours.

Tomato Sauce: Because the flavor of fresh tomatoes varies, I also use canned tomato sauce in recipes to control the tomato taste. I recommend *unseasoned* canned crushed tomatoes or tomato sauce.

VEGETABLES

Cooking and Serving Fresh Vegetables: You may wonder why there is no chapter of vegetable recipes in this book. That's because what we do at K-Paul's is so simple that you really don't need recipes. We just season vegetables lightly and sauté them briefly over very high heat in butter. We usually adjust the size of vegetable pieces, or add the tougher kinds to the pan first, so they will all cook at the same rate. I consider vegetables an *essential* part of a meal, both for their taste and for their beauty.

It's extremely important to me to retain the flavors and many of the cooking methods from the past. Almost all the recipes in this book in some way reflect old-fashioned Cajun and Creole cooking styles. But the one time I *don't* try to keep to the old style is with vegetables—because the old way of doing vegetables was to cook the daylights out of them! So with vegetables that are to be eaten as a side dish—rather than as an element of a main-course recipe, such as mirlitons and eggplant in stuffings—the old cooking methods simply don't work. Taking a fresh, just-picked vegetable that has a lot of color and juice, then lightly seasoning it and sautéing it very quickly, will brighten its natural color even more, maintain a crispy texture and "turn loose the juices"! One of the wonderful things that happens when you serve them this way is that the vegetables refresh and cleanse your palate. Their simplicity provides a light, fresh contrast to our K-Paul's main dishes, which are usually highly seasoned and very complex in taste. Even with strongly flavored vegetables such as Swiss chard, poke, mustard greens and collard greens (which are usually cooked for long lengths of time), the quick cooking method over very high heat really brings out the clear, colorful taste of each one.

Be sure to use whatever vegetables are in season in your part of the country. (What we have available here includes zucchini, yellow squash, squash, summer squash (pattypan or custard), okra, tomatoes, Swiss chard, mustard and collards, nasturtiums and carrots, as well as baby yellow squash, baby zucchini and baby corn on the cob.) Serve your simply seasoned and cooked vegetables as side dishes, or as garnishes, and they will enhance your main course every time.

Leftover Eggplant, Mirliton or Zucchini: In a number of recipes in this book, you will end up with a portion of these vegetables which will not have been all used in the recipes. Some examples are hollowed-out eggplant and mirliton pirogues and also the zucchini (and yellow squash) left over from making a julienne of the tender peelings. Here is a recipe for using what you have left, to serve with simply broiled or roasted meats and poultry or a simply cooked fish.

You may also add the leftover pulp of these vegetables to jambalayas, soups, or Dirty Rice.

Fried Eggplant, Mirliton or Zucchini

Makes 1 to 2 side-dish servings

Seasoning mix:
1⅛ teaspoons salt
¾ teaspoon sweet paprika
½ teaspoon white pepper
¼ teaspoon onion powder
¼ teaspoon garlic powder

¼ teaspoon ground red pepper (preferably cayenne)
¼ teaspoon black pepper
¼ teaspoon dried thyme leaves
⅛ teaspoon dried sweet basil leaves

1 cup peeled and coarsely chopped raw eggplant or zucchini, or 1 cup peeled and coarsely chopped cooked mirliton
½ cup all-purpose flour
½ cup very fine dry bread crumbs
½ cup milk
1 egg
Vegetable oil for deep frying
Powdered sugar, optional

Combine the seasoning mix ingredients in a small bowl, mixing thoroughly. Sprinkle the vegetables evenly with about *½ teaspoon* of the mix. Place the flour in a small bowl and the bread crumbs in another. Add *1 teaspoon* of the seasoning mix to the flour and *1 teaspoon* to the bread crumbs, mixing each well. (Use any leftover seasoning mix to season other vegetables before cooking.) In a separate small bowl combine the milk and egg until well blended.

Heat 1 inch oil in a 2-quart saucepan or deep fryer to 350°. Just before frying, dredge the chopped vegetables in the seasoned flour, shaking off excess. (Work quickly so flour doesn't get too moist; it's best to use your hands for this, but a slotted spoon will also do.) Then coat well with the milk mixture, and then quickly with the bread crumbs, shaking off excess. Cook vegetables in the hot oil until dark golden brown, about 2 to 3 minutes, making sure to separate vegetable pieces as you drop them into the oil. (Adjust heat as necessary to maintain oil's temperature at about 350°.) Drain on paper towels and serve immediately. If serving eggplant or zucchini, sprinkle lightly with powdered sugar if desired.

Utensils

I can think of very few occasions for which the pot or pan is going to make a tremendous difference in the quality of the finished dish. The recipes give advice when necessary, and cast-iron skillets are often recommended. No cook likes thin "tinny" equipment, but my advice to a new beginning cook in the kitchen is to spend more time and money looking for better ingredients. Then, as you become more at ease with cooking and with handling ingredients, you can consider more expensive and sophisticated cooking equipment. I personally think that if you're accustomed to your pots and pans—whatever they're made of—these will be the most successful to use in your own kitchen. However, don't use nonstick skillets and pans unless specifically recommended.

There are particular things that an expensive pot or pan will accomplish more easily than an inexpensive pot or pan will; however, it's been my experience that personal time and attention to the food in the pot, as well as the knowledge and security of having used the pot in the past, is the most important consideration.

BREADS

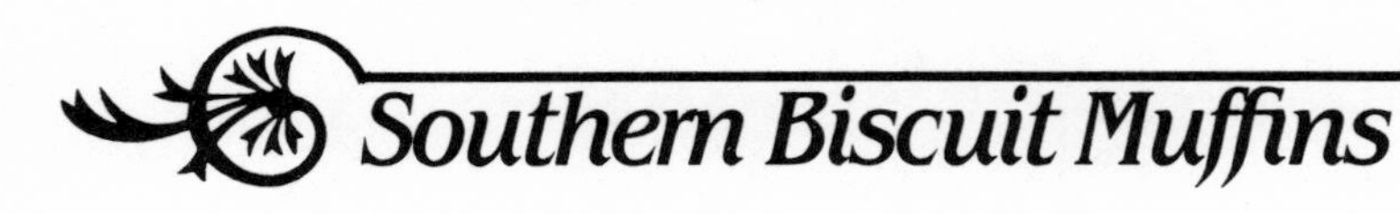

Southern Biscuit Muffins

Color Picture 3

Makes 1 dozen muffins

2½ cups all-purpose flour
¼ cup sugar
1½ tablespoons baking powder
¼ teaspoon salt
¼ pound (1 stick) plus 2 tablespoons unsalted butter, softened
1 cup cold milk

In a bowl, combine the flour, sugar, baking powder and salt; mix well, breaking up any lumps. Work the butter in by hand until the mixture resembles coarse cornmeal, making sure no lumps are left. Gradually stir in the milk, mixing just until dry ingredients are moistened. *Do not overbeat.* Spoon the batter into 12 greased muffin cups. Bake at 350° until golden brown, about 35 to 40 minutes. The finished muffins should have a thick crust with a cakelike center.

Banana Bread or Muffins

Color picture 3

Makes 2 loaves or 1 dozen muffins

Here's a tasty recipe for those overripe bananas with black skins.

2 cups (about 3 large) well-mashed overripe bananas
1 cup sugar
2 eggs
⅜ pound (1½ sticks) unsalted butter, melted and cooled
2 cups all-purpose flour
2 teaspoons baking soda

3 tablespoons buttermilk (or a mixture of 3 tablespoons
milk and ½ teaspoon vinegar which has been set out
for 1 hour)
1 cup coarsely chopped pecans, dry roasted

In a large bowl combine the bananas, sugar and eggs with a spoon until well blended. Gradually add the butter, mixing well. Stir in the flour and baking soda until well mixed and creamy. Stir in the buttermilk, then fold in the pecans.

For the bread: Spoon batter into two 8½x4½-inch greased loaf pans. Bake at 350° for 30 minutes, then reduce heat to 300° and bake until dark brown and cooked through, about 45 minutes. Remove from pan immediately and cool on a wire rack about 30 minutes before serving.

For the muffins: Spoon batter into 12 greased muffin cups (they will be very full). Bake at 300° until dark brown and done, about 65 minutes. Let sit about 5 minutes, then remove from pan and cool as directed for the bread.

Bran Muffins

Color picture 3

Makes 1 dozen muffins

1 cup milk
¾ cup raisins
2 small eggs or 1 large egg, beaten
¼ cup molasses
1½ teaspoons vanilla extract
2 cups all-purpose flour
½ cup sugar
6 tablespoons bran
1 tablespoon plus 1½ teaspoons baking powder
¼ teaspoon salt

In a medium-size bowl combine the milk, raisins, egg(s), molasses and vanilla; let sit 45 minutes.

Combine the dry ingredients in a large bowl, mixing well and breaking up any lumps.

Fold milk mixture into the dry ingredients with a rubber spatula just until flour is thoroughly incorporated; do not overmix. Spoon into 12 greased muffin cups. Bake at 300° until well browned, about 1 hour. Remove from pan immediately and serve while still hot.

Carrot Muffins or Bread

Makes 1 dozen muffins or 1 loaf bread

These are at their best if allowed to sit uncovered about 2 hours before serving.

2 cups all-purpose flour
¾ cup, packed, light brown sugar
¾ cup coarsely grated carrots
½ cup coarsely chopped pecans or walnuts, dry roasted
2 teaspoons baking powder
¾ teaspoon ground cinnamon
¼ teaspoon salt
1 egg plus 1 egg yolk, beaten
⅔ cup milk
¼ pound (1 stick) unsalted butter, melted and cooled

Combine the flour, sugar, carrots, nuts, baking powder, cinnamon and salt in a large bowl; mix thoroughly with a spoon, breaking up any lumps. Add the remaining ingredients and mix just until blended; do not overbeat.

For the muffins: Spoon batter into 12 greased muffin cups. Bake at 350° until golden brown and tops spring back when gently touched, about 45 minutes. Remove from pan immediately.

For the bread: Spoon batter into a greased 8½x4½-inch loaf pan. Bake at 350° until dark golden brown and done, about 1 hour, 30 minutes.

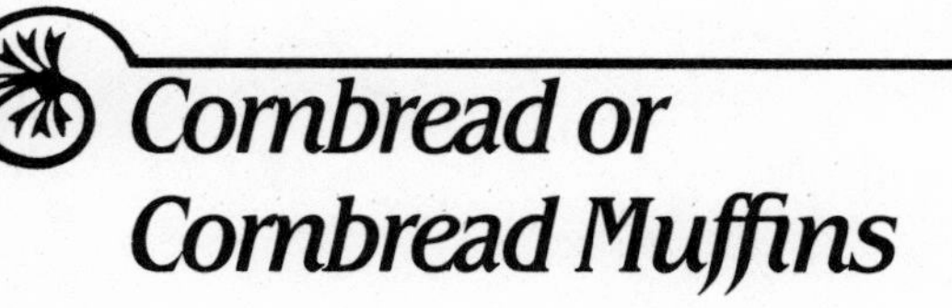

Cornbread or Cornbread Muffins

Makes 1 loaf bread or 1 dozen muffins

You can make your cornbread without sugar if you prefer. Cajuns like it sweet.

1⅓ cups all-purpose flour
⅔ cup cornmeal
⅔ cup sugar (optional)
½ cup corn flour (see **Note**)
5 teaspoons baking powder
½ teaspoon salt
1⅓ cups milk
5 tablespoons unsalted butter, melted
1 small egg, beaten

Note: Available at many health food stores.

In a large bowl combine the flour, cornmeal, sugar, corn flour, baking powder, and salt; mix well, breaking up any lumps. In a separate bowl combine the milk, butter and egg and add to the dry ingredients; blend just until mixed and large lumps are dissolved. Do not overbeat.

For bread: Pour mixture into a greased 8x8-inch baking pan and bake at 350° until golden brown, about 55 minutes. Remove from pan and serve immediately.

For muffins: Spoon mixture into 12 greased muffin cups. Bake at 350° until golden brown, about 45 minutes. Remove from pan immediately and serve while hot.

Honey Bread

Makes 3 loaves

½ cup plus 1 tablespoon honey *in all*
1 cup hot water (105° to 115°)
3 packages dry yeast
About 5½ cups all-purpose flour *in all*
½ teaspoon salt
1 cup evaporated milk
3 tablespoons pork lard, chicken fat or vegetable oil
1 tablespoon unsalted butter

In a medium-size bowl stir *1 tablespoon* of the honey into the water until dissolved. Stir in the yeast and let sit until yeast granules are totally dissolved, about 10 minutes.

Meanwhile, sift *4½ cups* of the flour and the salt into a large bowl. Set aside.

In a 2-quart saucepan bring the milk, lard and butter to a boil over high heat, stirring once or twice; reduce heat to very low and cook until reduced to 1 cup, about 5 to 10 minutes, stirring occasionally. Stir the hot liquid into the flour. Add the yeast mixture and beat with a spoon until well mixed, about 3 minutes. Stir in the remaining ½ cup honey. Continue mixing with a spoon or by hand until mixture forms a moist dough, about 5 minutes.

Place the dough on a well-floured surface. Knead until smooth and elastic to the touch, about 10 minutes, adding only enough additional flour (up to about 1 cup) to keep dough from sticking. Place in a large greased bowl and then invert dough so top is greased; cover with a dry towel and let stand in a warm place (90° to 100°) until doubled in size, about 30 to 45 minutes. (Place in a slightly warmer place if dough hasn't doubled in 1 hour.)

Punch down dough and knead on a floured surface for 2 minutes. Divide into 3 equal portions and form each into a loaf, stretching the top and tucking edges under to form as smooth a surface as possible; pop any large air bubbles by pinching them. Place in 3 greased 8½x4½-inch loaf pans. Cover with the towel again and let rise until almost doubled in size, about 45 minutes. Bake at 350° until done (see

Lagniappe), about 40 minutes, rotating the pans after 25 minutes for more even browning. Remove from pan immediately. Let cool on a wire rack about 1 hour before slicing.

LAGNIAPPE

To test doneness, carefully remove one loaf from pan; bottom should be evenly golden brown, and when bottom and sides are gently squeezed they should spring back into place. In high-humidity areas, store in paper bags or bread box (instead of airtight containers) so the bread can breathe.

New Orleans Black Muffins

Makes 1 dozen muffins

¾ cup hot water
½ cup molasses
¼ cup milk
2 cups whole wheat flour
1 cup all-purpose flour
¾ cup sugar
3 tablespoons baking powder
1 teaspoon baking soda
1 teaspoon salt
1½ cups coarsely chopped pecans, dry roasted

In a medium-size bowl combine the hot water and molasses, stirring until well blended. Stir in the milk until blended.

In a large bowl sift together the flours, sugar, baking powder, baking soda and salt.

With a rubber spatula, fold the liquid mixture and pecans into the dry ingredients just until flour is thoroughly incorporated; do not over-mix. Spoon into 12 greased muffin cups. Bake at 300° until done, 45 minutes to about 1 hour. Remove from pan immediately and serve while hot.

Mama's Yeast Bread or Rolls

Color pictures 3 and 4

Makes 3 loaves or 2 dozen rolls

About 7 cups all-purpose flour, *in all*
6 tablespoons sugar, *in all*
1¼ teaspoons salt
2½ packages dry yeast
2¼ cups hot water (105° to 115°)
¼ cup pork lard or vegetable oil
1 tablespoon unsalted butter, melted

In a large bowl mix *6 cups* of the flour, *5 tablespoons* of the sugar and the salt.

In a separate bowl combine the yeast and the remaining 1 tablespoon sugar with the hot water. Let sit 5 to 10 minutes; stir until yeast granules thoroughly dissolve. Add lard or oil to liquid mixture, stirring until lard is melted. Add half of liquid mixture to flour. Mix with hands to moisten flour as much as possible. Add remainder of liquid mixture to dough and mix until flour is thoroughly incorporated. Turn onto a lightly floured surface and knead by hand until smooth and elastic to the touch, about 15 minutes, gradually adding about ½ to 1 cup additional flour (add only enough to keep dough from sticking). Place in a large greased bowl and then invert dough so top is greased; cover with a dry towel and let stand in a warm place (90° to 100°) until doubled in size, about 1 hour. (Place in a slightly warmer place if dough hasn't doubled in 1 hour.) Punch down dough.

To make the bread: Divide dough into 3 equal portions. Form each into a ball, then shape each into a loaf, stretching top and tucking edges under to form as smooth a surface as possible; pop any large air bubbles by pinching them. Place in 3 greased 8½x4½-inch loaf pans. Cover with the towel again and let rise until almost doubled in size, about 30 to 45 minutes. Bake at 325° until lightly browned, about 45 to 50 minutes, rotating the pans after 25 minutes for more even browning; brush tops with melted butter and bake until done (see Lagniappe), about 5 to 10 minutes more. Cool 5 to 10 minutes before removing from pan. Let cool about 1 hour more before slicing.

To make rolls: Pinch off enough to make about 1½-inch balls. Roll dough into smooth balls with hands. Pop any large air bubbles by pinching them. Place in a greased 13x9-inch baking pan, with rolls fitted snugly against each other and sides of pan. Cover and let rise until doubled in size, about 35 to 45 minutes. Bake as for bread.

LAGNIAPPE

To test doneness, carefully remove one loaf or roll from pan; bottom should be evenly golden brown, and when bottom and sides are gently squeezed they should spring back into place. In high-humidity areas store in paper bags or bread box (instead of airtight containers) so the bread can breathe.

Jalapeño and Cheese Bread or Rolls

Color picture 3

Makes 3 loaves or about 2½ dozen rolls

About 8 cups all-purpose flour, *in all*
1 pound cheddar cheese, grated (about 5 cups)
¾ cup minced jalapeño peppers (see **Note**)
½ cup sugar, *in all*
1½ teaspoons salt
2 cups hot water (105° to 115°)
3 packages dry yeast
2 tablespoons plus 2 teaspoons pork lard or vegetable oil

Note: If your jalapeños are fairly mild, increase amount used by about ¼ cup. Fresh jalapeños are preferred; if you have to use pickled ones, rinse as much vinegar from them as possible.

In a very large bowl combine *7 cups* of the flour, the cheese, jalapeño peppers, *7 tablespoons* of the sugar and the salt; mix well.

In a separate bowl combine the water, yeast and remaining 1 tablespoon sugar. Let sit about 10 minutes; stir until all yeast granules are thoroughly dissolved. Add the lard or oil to the liquid mixture, stirring until lard is melted. Then add half of the liquid mixture to the flour mixture. Mix with hands to moisten flour as much as possible. Add remaining liquid mixture to dough and mix until flour is thoroughly incorporated. Turn onto a lightly floured surface and knead by hand until smooth and elastic to the touch, about 15 minutes, gradually adding only enough additional flour to keep dough from sticking. Place in a large greased bowl and then invert dough so top is greased; cover with a dry towel and let stand in a warm place (90° to 100°) until doubled in size, about 1 hour (if dough hasn't doubled in size after 1 hour, place in slightly warmer place). Punch down dough.

To make the bread: Divide dough into 3 equal portions. Form each into a ball, then stretch out dough with both hands and tuck edges under to form a smooth surface; pop any large air bubbles by pinching them. Place in 3 greased 8½x4½-inch loaf pans. Cover with towel again and allow to rise until almost doubled in size, about 45 minutes to 1 hour. Bake at 325° until dark brown and done (see Lagniappe), about 1 hour, rotating the pans after 25 minutes for more even browning. Remove from pan as soon as bread will easily lift out, after about 5 to 10 minutes. Let cool about 1 hour before slicing.

To make rolls: Pinch off dough and roll into 1½-inch balls until very smooth. Place in a greased 13x9-inch baking pan with rolls snugly touching each other and the sides of the pan. Cover and let rise again until doubled in size, about 45 minutes to 1 hour. Bake as directed above.

LAGNIAPPE

To test doneness, carefully remove one loaf or roll from pan; bottom should be evenly dark golden brown, and when bottom and sides are gently squeezed they should spring back into place. In high-humidity areas, store in paper bags or bread box (instead of airtight containers) so the bread can breathe.

Crêpes

Makes 12 to 14 (6-inch) entrée crêpes

The batter may be made ahead of time and refrigerated. Let it return to room temperature before using.

1 cup milk
2 eggs
1½ tablespoons vegetable oil
1 teaspoon sugar
¼ teaspoon ground nutmeg
Pinch of salt
¾ cup plus 1 tablespoon sifted all-purpose flour

In a medium-size bowl combine the milk, eggs, oil, sugar, nutmeg and salt; mix well with a metal whisk. Add the flour and whisk again just until blended and no lumps of flour remain; do not overbeat.

Very lightly oil an 8-inch slope-sided crêpe pan, then wipe it with a towel until the pan has only enough oil on it to be shiny. Heat the pan over medium heat about 2 minutes or until a drop of batter sizzles as soon as it's dropped in the pan. Then pick up the pan and slant it away from you. Pour 2 tablespoons batter into the pan, quickly rolling the batter so it thoroughly coats the bottom and slightly up the sides of the pan; make the crêpe as thin as possible. Cook until the edges and bottom are golden brown, about 30 seconds to 1 minute; brown only one side of the crêpe. Remove the crêpe from the pan and place it on a plate to cool, browned side up. Heat the pan about 15 seconds before cooking the next crêpe. Repeat with remaining batter, re-oiling pan if necessary. Keep the crêpes covered with a damp cloth at room temperature until ready to serve. They should be used within 2 hours.

FISH & SEAFOODS

Blackened Redfish

Color pictures 5a–5g

Makes 6 servings

See the color pictures! They show just what happens when you use this special method of cooking fish.

¾ pound (3 sticks) unsalted butter, melted in a skillet

Seasoning mix:
1 tablespoon sweet paprika
2½ teaspoons salt
1 teaspoon onion powder
1 teaspoon garlic powder
1 teaspoon ground red pepper (preferably cayenne)
¾ teaspoon white pepper
¾ teaspoon black pepper
½ teaspoon dried thyme leaves
½ teaspoon dried oregano leaves

6 (8- to 10-ounce) fish fillets (preferably redfish, pompano or tilefish), cut about ½ inch thick (see **Note**)

Note: Redfish and pompano are ideal for this method of cooking. If tilefish is used, you may have to split the fillets in half horizontally to have the proper thickness. If you can't get any of these fish, salmon steaks or red snapper fillets can be substituted. In any case, the fillets or steaks must not be more than ¾ inch thick.

Heat a large cast-iron skillet over very high heat until it is beyond the smoking stage and you see white ash in the skillet bottom (the skillet cannot be too hot for this dish), at least 10 minutes.

Meanwhile, pour 2 tablespoons melted butter in each of 6 small ramekins; set aside and keep warm. Reserve the remaining butter in its skillet. Heat the serving plates in a 250° oven.

Thoroughly combine the seasoning mix ingredients in a small bowl. Dip each fillet in the reserved melted butter so that both sides are well coated; then sprinkle seasoning mix generously and evenly on both sides of the fillets, patting it in by hand. Place in the hot skillet and pour 1 teaspoon melted butter on top of each fillet (be careful, as the butter may flame up). Cook, uncovered, over the same high heat until the underside looks charred, about 2 minutes (the time will vary according to the fillet's thickness and the heat of the skillet). Turn the fish over and again pour 1 teaspoon butter on top; cook until fish is done, about 2 minutes more. Repeat with remaining fillets. Serve each fillet while piping hot.

To serve, place one fillet and a ramekin of butter on each heated serving plate.

Seafood Dirty Rice

Makes 6 main-dish servings

1¾ pounds small shrimp with heads and shells (see **Note**)
2 tablespoons unsalted butter
1 tablespoon vegetable oil
½ cup canned tomato sauce
3 tablespoons very finely chopped onions
2½ tablespoons very finely chopped green bell peppers
2 tablespoons very finely chopped celery
1 teaspoon minced garlic
1 teaspoon salt
1 teaspoon white pepper
1 teaspoon dried thyme leaves
½ teaspoon ground red pepper (preferably cayenne)
1½ cups **Basic Shrimp Stock** (page 32)
½ cup heavy cream
3½ cups **Basic Cooked Rice** (page 224)
¾ cup very finely chopped green onions
1 cup, packed, lump crabmeat (picked over), about ½ pound

Note: If shrimp with heads are not available, buy 1 pound shrimp with shells and substitute other seafood ingredients for the heads in making the seafood stock.

Peel the shrimp and use the heads and shells to make the stock; refrigerate shrimp until ready to use.

In a large skillet melt the butter with the oil. Add the tomato sauce, onions, bell peppers, celery, garlic, salt, white pepper, thyme and red pepper; sauté over medium heat 5 minutes, stirring frequently. Add the stock and continue cooking over high heat for 10 minutes, stirring occasionally. Stir in the cream and simmer about 4 minutes. Add the shrimp and simmer 3 minutes longer, stirring occasionally. Stir in the rice, green onions and crabmeat, keeping the lumps of crabmeat intact as much as possible. Heat through and serve immediately.

Seafood Crêpes

Color picture 6

Makes 6 main-dish or 12 appetizer servings

Seasoning mix:
1 teaspoon salt
½ teaspoon white pepper
½ teaspoon ground red pepper (preferably cayenne)
¼ teaspoon dried sweet basil leaves
⅛ teaspoon dried thyme leaves
⅛ teaspoon dried oregano leaves

4 tablespoons unsalted butter
¼ cup finely chopped onions
½ cup finely chopped green onions
1 tablespoon all-purpose flour
1¼ cups heavy cream
½ pound lump crabmeat (picked over)

1 pound peeled crawfish tails
¾ pound peeled medium shrimp
12 **Crêpes** (page 47)

Prepare crêpes up to 2 hours ahead.

Combine the seasoning mix ingredients in a small bowl and set aside.

Heat the serving plates in a 250° oven.

Melt the butter in a 2-quart saucepan over high heat. Add the onions and sauté until they start getting tender, about 2 to 3 minutes, stirring occasionally. Add the seasoning mix and cook about 1 minute, stirring occasionally. Add the green onions and flour, stirring until flour is completely blended into the butter. Then stir in the cream and bring to a boil, stirring frequently. Add the crabmeat; return to a boil, stirring often and leaving crabmeat lumps intact as much as possible. Reduce heat and simmer until sauce has thickened slightly, about 1 minute, stirring almost constantly. Return heat to high. Add the crawfish and shrimp and cook just until shrimp are plump and pink, about 2 to 4 minutes, stirring often; remove from heat and serve immediately.

To serve for a main course, one at a time place 2 crêpes on each heated plate; fill each crêpe with a scant ⅓ cup filling, then fold crêpe in thirds. Spoon a little extra filling on top. For an appetizer, serve 1 crêpe per person. These crêpes may also be topped with a spoonful of **Hollandaise Sauce** (page 258).

Fish with Pecan Butter Sauce and Meunière Sauce

Color picture 7

Makes 6 servings

The fish are pan fried in this dish. See page 25 for more about pan frying.

Pecan Butter Sauce (recipe follows)
Meunière Sauce (page 243)
½ cup milk
1 egg, beaten

Seasoning mix:
1 tablespon salt
1 teaspoon onion powder
1 teaspoon sweet paprika
¾ teaspoon ground red pepper (preferably cayenne)
½ teaspoon white pepper
½ teaspoon garlic powder
½ teaspoon black pepper
¼ teaspoon dry mustard
¼ teaspoon dried oregano leaves
¼ teaspoon dried thyme leaves

1 cup all-purpose flour
6 (4-ounce) trout, redfish or other firm-fleshed fish fillets
Vegetable oil for pan frying
6 tablespoons coarsely chopped pecans, dry roasted

Make the Pecan Butter Sauce and the Meunière Sauce and set aside.

Combine the milk and egg in a pan (loaf, cake and pie pans work well) until well blended. In a small bowl thoroughly combine the seasonings. In a separate pan add *1 tablespoon* of the seasoning mix to the flour; mix well. Sprinkle some of the remaining seasoning mix lightly and evenly on both sides of the fish, patting it in by hand (use any remaining seasoning mix in another recipe).

Warm the serving plates in a 250° oven.

Heat about ¼ inch oil in a very large heavy skillet to about 350°. Meanwhile, dredge each fillet in the seasoned flour, shaking off excess; soak in the egg mixture; then, just before frying, drain off egg mixture and dredge fillets once more in the flour, shaking off excess. Fry the fillets in the hot oil until golden brown, about 2 to 3 minutes per side (adjust heat as necessary to maintain the oil's temperature). Drain on paper towels and, while still on the towels and very hot, spread a scant 2 tablespoons of the Pecan Butter Sauce over the top of each fillet. Serve immediately.

To serve, spoon a scant ⅓ cup Meunière Sauce onto each heated serving plate and place a fillet on top. Sprinkle each fillet with about 1 tablespoon pecans.

Pecan Butter Sauce

4 tablespoons unsalted butter, softened
½ cup coarsely chopped pecans, dry roasted
2 tablespoons very finely chopped onion
1 teaspoon lemon juice
½ teaspoon Tabasco sauce
¼ teaspoon minced garlic

Place all ingredients in a blender or food processor and process until creamy and smooth, about 2 to 3 minutes, pushing down sides a few times with a rubber spatula. Makes about ⅔ cup.

Fried Catfish with Hushpuppies

Makes 6 servings

Fry the hushpuppies first and set aside while frying the catfish.

Hushpuppies (recipe follows)

Seasoning mix:
1 tablespoon salt
1 tablespoon ground red pepper (preferably cayenne)
1 tablespoon sweet paprika
2¾ teaspoons garlic powder
2¾ teaspoons black pepper
1½ teaspoons onion powder
1½ teaspoons dried oregano leaves
1½ teaspoons dried thyme leaves

2½ cups all-purpose flour, *in all*
1½ cups cornmeal
1½ cups corn flour (see **NOTE**)
1 cup milk
2 eggs
¼ cup Creole mustard (preferred) or brown mustard
3 pounds freshwater catfish fillets
Vegetable oil for deep frying

NOTE: Corn flour is available at many health food stores.

Combine the seasoning mix ingredients in a small bowl and set aside. In a pan (loaf, cake and pie pans work well) combine *1½ teaspoons* of the mix with *1 cup* of the flour. In another pan, combine *2 tablespoons plus 1 teaspoon* of the seasoning mix with the remaining 1½ cups flour and the cornmeal and corn flour. In a third pan beat together the milk, eggs and mustard. Cut the catfish fillets into pieces about 2 inches long, 1 inch wide and ¼ inch thick.

Reheat the oil used for the hushpuppies to 350°. Meanwhile, sprinkle the remaining seasoning mix on each side of the fish fillets. Dredge the fillets in the flour first, then coat with the egg mixture, and then dredge in the cornmeal mixture, pressing the mixture firmly into the fish with your fingers; then pick up fillets and shake off excess coating. Fry the fish in the hot oil until golden brown and crispy. Do not crowd. Drain on paper towels. Serve immediately with hushpuppies.

Hushpuppies

Makes about 30 hushpuppies

1 cup cornmeal
½ cup all-purpose flour
½ cup corn flour (see **Note**)
1 tablespoon baking powder
¾ teaspoon ground red pepper (preferably cayenne)
½ teaspoon salt
½ teaspoon black pepper
½ teaspoon dried thyme leaves
¼ teaspoon white pepper
⅛ teaspoon dried oregano leaves

¼ cup very finely chopped green onions (tops only)
1½ teaspoons minced garlic
2 eggs, beaten
1 cup milk
2 tablespoons pork lard, unsalted butter, vegetable oil, chicken fat or bacon drippings
Vegetable oil for deep frying

Note: Corn flour is available at health food stores.

Combine all the dry ingredients in a large bowl, breaking up any lumps. Stir in the green onions and garlic. Add the eggs and blend well.

In a small saucepan bring the milk and lard (or other fat) to a boil; remove from heat and add to flour mixture, half at a time, stirring well after each addition. Refrigerate 1 hour.

In a large skillet or deep fryer, heat 4 inches of oil to 350°. Drop the batter by tablespoonfuls into the hot oil. Do not crowd. Cook until dark golden brown on each side and cooked through, about 1 minute per side. Drain on paper towels.

Sautéed Seafood Platter with Meunière Sauce

Color picture 8

Makes 6 servings

The fish are pan fried in this dish. See page 25 for more about pan frying.

Meunière Sauce (page 243)

Seasoning mix:
1 tablespoon salt
1½ teaspoons sweet paprika
1 teaspoon white pepper
1 teaspoon onion powder
1 teaspoon garlic powder
½ teaspoon ground red pepper (preferably cayenne)
½ teaspoon dried thyme leaves
¼ teaspoon black pepper
¼ teaspoon dried oregano leaves

1½ cups all-purpose flour
1 egg, beaten
1 cup milk
6 (4-ounce) fish fillets (preferably speckled trout, redfish or red snapper, or use your favorite)
Vegetable oil for pan frying
¼ pound (1 stick) unsalted butter, *in all*
8 ounces lump crabmeat (picked over)
½ cup finely chopped green onions, *in all*
2 tablespoons finely chopped fresh parsley, *in all*
½ teaspoon Worcestershire sauce
1½ dozen peeled medium to large shrimp, about ½ pound
1½ dozen medium to large shucked oysters, about 1 pound

Make the Meunière Sauce and set aside.

Combine the seasoning mix ingredients thoroughly in a small bowl. In a pan (loaf, cake and pie pans work well) combine the flour and 2 *teaspoons* of the seasoning mix. In a separate pan combine the egg and milk until well blended. Season the fillets by sprinkling about ¼ *teaspoon* of the seasoning mix on each.

In a large skillet heat about ¼ inch oil to about 350°. Meanwhile, dredge the fillets in the seasoned flour, shaking off excess, and coat well with the milk mixture. Just before frying, dredge again in the flour, shaking off excess. Fry the fillets in the hot oil until golden brown, about 1 to 2 minutes per side (adjust heat as necessary to maintain oil's temperature at about 350°). Drain on paper towels.

Heat the serving plates in a 250° oven.

In a 2-quart saucepan melt 4 *tablespoons* of the butter over medium heat. Add the crabmeat, 2 *tablespoons* of the green onions, 1 *tablespoon* of the parsley, 1 *teaspoon* of the seasoning mix and the Worcestershire; sauté just until crabmeat is heated through, about 2 minutes, stirring frequently and keeping crabmeat lumps intact as much as possible. Remove from heat.

In a large skillet melt 2 *tablespoons* of the butter over medium heat. Add the shrimp, 3 *tablespoons* of the green onions, the remaining 1 tablespoon parsley and 1½ *teaspoons* of the seasoning mix; sauté just until shrimp are plump and pink, about 2 minutes, stirring frequently. Remove from heat.

In a 1-quart saucepan melt the remaining 2 tablespoons butter over medium heat. Add the oysters, the remaining 3 tablespoons green onions and 1 *teaspoon* of the seasoning mix (use any remaining seasoning mix in another recipe); sauté just until oysters are plump and their edges curl, about 2 to 3 minutes, stirring occasionally. Remove from heat. Serve immediately.

To serve, place about ¼ cup Meunière Sauce on each heated serving plate and a fried fillet on top; spoon a portion of the crabmeat mixture on top of the fillet. Using a slotted spoon, arrange 3 drained shrimp on one side of the fish and 3 drained oysters on the other.

Seafood Stuffed Whole Fish

Color picture 9

Makes 6 servings

I like to use margarine to start this dish because it has more oil, which is needed in the stuffing, than butter. I also let the seafood cook longer than usual so it caramelizes; this intensifies and enhances the stuffing flavor.

Seasoning mix:
1 teaspoon salt
1 teaspoon white pepper
¾ teaspoon ground red pepper (preferably cayenne)
¾ teaspoon black pepper
½ teaspoon onion powder
¼ teaspoon dried thyme leaves
⅛ teaspoon dried oregano leaves

¼ pound (1 stick) margarine
1 cup finely chopped onions
½ cup finely chopped celery
½ cup finely chopped green bell peppers
½ cup finely chopped green onions
1½ teaspoons minced garlic
½ pound peeled shrimp, chopped (unless already small)
½ pound peeled crawfish tails (preferred) or additional shrimp or crabmeat (picked over)
1 cup very fine dry bread crumbs, *in all*
4 tablespoons unsalted butter
2 eggs, *in all*
3 tablespoons finely grated Parmesan cheese (preferably imported)
6 (8- to 10-ounce) whole speckled trout, salmon trout, redfish or any other small freshwater or saltwater fish, cleaned and boned from the stomach

½ teaspoon salt
½ teaspoon white pepper
1½ cups milk

Seasoned flour:
1 cup all-purpose flour
1 teaspoon white pepper
1 teaspoon onion powder
1 teaspoon ground red pepper (preferably cayenne)
½ teaspoon garlic powder
½ teaspoon dried thyme leaves
⅛ teaspoon oregano leaves

Vegetable oil for pan frying

Thoroughly combine the seasoning mix ingredients in a small bowl; set aside.

Place the margarine in a large skillet (preferably nonstick) over high heat; when half melted, add the onions, celery and bell peppers; sauté about 4 minutes, stirring occasionally. Add the seasoning mix, green onions and garlic; cook about 3 minutes, stirring occasionally. Add the shrimp and crawfish and continue cooking about 5 to 7 minutes, stirring infrequently (let sediment coat pan bottom, then scrape bottom well). Add *½ cup* bread crumbs; stir well and then let cook without stirring until mixture sticks, about 1 minute. Stir and scrape pan bottom well, then add the butter and continue cooking until the butter melts, stirring and scraping pan bottom continuously. Stir in the remaining ½ cup bread crumbs and remove from heat; cool slightly. Combine *1 egg*, beaten, with the Parmesan; add to mixture in skillet, mixing well. Transfer to a shallow pan and refrigerate until well chilled.

Meanwhile, sprinkle the inside surfaces of the fish with the salt and pepper.

Combine the milk and the remaining egg in a loaf pan or similarly shaped container. In a 13x9-inch pan, combine the seasoned flour ingredients, mixing well.

Stuff each fish with ½ cup cold stuffing; close fish and refrigerate until well chilled.

In a very large skillet heat ½ inch oil to 350°. Dredge the fish in the seasoned flour, then soak in the milk mixture. Just before frying, dredge again in the seasoned flour. Fry the fish in the hot oil, first with the fish stuffing side down, so the exposed stuffing fries; as soon as the stuffing side is crispy, about 30 seconds, fry each side of the fish until golden brown, about 1 to 2 minutes per side. Transfer to a large baking pan and bake at 350° until stuffing is heated through, about 20 minutes. Heat the serving plates during the last 5 minutes of cooking time. Remove from oven and serve immediately.

To serve, place each fish on a heated serving plate. Eat as is, or spoon **Béarnaise Sauce** (page 306), **Hollandaise Sauce** (page 258) or **Shrimp and Crab Butter Cream Sauce** (page 254) under or over the fish.

Seafood Stuffed Flounder

Makes 6 servings

Seasoning mix:
1 teaspoon salt
½ teaspoon sweet paprika
½ teaspoon black pepper
½ teaspoon dried thyme leaves
½ teaspoon dried sweet basil leaves
½ teaspoon gumbo filé (filé powder), optional

3 slices bacon, diced
1½ cups very finely chopped onions
1 cup very finely chopped celery
1 cup very finely chopped green bell peppers
¼ pound (1 stick) plus 1 tablespoon unsalted butter, *in all*
¾ teaspoon white pepper
¾ teaspoon ground red pepper (preferably cayenne)
½ pound peeled small shrimp
1½ cups **Basic Seafood Stock** (page 32)
6 shucked oysters (we use medium-size ones), about 3 ounces
¾ cup all-purpose flour, *in all*
½ cup very finely chopped green onions

¼ cup finely grated Parmesan cheese (preferably imported)

Flounder seasoning mix:
2 teaspoons salt
1 teaspoon sweet paprika
½ teaspoon white pepper
½ teaspoon onion powder
½ teaspoon garlic powder
½ teaspoon dry mustard
¼ teaspoon ground red pepper (preferably cayenne)
¼ teaspoon dried thyme leaves
¼ teaspoon dried sweet basil leaves

6 (1- to 1¼-pound) flounders, boned, heads removed, and brown side split down the center
1½ cups grated cheddar cheese
Vegetable oil for pan frying

Combine the first seasoning mix ingredients in a small bowl; mix well and set aside.

In a large skillet fry the bacon over high heat until crisp. Add the onions, celery and bell peppers. Stir well and sauté until vegetables start to get tender, about 5 minutes, stirring occasionally. Add *3 tablespoons* of the butter and the white and red peppers; stir until butter is melted. Stir in the shrimp and the first seasoning mix. Continue cooking about 3 to 5 minutes, stirring occasionally and scraping pan bottom well. Stir in the stock and the oysters; cook and stir about 6 to 8 minutes. Remove from heat. Use a slotted spoon to spoon the seafood-vegetable mixture into a food processor or blender, leaving the liquid in the skillet; process mixture until smooth, about 15 to 30 seconds. Return mixture to skillet, stirring to blend with liquid; turn heat to high, and cook until mixture starts sticking excessively, about 5 minutes, stirring occasionally and scraping pan bottom well. Remove from heat.

Meanwhile, in a 1-quart saucepan melt the remaining 6 tablespoons butter over high heat; when almost melted, remove from heat, then add *¼ cup* of the flour and stir until mixture is smooth. Return to high heat for 1 minute, stirring constantly.

Turn heat to high under the stuffing mixture; gradually add the butter-flour mixture, stirring constantly until well blended. (If mixture starts "weeping" oil at this point, stir in about 2 tablespoons more stock or water.) Continue cooking until very thick, about 1 to 2 minutes, stirring constantly. Add the green onions and cook 1 minute more, stirring constantly. Remove from heat and stir in the Parmesan. Cool slightly, then refrigerate until chilled, about 30 minutes.

In a small bowl thoroughly combine the flounder seasoning mix ingredients. Open the flounders for stuffing. Sprinkle ¼ *teaspoon* of the seasoning mix on the inside of each flounder. Mound ¼ cup of the cheddar cheese in the center of each, then spoon a scant ½ cup chilled stuffing on top of the cheese. Close the fish so the stuffing doesn't show. Cover and refrigerate for 1 to 2 hours.

Sprinkle ¼ *teaspoon* of the seasoning mix on each side of each chilled flounder, patting it in with your hands. In a pan (cake and pie pans work well) combine the remaining seasoning mix with the remaining ½ cup flour.

In a large, heavy skillet heat ¼ inch oil over high heat to about 350°. Meanwhile, place each flounder (split side up) in the seasoned flour to coat *only* the bottom surface. Carefully slide each flounder into the hot oil and fry the bottom until it's crispy, crunchy and brown-brown!—about 3 to 4 minutes. Without draining, place flounder, still split side up, on an ungreased cookie sheet. Bake at 550° until the fish are cooked and well browned on top, about 10 minutes (after about 4 minutes, drape a piece of aluminum foil over the tails so they won't burn). Serve immediately as is, or topped with **Hollandaise Sauce** (page 258), **Shrimp and Crab Butter Cream Sauce** (page 254) or **Béarnaise Sauce** (page 306).

Eggplant Bayou Teche

Color picture 10

Makes 6 servings

A pirogue is a canoe commonly used to travel many south Louisiana bayous. The pirogues can be hollowed out ahead of time; cover well and refrigerate until ready to use.

3 medium eggplants, halved lengthwise and peeled

Seasoning mix:
1 tablespoon plus 1½ teaspoons salt
1 tablespoon sweet paprika
2 teaspoons white pepper
1½ teaspoons onion powder
1 teaspoon garlic powder
1 teaspoon ground red pepper (preferably cayenne)
1 teaspoon black pepper
1 teaspoon dried thyme leaves
½ teaspoon dried sweet basil leaves

¼ cup finely chopped onions
¼ cup finely chopped celery
¼ cup finely chopped green bell peppers
¼ cup vegetable oil
1 cup all-purpose flour, *in all*
1½ cups **Basic Seafood Stock** (page 32)
¾ cup very fine dry bread crumbs
¾ cup milk
2 small eggs or 1 large egg
Vegetable oil for frying
6 tablespoons unsalted butter, *in all*
½ pound lump crabmeat (picked over)
¼ cup plus 2 tablespoons finely chopped green onions, *in all*
⅛ teaspoon minced garlic
1½ pounds peeled medium shrimp
1 tablespoon Pernod

Cut a thin slice from the rounded side of each eggplant half so it will sit level. Carefully carve out the center, leaving ¼-inch-thick sides and bottom. (**Note:** Use a paring knife to cut a neat ¼-inch wall all around the cut sides of the eggplant halves. Then with the knife or a spoon whittle out the pulp, being careful not to pierce through the bottom. Use the pulp in another recipe.) Cover shells well and refrigerate until ready to use.

In a small bowl combine the seasoning mix ingredients thoroughly. In a separate bowl combine the onions, celery and bell peppers. Set aside.

In a large heavy skillet heat the ¼ cup oil over high heat until it begins to smoke, about 3 to 5 minutes. Gradually add *¼ cup* of the flour, whisking constantly with a long-handled metal whisk until smooth; continue cooking, whisking constantly, until the roux is medium brown, about 1 minute, being careful not to let it scorch or splash on your skin. Remove from heat. Immediately stir in the reserved vegetable mixture and *1½ teaspoons* of the seasoning mix until well mixed (switch to a wooden spoon if necessary).

✸ See page 26 for more about making roux.

In a 1-quart saucepan bring the stock to a boil over high heat. Gradually add the roux mixture, stirring until dissolved between each addition. Cook about 5 minutes, stirring frequently. Reduce heat to a simmer and cook about 5 minutes more, stirring frequently. Remove from heat and strain liquid into a glass or ceramic container (discard vegetables); set this sauce aside.

Place the remaining ¾ cup flour in a pan (loaf, cake and pie pans work well); add *1 tablespoon* of the seasoning mix, blending well. In a separate pan mix together well the bread crumbs and *1 tablespoon* of the seasoning mix. In a third pan beat the milk and egg(s) together until well blended.

In a large skillet or deep fryer, heat ¾ inch oil to 350°. Meanwhile, sprinkle each eggplant pirogue evenly with a scant ¾ teaspoon of the seasoning mix, patting it in by hand. Just before frying, dredge the pirogues on both sides in the seasoned flour, shaking off excess; coat with the milk mixture and then dredge in the seasoned bread crumbs. Fry in the hot oil until golden brown, about 1 to 2 minutes per side (adjust heat as necessary to maintain the oil's temperature at about 350°). Do not crowd. Drain on paper towels and set aside.

Heat the serving plates in a 250° oven.

In a 1-quart saucepan melt *2 tablespoons* of the butter over medium heat. Turn heat to high. Stir in the crabmeat, *¼ cup* of the green onions, the garlic and *¼ teaspoon* of the seasoning mix. Continue cooking about 2 minutes, stirring occasionally. Remove from heat.

In a 2-quart saucepan melt the remaining 4 tablespoons butter over high heat. Add the shrimp, the remaining 2 tablespoons green onions and *1½ teaspoons* of the seasoning mix (use any remaining seasoning mix in another recipe). Cook about 1 minute, stirring occasionally. Add the Pernod and ½ cup of the strained sauce (use any remaining in another dish). Cook until shrimp are plump and pink, about 1 minute more. Remove from heat. Serve immediately.

To serve, place each fried pirogue on a heated serving plate. Spoon about ¼ cup of the crabmeat mixture in the center, then top with about ½ cup shrimp in their sauce.

Seafood Stuffed Eggplant with Shrimp Butter Cream Sauce

Makes 6 servings

Seasoning mix:
2 teaspoons salt
1½ teaspoons ground red pepper (preferably cayenne)
1¼ teaspoons black pepper
1 teaspoon onion powder
1 teaspoon garlic powder
1 teaspoon dried thyme leaves
¾ teaspoon white pepper
½ teaspoon dried oregano leaves

3 large eggplants (about 1 pound each)
3 quarts, *in all*, **Basic Seafood Stock** (page 32)
⅜ pound (1½ sticks) unsalted butter
¼ pound (1 stick) margarine
2¾ cups finely chopped onions, *in all*
2 cups finely chopped green bell peppers, *in all*
1 cup finely chopped celery, *in all*
1 tablespoon plus 1 teaspoon minced garlic, *in all*
2 bay leaves
1 cup very fine dry bread crumbs
2 dozen peeled small shrimp, about 4 ounces
¾ cup, packed, crabmeat (picked over), about 4 ounces
Shrimp Butter Cream Sauce (recipe follows)

Thoroughly combine the seasoning mix ingredients in a small bowl and set aside.

Remove stems from eggplants and slice each in half lengthwise. Place eggplants and stock in a large pot over high heat; cover and cook till fork tender, about 15 minutes. Drain well and reserve *4½ cups* of the stock. Remove pulp from eggplants with a spoon, being careful to keep skins intact; reserve pulp and skins.

In a large, heavy, ovenproof skillet, melt the butter with the margarine over medium heat. Add *1 cup* of the onions, *¾ cup* of the bell peppers and *½ cup* of the celery; sauté until onions are dark brown but not burned, about 25 minutes, stirring occasionally. Add *1 cup* more onions, *¾ cup* more bell peppers, the remaining ½ cup celery, *1 tablespoon* of the minced garlic and the bay leaves; sauté about 12 minutes. Turn heat to high. Add all but ½ cup of the eggplant pulp (reserve the ½ cup for the sauce), *1 cup* of the reserved stock and all the seasoning mix; cook 5 minutes, stirring frequently and scraping pan bottom well. Add the remaining ¾ cup onions, ½ cup bell peppers and 1 teaspoon minced garlic; cook 6 minutes, stirring occasionally. Add *1 cup* stock; cook 15 minutes, stirring occasionally and scraping pan bottom as needed. Stir in another *1 cup* stock (reserve the remaining 1½ cups for the sauce) and continue cooking 8 minutes, stirring occasionally. Add the bread crumbs; stir well and cook 1 minute.

Place skillet in oven and bake at 350° for 15 minutes. Then stir in the shrimp and crabmeat, return to oven and bake at 250° for 10 minutes. Remove bay leaves and serve immediately.

To serve, fill each eggplant skin with about ⅔ cup stuffing and top with about ⅓ cup Shrimp Butter Cream Sauce.

Shrimp Butter Cream Sauce

5½ tablespoons unsalted butter, *in all*
2 tablespoons all-purpose flour
½ cup very finely chopped reserved eggplant pulp
(preceding recipe)
¼ cup finely chopped onions
1½ cups reserved stock (preceding recipe)

¾ teaspoon salt
½ teaspoon ground red pepper (preferably cayenne)
¼ teaspoon white pepper
½ cup heavy cream
1 dozen peeled small shrimp, about 2 ounces

In a 1-quart saucepan melt *4 tablespoons* of the butter over medium heat. Whisk in the flour with a metal whisk until well blended. Remove from heat and set aside.

Place the remaining 1½ tablespoons butter, the eggplant pulp and onions in a 2-quart saucepan. Sauté over high heat until onions are wilted, about 2 minutes, stirring occasionally. Add the stock and bring to a boil. Whisk in the salt and red and white peppers, then the butter-flour mixture; cook over high heat 4 minutes, whisking frequently. Add the cream and continue cooking 1 minute, whisking constantly. Add the shrimp and continue cooking and stirring just until the shrimp turn pink, about 30 seconds. Remove from heat. Makes about 2 cups.

Seafood Stuffed Zucchini with Seafood Cream Sauce

Color picture 11

Makes 6 servings

The zucchini shells and pulp can be prepared ahead of time and refrigerated until ready to use.

10 (5- to 6-inch) zucchini, *in all*
1¼ cups minced celery
1 cup minced onions
1 cup minced green bell peppers

Seasoning mix:
1½ teaspons salt
¾ teaspoon sweet paprika

½ teaspoon black pepper
¼ teaspoon white pepper
¼ teaspoon onion powder
¼ teaspoon garlic powder
¼ teaspoon dry mustard
¼ teaspoon ground red pepper (preferably cayenne)
¼ teaspoon gumbo filé (filé powder), optional
Pinch of dried sweet basil leaves
Pinch of dried thyme leaves

⅜ pound (1½ sticks) margarine, *in all*
4 tablespoons unsalted butter
1 tablespoon minced garlic
3 bay leaves
3 cups, *in all*, **Basic Seafood Stock** (page 32)
1 cup very fine dry bread crumbs, *in all*
½ cup finely chopped green onions
½ teaspoon white pepper
½ teaspoon ground red pepper (preferably cayenne)
½ pound, *in all*, peeled shrimp or crawfish tails, coarsely chopped
6 ounces, *in all*, crabmeat (picked over) or fish, cut in small pieces
½ cup chopped onions
3½ tablespoons unsalted butter, softened
2 tablespoons all-purpose flour
1 cup heavy cream
Vegetable oil for frying

Cut 6 of the zucchini in half lengthwise, leaving up to ¾ inch of the stem on. Cut a thin slice from the rounded side of each half so it will sit level. Scoop out 36 small balls of the pulp with a melon baller and reserve. With the melon baller or a teaspoon carefully remove the remaining pulp, leaving a ⅛-inch shell. Coarsely grate enough of the pulp to obtain 6 cups (you will need the remaining 4 zucchini to have enough pulp); set aside.

Thoroughly combine the celery, minced onions and bell peppers in a medium-size bowl and set aside. In a small bowl combine the seasoning mix ingredients; mix well and set aside.

In a large ovenproof skillet melt *4 tablespoons* of the margarine and the 4 tablespoons butter over high heat. Add about *half* the vegetable mixture and sauté about 2 minutes, stirring occasionally. Stir in the garlic, bay leaves, remaining 1 stick margarine and *1 tablespoon* of the seasoning mix. Cook until mixture browns, about 10 minutes, stirring occasionally. Add the remaining vegetable mixture and *5 cups* of the grated zucchini; stir well and scrape the pan bottom. Continue cooking for about 2 minutes, stirring occasionally.

Place the skillet in a 450° oven and bake until the surface is somewhat oily and edges are browned and crispy, about 20 minutes. Stir in *1 cup* of the stock; continue baking until oil has reappeared on the surface, about 15 minutes. Sprinkle *½ cup* of the bread crumbs on the oil, then stir well into the mixture. Continue baking 15 minutes. Stir in the remaining bread crumbs and cook 15 minutes more, stirring once after 10 minutes. Remove from oven. Discard bay leaves. Stir in the green onions, white and red peppers, *half* the shrimp or crawfish and *half* the crabmeat or fish. Fill the zucchini halves with 3 to 4 tablespoons of this stuffing and place in a single layer in an ungreased baking pan that is just big enough for the shells to fit in it snugly, about 13x9 inches. Bake at 450° for 15 minutes.

Begin the rest of the recipe when you first put the stuffing skillet in the oven. In a 1-quart saucepan combine the remaining 2 cups stock, remaining 1 cup grated zucchini and the chopped onions. Bring to a boil over high heat; continue boiling until vegetables are soft and liquid has reduced some, about 15 minutes, stirring occasionally. Set aside.

In a small bowl combine the 3½ tablespoons softened butter and the flour with a fork until smooth. Return stock mixture to high heat and add the flour mixture by spoonfuls, whisking in each addition with a metal whisk until dissolved. Then add the cream, the remaining seasoning mix and the remaining shrimp or crawfish. Bring to a slow boil, whisking constantly. Reduce heat and simmer 1 minute, whisking almost constantly. Stir in the remaining crabmeat or fish. Cook 1 minute more, whisking constantly. Remove from heat. Set aside.

Five minutes before the zucchini are done, heat the serving plates in a 250° oven.

Meanwhile, in a 2-quart saucepan heat ¼ inch oil to about 350°. Fry the zucchini balls until brown, about 1 to 2 minutes per side. Drain on paper towels. Serve immediately.

To serve, place 2 zucchini halves on each heated serving plate; arrange 3 fried zucchini balls on each half and top with about ½ cup seafood cream sauce, pouring most of the sauce on the plate so that the stuffed zucchini shows through the sauce.

Stuffed Mirliton with Shrimp and Crab Butter Cream Sauce

Makes 6 servings

I like to use margarine in this dish because it has more oil than butter and reacts better in the caramelization process.

Seasoning mix:
2 whole bay leaves
2 teaspoons white pepper
2 teaspoons ground red pepper (preferably cayenne)
1 teaspoon dried thyme leaves
1 teaspoon dried sweet basil leaves
½ teaspoon black pepper

7 medium-size mirlitons (chayotes), or substitute zucchini or yellow squash
¼ pound (1 stick) margarine
2 cups finely chopped onions, *in all*
1¼ cups finely chopped green bell peppers, *in all*
1 cup finely chopped celery, *in all*
6¼ cups, *in all*, **Basic Seafood Stock** (page 32)
1 tablespoon minced garlic
¼ pound (1 stick) unsalted butter
2 teaspoons salt

1½ cups very fine dry bread crumbs
Shrimp and Crab Butter Cream Sauce (see page 254)
6 tablespoons finely chopped green onions

Combine the seasoning mix ingredients in a small bowl and set aside.

Peel and finely chop 4 of the mirlitons. Peel, cut in half lengthwise, and remove the seeds from the remaining 3 mirlitons. (Eat the seeds or save to put in a salad.) Set aside.

In a large skillet combine the margarine with *1 cup* of the onions, *¾ cup* of the bell peppers and *½ cup* of the celery. Sauté over high heat until most of the onions are browned, about 15 minutes, stirring occasionally. Add *¼ cup* of the stock, the remaining 1 cup onions, ½ cup bell peppers and ½ cup celery, the seasoning mix and garlic; stir well and continue cooking 2 minutes, stirring frequently. Add the butter and continue cooking until it melts, constantly stirring and scraping the pan bottom well. Stir in the chopped mirlitons and cook 5 minutes, stirring occasionally. Stir in the salt and continue cooking about 2 minutes to reduce some of the liquid. Remove from heat and transfer mixture to an ungreased 13x9-inch baking pan. Bake in a 350° oven until mushy, about 35 minutes. Stir in bread crumbs and continue baking until browned, about 30 minutes. Remove from oven and discard bay leaves.

Meanwhile, place the mirliton halves and the remaining 6 cups stock in a 4-quart saucepan. Boil mirlitons until tender, about 40 minutes. (Add water to pan as necessary to keep mirlitons covered with liquid.) Drain mirlitons, reserving *1½ cups* of the stock to make the Shrimp and Crab Butter Cream Sauce. Shave a thin slice from the rounded side of each mirliton half so it will sit level (seed side up) on a plate.

Warm the plates in a 250° oven. Make the sauce and serve immediately. (**Note:** When making the Shrimp and Crab Butter Cream Sauce, substitute the 1½ cups reserved stock for the Basic Seafood Stock, since this will add a bit of mirliton flavor to the sauce.)

To serve, place a mirliton half on each heated plate; mound ⅔ cup stuffing on the top; spoon about ⅔ cup Shrimp and Crab Butter Cream Sauce over the stuffing and sprinkle each with 1 tablespoon green onions.

Crawfish Enchiladas con Queso

Makes 10 servings

This recipe works equally well substituting 3 pounds of peeled medium-size shrimp for the crawfish. The sauce is also great over spaghetti or rice.

½ pound (2 sticks) unsalted butter, *in all*
1 cup finely chopped onions
1 cup canned green chilies, drained and chopped
¾ cup finely chopped green bell peppers.
2¾ teaspoon salt, *in all*
2¾ teaspoons white pepper, *in all*
1½ teaspoons, *in all*, ground red pepper (preferably cayenne)
¾ teaspoon dried oregano leaves, *in all*
½ teaspoon minced garlic
3 cups heavy cream
1 cup dairy sour cream
8 cups, *in all*, grated Monterey Jack cheese or other white (nonprocessed) cheese, 2 pounds
2 pounds peeled crawfish tails
⅔ cup very finely chopped green onions
½ cup vegetable oil
20 (6-inch) corn tortillas

In a large skillet melt *1 stick* of the butter. Add the onions, green chilies, bell peppers, *1¼ teaspoons* of the salt, *¾ teaspoon* of the white pepper, *½ teaspoon* of the red pepper, *¼ teaspoon* of the oregano and the garlic. Sauté over medium heat for 10 minutes, stirring often. Stir in the heavy cream and bring mixture to a rapid boil; then reduce the heat and simmer uncovered 10 minutes, stirring constantly. Add the sour cream; with a metal whisk, beat continuously until the sour cream is dissolved, about 3 minutes. Add *3 cups* of the cheese and stir until melted. Set the sauce aside.

In a 4-quart saucepan melt the remaining 1 stick butter. Add the crawfish, green onions and the remaining 1½ teaspoons salt, 2 teaspoons white pepper, 1 teaspoon red pepper and ½ teaspoon oregano. Sauté over medium heat for about 6 minutes, stirring occasionally. Add the cheese sauce to the crawfish mixture and stir well. Simmer until the flavors are well blended, about 6 to 10 minutes, stirring occasionally. Set aside.

In a small skillet heat the oil to about 325°. Holding tortillas one at a time with metal tongs, dip each into the hot oil just long enough to soften, about 1 second on each side; drain on paper towels. Spoon about ⅓ cup crawfish sauce on each tortilla and roll up tortilla.

For the prettiest presentation, broil the enchiladas: Put them all, seam side down, in a flameproof baking dish; or place two on each individual (flameproof) serving plate. Cover each enchilada from end to end with a generous amount of additional sauce, then sprinkle each with ¼ cup cheese. Place the baking dish (or two or three individual plates at a time) under a broiler near the flame until the cheese melts and begins to brown, about 2 minutes. Or, bake the enchiladas in a 350° oven until the cheese melts, about 5 to 8 minutes. Serve immediately. **Note:** If you choose to finish the enchiladas in one large baking dish, serve them on *heated* plates.

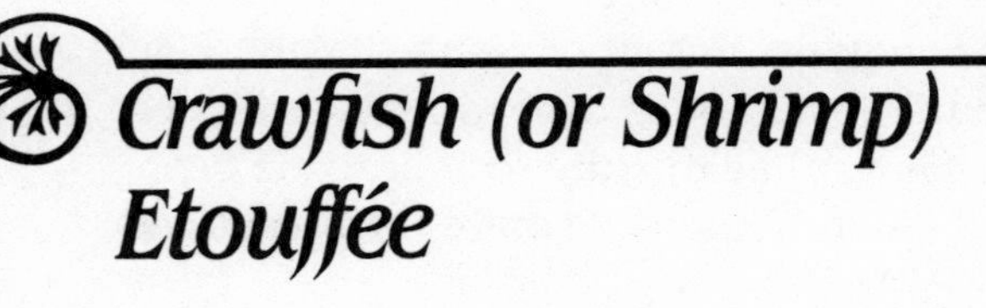

Crawfish (or Shrimp) Etouffée

Color Pictures 1 and 12

Makes 8 servings

Seasoning mix:
2 teaspoons salt
2 teaspoons ground red pepper (preferably cayenne)
1 teaspoon white pepper
1 teaspoon black pepper
1 teaspoon dried sweet basil leaves
½ teaspoon dried thyme leaves

¼ cup chopped onions
¼ cup chopped celery
¼ cup chopped green bell peppers
7 tablespoons vegetable oil
¾ cup all-purpose flour
3 cups, *in all*, **Basic Seafood Stock** (page 32)
½ pound (2 sticks) unsalted butter, *in all*
2 pounds peeled crawfish tails or medium shrimp
1 cup very finely chopped green onions
4 cups hot **Basic Cooked Rice** (page 224)

Thoroughly combine the seasoning mix ingredients in a small bowl and set aside. In a separate bowl combine the onions, celery and bell peppers.

In a large heavy skillet (preferably cast iron), heat the oil over high heat until it begins to smoke, about 4 minutes. With a long-handled metal whisk, gradually mix in the flour, stirring until smooth. Continue cooking, whisking constantly, until roux is dark red-brown, about 3 to 5 minutes (be careful not to let it scorch in the pan or splash on your skin). Remove from heat and immediately stir in the vegetables and *1 tablespoon* of the seasoning mix with a wooden spoon; continue stirring until cooled, about 5 minutes.

✸ See page 26 for more about making roux.

In a 2-quart saucepan bring *2 cups* of the stock to a boil over high heat. Gradually add the roux and whisk until thoroughly dissolved. Reduce heat to low and cook until flour taste is gone, about 2 minutes, whisking almost constantly (if any of the mixture scorches, don't continue to scrape that part of the pan bottom). Remove from heat and set aside.

Heat the serving plates in a 250° oven.

In a 4-quart saucepan melt *1 stick* of the butter over medium heat. Stir in the crawfish (or shrimp) and the green onions; sauté about 1 minute, stirring almost constantly. Add the remaining stick of butter, the stock mixture and the remaining 1 cup stock; cook until butter melts and is mixed into the sauce, about 4 to 6 minutes, constantly shaking the pan in a back-and-forth motion (versus stirring). Add the remaining seasoning mix; stir well and remove from heat (if sauce starts separating, add about 2 tablespoons more of stock or water and shake pan until it combines). Serve immediately.

To serve, mound ½ cup rice on each heated serving plate. Surround the rice with ¾ cup of the etouffée.

LAGNIAPPE

A certain percentage of oil is released when butter is melted; shaking the pan in a back-and-forth motion and the addition of stock keep the sauce from separating and having an oily texture—stirring doesn't produce the same effect.

Sautéed Crawfish

Makes 3 servings

The sauce for this dish is best if made only three servings at a time. If you want to make more than three servings, do so in separate batches but serve while piping hot.

Seasoning mix:
1 teaspoon white pepper
½ teaspoon salt
½ teaspoon ground red pepper (preferably cayenne)
½ teaspoon black pepper
½ teaspoon dried sweet basil leaves
¼ teaspoon dry mustard

½ pound (2 sticks) unsalted butter, *in all*
½ cup finely chopped green onions (tops only)
1 teaspoon minced garlic
1 pound peeled crawfish tails
1 teaspoon Tabasco sauce
½ cup **Basic Seafood Stock** (page 32)
1½ cups hot **Basic Cooked Rice** (page 224)

Combine the seasoning mix ingredients in a small bowl and set aside. Heat the serving plates in a 250° oven.

Place *1 stick* of the butter, the onions and garlic in a large deep skillet. Sauté 1 minute over high heat; turn off heat. Add the crawfish, Tabasco and seasoning mix; turn heat to high and sauté about 3 minutes, stirring occasionally. Add the remaining stick of butter, breaking it into chunks in the pan; then slowly add the stock while moving the pan back and forth on the burner; shake the pan hard enough to toss but not spill the ingredients (see Lagniappe). Cook over high heat 6 minutes, shaking the pan constantly. Serve immediately.

To serve, mound ½ cup rice in the middle of each heated serving plate. Encircle the rice with 1 cup sautéed crawfish and their sauce.

LAGNIAPPE

A certain percentage of oil is released when butter is melted; shaking the pan in a back-and-forth motion and the addition of stock to the melting butter keep the sauce from separating and having an oily texture—stirring doesn't produce the same effect.

Crawfish Magnifique
in a Mirliton Pirogue

Makes 6 servings

We've filled these pirogues with wonderful Louisiana crawfish. The pirogues can be hollowed out ahead of time; cover well and refrigerate until ready to use.

3 medium-size mirlitons (chayotes)

Crawfish Magnifique:

¼ cup vegetable oil
¾ cup all-purpose flour, *in all*
½ cup minced green bell peppers
⅓ cup minced onions
¼ cup minced celery
1½ cups heavy cream

Seasoning mix:
1 tablespoon salt
2 teaspoons sweet paprika
¾ teaspoon white pepper
¾ teaspoon ground red pepper (preferably cayenne)
¾ teaspoon black pepper
½ teaspoon onion powder
½ teaspoon garlic powder
½ teaspoon dry mustard
½ teaspoon gumbo filé (filé powder), optional
¼ teaspoon dried thyme leaves
¼ teaspoon dried sweet basil leaves

⅜ pound (1½ sticks) unsalted butter
¾ cup finely chopped green onions
1 teaspoon minced garlic
1½ pounds peeled crawfish tails

¾ cup very fine dry bread crumbs
½ cup milk
1 egg
Vegetable oil for deep frying

Boil the mirlitons just until fork tender. Cool and peel. Cut each in half lengthwise and trim off the tough pulp at the end closest to the seed. Remove seed (eat or save to put in a salad). Cut a thin slice from the rounded side of each mirliton half so it will sit level. Carefully spoon out pulp from inside, leaving a ¼-inch-thick shell. (Use pulp in another recipe.) Set aside.

In a heavy 1-quart saucepan heat the vegetable oil until it begins to smoke, about 2 minutes. With a long-handled metal whisk or a wooden spoon, gradually stir in *¼ cup* of the flour and cook, whisking constantly or stirring briskly, until roux is a dark red-brown, about 2 to 3 minutes; remove pan momentarily from heat if the roux is browning too quickly for you to keep it from scorching (be careful not to splash it on your skin). Remove from heat and immediately add the bell peppers, onions and celery. Continue whisking constantly until mixture cools, about 3 minutes. Set aside.

✱ See page 26 for more about making roux.

In a 2-quart saucepan heat the cream to a quick simmer over high heat, whisking almost constantly. Gradually add the roux, stirring until dissolved between each addition. Bring to a boil, whisking constantly so mixture doesn't scorch. Remove from heat and set aside.

Thoroughly combine the seasoning mix ingredients in a small bowl and set aside.

In a large skillet combine the butter with the green onions and garlic; cook over low heat until butter melts, stirring occasionally. Add the crawfish and *1½ tablespoons* of the seasoning mix; turn heat to high and sauté until crawfish are hot, about 3 minutes, stirring almost constantly. Stir the cream mixture into the crawfish mixture.

Reduce heat to *very* low to keep crawfish sauce hot while frying the mirlitons; stir occasionally. Heat the serving plates in a 250° oven.

Place the remaining ½ cup flour in a pan (loaf, cake and pie pans work well). Place the bread crumbs in another. Add *1¾ teaspoons* of the seasoning mix to the flour and *2 teaspoons* to the bread crumbs, mixing each well. Sprinkle a total of about *¼ teaspoon* seasoning mix on both sides of the mirlitons. In a separate pan combine the milk and egg until well blended. Heat 1 inch of oil in a 2-quart saucepan or deep fryer to 350°. Meanwhile, dredge each mirliton in the seasoned flour, shaking off excess; then coat well with the milk mixture and then with the bread crumbs. Fry the mirlitons in the hot oil until golden brown, about 1 to 2 minutes per side (adjust heat as necessary to maintain oil's temperature at about 350°). Do not crowd. Drain on paper towels. Serve immediately.

To serve, place a pirogue on each heated serving plate and spoon in about ¾ cup crawfish sauce.

Crawfish Pie

Color Picture 13

Makes 6 main-dish individual pies

When I was a boy, my family always used semisweet crusts for crawfish dishes, so this crust recipe is semisweet. You can make the dough a day ahead and refrigerate (covered) until ready to use.

Crawfish Pie Crusts (recipe follows)
Crawfish Magnifique (preceding recipe)

Seasoning mix:
1½ teaspoons salt
1 teaspoon sweet paprika
½ teaspoon white pepper
¼ teaspoon onion powder
¼ teaspoon garlic powder
¼ teaspoon dry mustard
¼ teaspoon ground red pepper (preferably cayenne)
¼ teaspoon black pepper
¼ teaspoon gumbo filé (filé powder), optional
⅛ teaspoon dried thyme leaves
⅛ teaspoon dried sweet basil leaves

Make the pie crusts and set aside.

Make the Crawfish Magnifique, starting with the roux made with the ¼ cup vegetable oil and *¼ cup* of flour. Use the smaller amounts of spices for the seasoning mix as listed here (use any remaining seasoning mix in another recipe). Follow the recipe to the point where the cream mixture is stirred into the crawfish mixture. Serve immediately.

To serve fill each crust with about ¾ cup of the crawfish sauce and arrange a few crawfish tails on top.

Crawfish Pie Crusts

NOTE: You will need at least 6 individual oval, ovenproof casserole dishes (about 1½-cup capacity) to bake all the crusts at once.

¾ pound (3 sticks) unsalted butter, very soft
¾ cup sugar
1½ teaspoons vanilla extract
½ teaspoon salt
3 eggs
½ cup milk
About 4 cups all-purpose flour

In a large bowl combine the butter, sugar, vanilla and salt; stir until creamy and smooth. Stir in the eggs and milk. Gradually add *3¾ cups* of the flour and stir until all the flour is mixed in.

On a surface floured with about ¼ cup more flour, knead the dough for 1 minute. Place in a bowl, cover, and refrigerate at least 1 hour. Then divide dough into 6 equal portions. Reflour surface and roll each piece into an oval shape about ¼ inch thick. Place a casserole dish face down over each piece of dough. With a knife cut around the shape of the casserole, leaving an additional ½-inch border. Flour the dough's surface lightly, fold into quarters, and carefully place dough so the corner of the fold is centered in the ungreased casserole. Unfold the dough and line the casserole with it, pressing it firmly against the bottom and sides. The dough should come slightly over the casserole top. Place an empty casserole of the same size (or use pie weights or dried beans) on top to hold dough in place while baking. Bake at 350° for 25 minutes. Remove top casserole or weights. Reduce temperature to 300° and continue baking until sides and bottom are browned, about 40 minutes more (baking time may vary about 10 to 15 minutes depending on what you used to weigh down the dough). Remove from oven and cool slightly; then remove from casseroles and set aside. (**NOTE:** You will have enough dough scraps left to make an extra crust, or you can use the scraps to make decorative strips to put across the tops of the pies.)

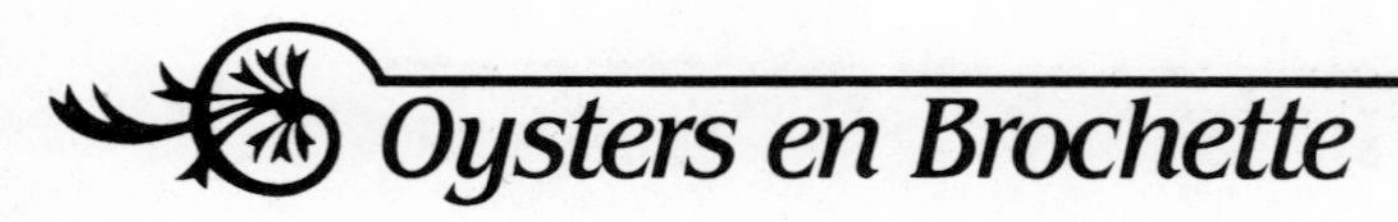

Oysters en Brochette

Makes 6 servings

This is best when served alongside another entrée such as **Seafood Dirty Rice** (page 51) or a dressing such as **Rice, Apple and Raisin Dressing** (page 229).

Seasoning mix:

1½ tablespoons salt
1½ teaspoons garlic powder
1½ teaspoons sweet paprika

1¼ teaspoons ground red pepper (preferably cayenne)
1 teaspoon black pepper
¾ teaspoon white pepper
¾ teaspoon onion powder
¾ teaspoon dried oregano leaves
½ teaspoon dried thyme leaves
¼ teaspoon dried sweet basil leaves

About ¾ pound sliced bacon, cut into 2½-inch pieces
12 mushroom caps
5 dozen medium to large shucked oysters (about 2¾ pounds)
¾ cup all-purpose flour
Vegetable oil for frying
Hot **Browned Garlic Butter Sauce** (page 242)

Thoroughly combine the seasonings in a small bowl. Set aside.

Blanch the bacon pieces in boiling water about 4 minutes. Rinse in cold water to cool, then drain.

Fill six 9- to 10-inch metal or wooden skewers as follows: Place one mushroom cap, then one piece of bacon, then one oyster (skewer through the firmest part); continue with bacon and oysters until skewer is almost full, ending with bacon. Then finish the skewer with another mushroom cap. (For each skewer you will use 2 mushroom caps, 10 oysters and 11 pieces of bacon.)

Place serving plates in a 250° oven to warm.

In a pan (loaf, cake or pie pans work well), thoroughly combine the flour and 2 *teaspoons* of the seasoning mix. Sprinkle 1 teaspoon of the remaining seasoning mix on each filled skewer. In a large heavy skillet heat ⅝ inch oil to 350°. Just before frying, dredge each skewer well in the seasoned flour, shaking off excess. Fry each skewer in the hot oil until golden brown and crispy, about 2 to 3 minutes per side. Do not crowd. Drain on paper towels.

Make the Browned Garlic Butter Sauce and serve immediately. To serve, place one brochette on each warmed plate, remove skewer, and drizzle with the hot, foamy sauce.

Tasso and Oysters in Cream on Pasta

Makes 8 servings

6 quarts hot water
¼ cup vegetable oil
3 tablespoons salt
1½ pounds fresh spaghetti, or 1 pound dry
¾ pound (3 sticks) unsalted butter, *in all*
2½ cups tasso (preferred) or other smoked ham
(preferably Cure 81), about 11 ounces, thinly sliced
and cut into ½-inch squares
1½ cups very finely chopped green onions
3 cups heavy cream
3½ dozen shucked oysters in their liquor, about 1 pound
(we use medium-size ones)
Finely chopped fresh parsley

Combine the hot water, oil and salt in a large pot over high heat; cover and bring to a boil. When water reaches a rolling boil, add small amounts of spaghetti at a time to the pot, breaking up oil patches as you drop spaghetti in. Return to boiling and cook uncovered to al dente stage (about 4 minutes if fresh, 7 minutes if dry); do not overcook. During this cooking time, use a wooden or spaghetti spoon to lift spaghetti out of the water by spoonfuls and shake strands back into the boiling water. (It may be an old wives' tale, but this procedure seems to enhance the spaghetti's texture.) Then immediately drain spaghetti into a colander; stop its cooking by running cold water over strands. (If you used dry spaghetti, first rinse with hot water to wash off starch.) After the spaghetti has cooled thoroughly, about 2 to 3 minutes, pour a liberal amount of vegetable oil in your hands and toss spaghetti. Set aside still in the colander.

Heat the serving plates in a 250° oven.

Melt 2 *sticks* of the butter with the tasso in a 4-quart saucepan over medium heat; simmer 3 minutes, stirring constantly with a wooden spoon and scraping the pan bottom well. Add the green onions and continue cooking and stirring for 2 minutes. Using a whisk, gradually beat in the cream, whisking constantly until the mixture reaches a boil, about 5 minutes. Add the remaining stick of butter; cook and stir constantly in a "figure-eight" motion until the sauce thickens, about 5 minutes. Add the oysters and liquor and stir until edges curl, about 1 minute. Then add the spaghetti to the sauce and toss with 2 wooden spoons in a turning, oval motion to completely coat the spaghetti. Serve immediately.

To serve, roll a portion of spaghetti onto a large fork and lift onto a heated serving plate. Arrange oysters and tasso on top and sprinkle with parsley.

LAGNIAPPE

To test doneness of spaghetti, cut a strand in half near the end of cooking time. When done, there should be only a speck of white in the center, less than one-fourth the diameter of the strand.

Fried Oysters Bayou Teche

Makes 5 main-dish or 10 appetizer servings

1 large egg, beaten
1 cup milk

Seasoned flour mix:
1 cup all-purpose flour
½ teaspoon salt
½ teaspoon garlic powder
½ teaspoon ground red pepper (preferably cayenne)
½ teaspoon sweet paprika
¼ teaspoon onion powder
¼ teaspoon black pepper
¼ teaspoon dried thyme leaves
¼ teaspoon dried oregano leaves

Bienville Stuffing, chilled (page 230)

10 large oysters, well drained (about 10 ounces in their liquor)
Vegetable oil for deep frying
1 cup heavy cream
3 tablespoons very finely chopped green onions

In a small bowl combine the egg and milk; mix well and set aside. In another bowl combine the flour and seasonings; mix well and set aside.

Reserve ½ cup of the Bienville Stuffing to make the cream sauce. Divide the remaining stuffing into 10 equal portions, about ⅓ cup each. Flatten each portion of stuffing on a well-floured surface to a round patty slightly more than twice the size of each oyster. Place an oyster on one side of each patty, then fold the stuffing in half over each so the oysters are covered. Seal the edges and, with floured hands, gently shape each again into a round patty. Set each patty on a well-floured plate until all have been prepared.

Heat 2 or more inches of oil in a deep fryer or deep-sided skillet to 375°. Meanwhile, dredge each oyster patty in the seasoned flour, then coat it thoroughly in the egg mixture; then just before frying dredge again in the seasoned flour. Fry patties in the hot oil until golden brown and oysters are hot, about 2 minutes. Do not crowd. Drain on paper towels.

For the sauce, bring the cream to a simmer over medium heat in a 1-quart saucepan, whisking frequently with a metal whisk. Add the reserved ½ cup Bienville Stuffing and the green onions. Simmer over low heat, whisking constantly, until sauce is smooth and thickened, about 7 minutes.

Serve immediately, allowing two patties per person for a main course or one for an appetizer; top each patty with about 2 tablespoons sauce.

Shrimp Diane

Color Picture 14

Makes 2 servings

This dish is best if made only two servings at a time. If you want to make more than two servings, do so in separate batches but serve while piping hot.

1¾ pounds medium shrimp with heads and shells (see **Note**)
6 tablespoons, *in all*, **Basic Shrimp Stock** (page 32)
⅜ pound (1½ sticks) unsalted butter, *in all*
¼ cup very finely chopped green onions
¾ teaspoon salt
½ teaspoon minced garlic
½ teaspoon ground red pepper (preferably cayenne)
¼ teaspoon white pepper
¼ teaspoon black pepper
¼ teaspoon dried sweet basil leaves
¼ teaspoon dried thyme leaves
⅛ teaspoon dried oregano leaves
½ pound mushrooms, cut into ¼-inch-thick slices
3 tablespoons very finely chopped fresh parsley
French bread, pasta or hot **Basic Cooked Rice** (page 224)

Note: If shrimp with heads are not available, buy 1 pound of shrimp without heads but with shells for making the stock.

Rinse and peel the shrimp; refrigerate until needed. Use shells and heads to make the shrimp stock.

In a large skillet melt *1 stick* of the butter over high heat. When almost melted, add the green onions, salt, garlic, the ground peppers, basil, thyme and oregano; stir well. Add the shrimp and sauté just until they turn pink, about 1 minute, shaking the pan (versus stirring) in a back-and-forth motion. Add the mushrooms and *¼ cup* of the stock; then add the remaining 4 tablespoons butter in chunks and continue cooking, continuing to shake the pan. Before the butter chunks are completely melted, add the parsley, then the remaining 2 tablespoons stock; continue cooking and shaking the pan until all ingredients are mixed thoroughly and butter sauce is the consistency of cream.

Serve immediately in a bowl with lots of French bread on the side, or serve over pasta or rice.

LAGNIAPPE

A certain percentage of oil is released when butter is melted; shaking the pan in a back-and-forth motion and the addition of stock to the melting butter keep the sauce from separating and having an oily texture—stirring doesn't produce the same effect.

Barbecued Shrimp

Color Picture 15

Makes 2 servings

If you want to make more than two servings of this, do so in separate batches (one recipe fills a large skillet), but serve while piping hot. Be sure to stir the sauce frequently while serving, since it separates easily. To eat this dish, everyone peels his own shrimp at the table (most people use their fingers, although one of our best customers insists on using a knife and fork!) and then stirs the shrimp in the sauce. You can also dip French bread in the sauce.

2 dozen large shrimp with heads and shells (about 1 pound)

Seasoning mix:

1 teaspoon ground red pepper (preferably cayenne)
1 teaspoon black pepper
½ teaspoon salt
½ teaspoon crushed red pepper
½ teaspoon dried thyme leaves
½ teaspoon dried rosemary leaves, crushed
⅛ teaspoon dried oregano leaves

¼ pound (1 stick) plus 5 tablespoons unsalted butter, *in all*
1½ teaspoons minced garlic
1 teaspoon Worcestershire sauce
½ cup **Basic Shrimp Stock** (page 32)
¼ cup beer at room temperature

Rinse the shrimp in cold water and drain well. Then pinch off and discard the portion of the head from the eyes forward (including the eyes, but not the protruding long spine above the eyes). Leave as much as possible of the orange shrimp fat from the head attached to the body. Set aside.

In a small bowl combine the seasoning mix ingredients. Combine *1 stick* of the butter, the garlic, Worcestershire and seasoning mix in a large skillet over high heat. When the butter is melted, add the shrimp. Cook for 2 minutes, shaking the pan (versus stirring) in a back-and-forth motion. Add the remaining 5 tablespoons butter and the stock; cook and shake pan for 2 minutes. Add the beer and cook and shake the pan 1 minute longer. Remove from heat.

Serve immediately in bowls with lots of French bread on the side, or on a platter with cooked rice mounded in the middle and the shrimp and sauce surrounding it.

LAGNIAPPE

A certain percentage of oil is released when butter is melted; shaking the pan in a back-and-forth motion and the addition of stock to the butter keep the sauce from separating and having an oily texture—stirring doesn't produce the same effect.

Garlic Shrimp and Oysters on Pasta

Makes 2 servings

The sauce for this dish is best if made only two servings at a time. If you want to make more than two servings, do so in separate batches but serve while piping hot.

2 quarts hot water
1 tablespoon salt
1 tablespoon vegetable oil
½ pound fresh spaghetti, or ⅓ pound dry

Seasoning mix:
¾ teaspoon salt
½ teaspoon white pepper
½ teaspoon onion powder
½ teaspoon ground red pepper (preferably cayenne)
½ teaspoon sweet paprika
½ teaspoon dried thyme leaves
¼ teaspoon black pepper

⅜ pound (1½ sticks) unsalted butter, *in all*
½ cup chopped green onions
8 peeled medium shrimp (about 3 ounces)
1 tablespoon minced garlic
8 shucked oysters, drained (we use medium-size ones), about 5 ounces
¾ cup warm **Basic Seafood Stock** (page 32)

Combine the hot water, salt and oil in a large pot over high heat; cover and bring to a boil. When water reaches a rolling boil, add small amounts of spaghetti at a time to the pot, breaking up oil patches as you drop spaghetti in. Return to boiling and cook uncovered to al dente stage (about 4 minutes if fresh, 7 minutes if dry); do not overcook. During this cooking time, use a wooden or spaghetti spoon to lift spaghetti out of the water by spoonfuls and shake strands back into the boiling water. (It may be an old wives' tale, but this procedure seems to enhance the spaghetti's texture.) Then immediately drain spaghetti into a colander; stop its cooking by running cold water over strands. (If you used dry spaghetti, first rinse with hot water to wash off starch.) After the spaghetti has cooled thoroughly, about 2 to 3 minutes, pour a liberal amount of vegetable oil in your hands and toss spaghetti. Set aside still in the colander.

Heat the serving plates in a 250° oven.

Combine the seasoning mix ingredients thoroughly in a small bowl and set aside.

Melt *6 tablespoons* of the butter in a large skillet over high heat.

Add the green onions, shrimp, garlic and seasoning mix; cook until shrimp turn pink while vigorously shaking the pan in a back-and-forth motion (versus stirring), about 1 minute. Add the oysters, stock and the remaining 6 tablespoons butter. Cook until butter melts and oysters curl, about 1 minute, continuing to shake the pan. Add the spaghetti; toss and cook the spaghetti just until heated through, about 1 minute. Remove from heat and serve immediately.

For each serving, roll spaghetti on a large fork and place on a heated serving plate. Top with remaining sauce and garnish with the shrimp and oysters.

LAGNIAPPE

To test doneness of spaghetti, cut a strand in half near the end of cooking time. When done, there should be only a speck of white in the center, less than one-fourth the diameter of the strand.

Shaking the pan in a back-and-forth motion and the addition of stock to the melting butter keep the sauce from separating and having an oily texture—stirring doesn't produce the same effect.

Shrimp Sauce Piquant

Makes 8 servings

The sauce is best if made a day or so in advance without the shrimp. When ready to serve, bring the sauce to a boil and add the shrimp.

2 tablespoons unsalted butter
2¼ cups chopped onions
1½ cups chopped green bell peppers
¾ cup chopped celery
3 cups peeled and chopped tomatoes
1 cup canned tomato sauce
3 tablespoons minced jalapeño peppers (see **NOTE**)
2 bay leaves

5½ teaspoons ground red pepper (preferably cayenne)
1½ teaspoons white pepper
1 teaspoon black pepper
1½ teaspoons minced garlic
2¼ cups **Basic Seafood Stock** (page 32)
1½ tablespoons dark brown sugar
¾ teaspoon salt
2 pounds peeled large shrimp
4 cups hot **Basic Cooked Rice** (page 224)

Note: Fresh jalapeños are preferred; if you have to use pickled ones, rinse as much vinegar from them as possible.

Melt the butter in a 4-quart saucepan over high heat. Add the onions, bell peppers and celery; sauté about 2 minutes, stirring occasionally. Add the tomatoes, tomato sauce, jalapeños, bay leaves, ground peppers and garlic; stir well. Continue cooking about 3 minutes, stirring often and scraping the pan bottom well. Stir in the stock, sugar and salt and bring to a boil. Reduce heat and simmer until flavors are married, about 20 minutes, stirring often and scraping pan bottom as needed. (If mixture scorches, quit stirring and pour mixture into a clean pot, leaving the scorched ingredients in the first pan.)

Add the shrimp to the hot (or reheated) sauce and stir. Turn heat up to high, cover pan, and bring mixture to a boil. Remove from heat. Let sit covered for 10 minutes. (Meanwhile, heat the serving plates in a 250° oven.) Stir, remove bay leaves, and serve immediately.

To serve, mound ½ cup rice in the center of each heated serving plate; then pour about ½ cup sauce around the rice and arrange about 8 shrimp on top of the sauce.

LAGNIAPPE

"Piquant" to a Cajun means "it's hot and 'hurts like a sticker in your tongue.'" If you want less "piquant," reduce the jalapeño peppers by half. Sauce Piquant is enjoyed with such gusto in Louisiana that the town of Raceland has a Sauce Piquant Festival every year dedicated to nothing but fish, meat, fowl and seafood made with variations of this sauce.

Seafood Stuffed Shrimp

Makes 6 main-dish or 16 appetizer servings

Seasoning mix:
1½ teaspoons garlic powder
1½ teaspoons ground red pepper (preferably cayenne)
1½ teaspoons black pepper
1½ teaspoons dried sweet basil leaves
¾ teaspoon salt
¾ teaspoon dried oregano leaves

½ pound (2 sticks) plus 5 tablespoons unsalted butter, *in all*
1 cup plus 2 tablespoons finely chopped celery
1 cup plus 2 tablespoons finely chopped green bell peppers
¾ cup finely chopped onions
1 tablespoon minced garlic
¾ cup very fine dry bread crumbs
1 tablespoon Worcestershire sauce
1½ teaspoons Tabasco sauce
1½ cups, packed, crabmeat (picked over), about 9 ounces
4 dozen large peeled shrimp, with tails on, about 1½ pounds

Shrimp seasoning mix:
2 tablespoons plus 1½ teaspoons ground red pepper (preferably cayenne)
1 tablespoon plus 2½ teaspoons salt
1 tablespoon plus ¾ teaspoon sweet paprika
1 tablespoon garlic powder
1 tablespoon black pepper
1¾ teaspoons onion powder
1¾ teaspoons dried thyme leaves
1¾ teaspoons dried oregano leaves

3¾ cups all-purpose flour
2¼ cups milk
2 eggs, beaten
Vegetable oil for deep frying
Tartar Sauce (page 240)

Combine the seasoning mix ingredients in a small bowl; mix well and set aside.

In a large skillet over high heat, melt *2 sticks plus 2 tablespoons* of the butter with the celery, bell peppers, onions and garlic; sauté until vegetables are wilted, about 5 to 7 minutes, stirring occasionally. Turn heat to low and add the seasoning mix, stirring well. Stir in the bread crumbs, Worcestershire and Tabasco. Add the crabmeat and mix thoroughly, breaking up large crabmeat lumps. Turn heat to high and cook 2 minutes, stirring constantly. Remove from heat and continue stirring 1 minute. Stir in the remaining 3 tablespoons butter until melted. Set aside.

Butterfly the shrimp (see Lagniappe). Combine the shrimp seasoning mix in a small bowl and sprinkle the shrimp on both sides with some of the mix, patting it in by hand. In a pan (loaf, cake and pie pans work well) combine the remaining mix with the flour; mix well. In a separate pan, beat the milk and eggs together until well blended. Meanwhile, heat 1 inch oil to 350° in a deep skillet or deep fryer. Dredge each shrimp lightly in the seasoned flour, then, with shrimp open and flat, mound 1 tablespoon crab mixture on top; dredge in the flour again, shaking off excess, then dip in the milk mixture, and then dredge again in the flour. Fry shrimp in the hot oil until golden brown, about 4 minutes. Do not crowd. Drain on paper towels and serve immediately with Tartar Sauce on the side.

LAGNIAPPE

To butterfly shrimp, slice down the length of each shrimp along the center line of the back, cutting as deeply as possible without going all the way through. Remove any exposed vein and open shrimp to lie flat.

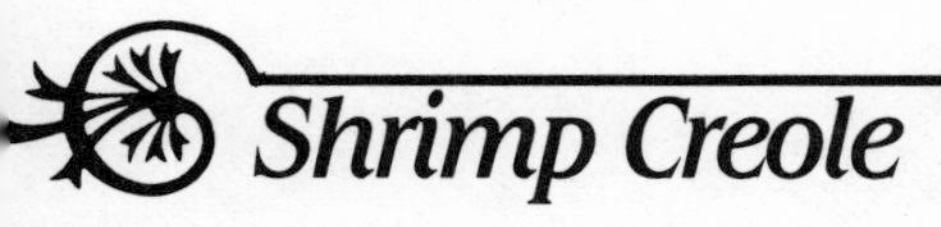

Shrimp Creole

Color Picture 17

Makes 10 servings

Shrimp Creole was created before the days of refrigeration. Like most great dishes of the world, it was made only during the season when fresh ingredients were available—in this case, whole fresh shrimp and Creole tomatoes. The fat in the shrimp heads is an important taste and color contributor. The fresh Creole tomatoes and fresh shrimp fat give the sauce a natural sweetness and an incredible flavor. Browning the onions until caramelized is also an integral part of the dish, as it brings the sugar in the onions to the surface. The use of butter enriches the sauce further, and the red and white ground peppers are important stimulators of the taste buds. The completed sauce may have white specks of shrimp fat in it and should be an antique red color. (In the old days, whole shrimp—heads, tails, shells and all—would go into the pot; then the shrimp fat really did show in the sauce.)

The sauce is best if made a day before serving. Make the shrimp stock first, then the sauce. When ready to serve, skim off the oil from the surface and reheat the sauce to a boil. Lower the heat to very low, add the peeled shrimp tails and cook covered just until the shrimp turn pink, about 5 minutes.

3½ pounds large shrimp with heads and shells, as fatty as possible (see **Note**)
2½ cups, *in all*, **Basic Shrimp Stock** (page 32)
¼ cup chicken fat, pork lard or beef fat
2½ cups finely chopped onions, *in all*
1¾ cups finely chopped celery
1½ cups finely chopped green bell peppers
4 tablespoons unsalted butter
2 teaspoons minced garlic
1 bay leaf
2 teaspoons salt
1½ teaspoons white pepper
1 teaspoon ground red pepper (preferably cayenne)
¾ teaspoon black pepper

1½ teaspoons Tabasco sauce
1 tablespoon dried thyme leaves
1½ teaspoons dried sweet basil leaves
3 cups finely chopped peeled tomatoes (preferably Creole)
1½ cups canned tomato sauce
2 teaspoons sugar
5 cups hot **Basic Cooked Rice** (page 224)

NOTE: Shrimp fat is the orange substance in the heads. If shrimp with heads are not available, buy 2 pounds of shrimp without heads (but with shells for making the stock).

Rinse and peel shrimp; refrigerate until needed. Use heads and shells to make the Basic Shrimp Stock.

Heat the chicken or other fat over high heat in a 4-quart saucepan until melted. Add *1 cup* of the onions and cook over high heat 3 minutes, stirring frequently. Lower the heat to medium-low and continue cooking, stirring frequently, until onions are a rich brown color but not burned, about 3 to 5 minutes. Add the remaining 1½ cups onions, the celery, bell peppers and butter. Cook over high heat until the bell peppers and celery start to get tender, about 5 minutes, stirring occasionally. Add the garlic, bay leaf, salt and peppers; stir well. Then add the Tabasco, thyme, basil and *½ cup* of the stock. Cook over medium heat about 5 minutes to allow seasonings to marry and vegetables to brown further, stirring occasionally and scraping pan bottom well. Add the tomatoes; turn heat to low and simmer 10 minutes, stirring occasionally and scraping pan bottom. Stir in the tomato sauce and simmer 5 minutes, stirring occasionally. Add the remaining 2 cups stock and the sugar. Continue simmering sauce for 15 minutes, stirring occasionally.

Cool and refrigerate if made the day before. Or, if serving immediately, turn heat off and add the shrimp; cover the pot and let sit just until shrimp are plump and pink, about 5 to 10 minutes. Meanwhile, heat the serving plates in a 250° oven. Serve immediately.

To serve, center ½ cup mounded rice on each heated serving plate; spoon 1 cup Shrimp Creole sauce around the rice and arrange 8 or 9 shrimp on the sauce.

7. Fish with Pecan Butter Sauce and Meunière Sauce

8. Sautéed Seafood Platter with Meunière Sauce

9. Seafood Stuffed Whole Fish

10. *Eggplant Bayou Teche*

11. Seafood Stuffed Zucchini with Seafood Cream Sauce

12. Shrimp Etouffée

13. *Crawfish Pie*

14. Shrimp Diane

Crab and Shrimp au Gratin in Eggplant Pirogue

Color Picture 16

Makes 6 servings

The pirogues can be hollowed out ahead of time; cover well and refrigerate until ready to use.

2 medium to large eggplants, peeled
1 cup plus 4 teaspoons all-purpose flour, *in all*
1½ cups very fine dry bread crumbs

Seasoning mix:
1 tablespoon plus 1½ teaspoons salt
1½ teaspoons onion powder
1½ teaspoons garlic powder
¾ teaspoon dry mustard
¾ teaspoon ground red pepper (preferably cayenne)
¾ teaspoon sweet paprika
¾ teaspoon dried sweet basil leaves
½ teaspoon white pepper
¼ teaspoon black pepper

2 eggs
2⅓ cups milk, *in all*
7 tablespoons unsalted butter, *in all*
⅓ cup very finely chopped onions
½ cup heavy cream
1¼ cups grated cheddar cheese
1 bay leaf
Vegetable oil for frying
¾ pound peeled medium shrimp
¾ pound lump crabmeat (picked over)

2 tablespoons plus 1 teaspoon white wine
⅓ cup finely chopped green onions
2 tablespoons finely grated Parmesan cheese (preferably imported)

Cut each eggplant in thirds lengthwise; cut a thin slice from the rounded side of each piece so it will sit level. With a knife and spoon, carve out pulp from inside, leaving a ¼-inch-thick shell (use pulp in another recipe). Set aside. (If you're short of time, substitute a ½-inch-thick lengthwise slice of eggplant for each pirogue.)

Place *1 cup* of the flour in a pan (loaf, cake and pie pans work well) and the bread crumbs in another. In a small bowl thoroughly combine the seasoning mix ingredients. Add *2 teaspoons* of the mix to the flour and *2 teaspoons* to the bread crumbs, mixing each well. In a third pan beat the eggs, then stir in *1 cup* of the milk, blending well.

In a 2-quart saucepan combine *2½ tablespoons* of the butter and the onions; sauté over high heat about 1 minute, stirring frequently. Stir in *1 teaspoon* of the seasoning mix and cook about 1 minute more, stirring frequently and scraping the pan bottom well. Reduce heat to low. Gradually stir in the remaining 4 teaspoons flour, mixing and scraping pan bottom well. Then stir in the remaining 1⅓ cups milk. Return heat to high. Bring mixture to a quick simmer while whisking frequently with a metal whisk (especially as milk heats up, since this is what makes the flour start thickening the mixture). Add the cream and bring to a boil, whisking constantly. Remove from heat and add the cheddar cheese, stirring until melted. Stir in the bay leaf and set this gratin sauce aside.

In a large skillet or deep fryer, heat ¾ inch oil to 350°. Meanwhile, season the eggplant pirogues with a generous amount of seasoning mix (use about *3½ to 4 teaspoons* in all). Just before frying, dredge the pirogues in the seasoned flour, shaking off excess; coat thoroughly with the egg mixture, then dredge in the seasoned bread crumbs (reserve ¼ cup of the remaining bread crumbs). Fry pirogues in the hot oil until golden brown, about 1 to 2 minutes per side (adjust heat as necessary to maintain oil's temperature at about 350°). Do not crowd. Drain on paper towels and set aside.

In a large skillet melt the remaining 4½ tablespoons butter over high heat. Add the shrimp and sauté until plump, about 1 minute, stirring occasionally. Stir in the crabmeat, *2¼ teaspoons* of the seasoning mix (use any leftover mix in another recipe), wine and green onions; continue cooking about 1 minute, stirring occasionally and leaving crabmeat lumps intact as much as possible. Stir in the gratin sauce. Bring mixture to a boil, stirring constantly. Remove from heat and discard bay leaf. Set aside.

In a small bowl combine the reserved ¼ cup seasoned bread crumbs with the Parmesan. Place each fried pirogue on a heatproof serving plate or individual oval gratin dish. Spoon about ¾ cup seafood mixture on top and sprinkle with about 1 tablespoon of the bread crumb mixture. Broil until bread crumbs are browned, about 1 to 2 minutes. Serve immediately.

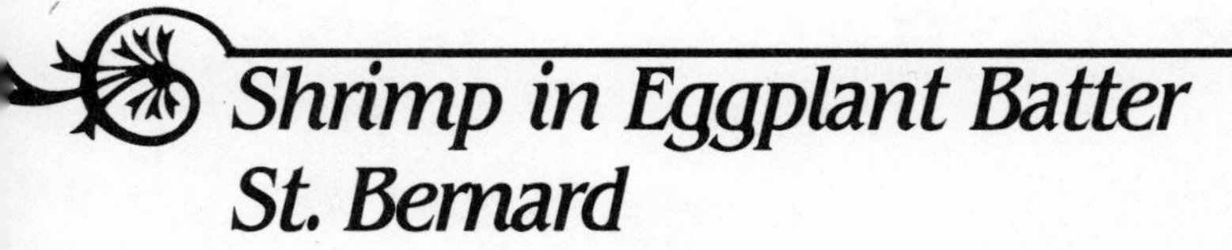

Shrimp in Eggplant Batter St. Bernard

Makes 4 main-dish or 12 appetizer servings

This makes a super hors d'oeuvre but may also be served as an appetizer or main course.

¾ cup beer
4 tablespoons unsalted butter
¼ cup cornmeal
¾ cup all-purpose flour, *in all*
½ cup plus 2 tablespoons corn flour (see **Note**)
2 eggs
½ cup heavy cream
1½ teaspoons ground red pepper (preferably cayenne), *in all*
1 teaspoon salt, *in all*
1 teaspoon onion powder
¾ teaspoon white pepper, *in all*
½ teaspoon garlic powder

3 tablespoons margarine
3 tablespoons vegetable oil
6 cups peeled and chopped eggplant
1 cup finely chopped onions
2 teaspoons minced garlic
1 teaspoon dried thyme leaves
1 teaspoon dried sweet basil leaves
½ teaspoon black pepper
¼ teaspoon dried oregano leaves
2 teaspoons dark brown sugar
½ cup finely chopped green onions

Shrimp seasoning mix:
2 teaspoons ground red pepper (preferably cayenne)
2 teaspoons dried thyme leaves
2 teaspoons dried sweet basil leaves
1½ teaspoons salt
1 teaspoon white pepper
1 teaspoon black pepper
½ teaspoon dried oregano leaves

4 dozen large peeled shrimp with tails on (about 1½ pounds)
Vegetable oil for deep frying
Garlic Mayonnaise (page 270)

NOTE: Corn flour is available at many health food stores.

Place the beer and butter in a small saucepan. Heat over low heat just until the butter melts, about 5 minutes. Remove from heat. Pour into a large mixing bowl with the cornmeal; beat well with a whisk and let sit 5 minutes. Then stir in *¼ cup* of the flour and the corn flour, then the eggs, and then the cream, mixing well after each addition. Add *½ teaspoon* of the red pepper, *¼ teaspoon* of the salt, the onion powder, *¼ teaspoon* of the white pepper and the garlic powder; mix well and set aside.

Place the margarine and 3 tablespoons vegetable oil in a large skillet with the eggplant. Sauté over low heat until eggplant is caramelized (dark in color), about 10 minutes, stirring occasionally. Add the onions and continue cooking 10 minutes, stirring occasionally and scraping pan bottom well. Add the minced garlic, thyme, basil, black pepper, oregano and the remaining 1 teaspoon red pepper, ¾ teaspoon salt and ½ teaspoon white pepper; stir well. Lower heat and continue cooking 5 minutes, stirring occasionally and scraping pan bottom as needed. Stir in the sugar and cook 3 minutes more, stirring occasionally. Stir in the green onions and continue cooking and stirring 2 minutes. Add the eggplant mixture to the bowl of cornmeal mixture; beat with a whisk until well mixed; set batter aside.

Combine ingredients of shrimp seasoning mix in a small bowl. In another small bowl combine *1 teaspoon* of the seasoning mix with the remaining ½ cup flour. Use the remaining seasoning mix to season the shrimp, sprinkling it evenly on each side.

In a deep skillet or deep fryer, heat 4 inches of oil to 350°. Meanwhile, dredge the shrimp in the seasoned flour, shaking off excess. Then coat the shrimp well with the batter. Fry until dark golden brown, about 1 minute per side. Do not crowd. Serve immediately with Garlic Mayonnaise on the side.

Eggplant Filled with Shrimp (or Crawfish) with Oyster Sauce

Makes 6 servings

The carved eggplant bowls and lids make a spectacular presentation, and you can prepare them a few hours ahead. If you prefer, substitute two peeled eggplant slices 1 inch thick and serve the stuffing between the slices like a sandwich, topped with the oyster sauce.

First seasoning mix:
2 whole bay leaves
1 teaspoon salt
¾ teaspoon ground red pepper (preferably cayenne)

½ teaspoon white pepper
½ teaspoon black pepper
½ teaspoon dried thyme leaves

3 plump eggplants (about 12 inches in circumference or 4 inches in diameter)
½ pound (2 sticks) unsalted butter, *in all*
1 cup chopped onions
½ cup chopped celery
½ cup chopped green bell peppers
1 pound peeled small shrimp or crawfish tails
1½ cups, *in all*, **Basic Seafood Stock** (page 32) or oyster water (see **NOTE**)
½ cup very finely chopped onions
1 teaspoon salt
¾ teaspoon white pepper
½ teaspoon ground red pepper (preferably cayenne)
½ teaspoon dried sweet basil leaves
⅛ teaspoon ground nutmeg
1 teaspoon lemon juice
¾ teaspoon minced garlic
1⅓ cups all-purpose flour, *in all*
1 cup heavy cream
3 dozen medium to large oysters in their liquor (about 1¾ pounds)
½ cup finely chopped green onions
1¼ cups very fine dry bread crumbs
1 cup milk
2 small eggs or 1 large egg

Second seasoning mix:
2 teaspoons salt
1½ teaspoons white pepper
1 teaspoon dry mustard
1 teaspoon ground red pepper (preferably cayenne)
1 teaspoon sweet paprika
¾ teaspoon onion powder
¾ teaspoon garlic powder

Vegetable oil for frying

NOTE: To make oyster water, add 1 cup cold water to the oysters; stir and refrigerate for 1 hour. Strain and reserve oysters and oyster water in the refrigerator until ready to use.

Combine the first seasoning mix ingredients thoroughly in a small bowl and set aside.

Remove stems from eggplants and discard. Cut each eggplant in half crosswise (not lengthwise). Then cut a 1½-inch slice from the cut end of each eggplant half. Peel each slice, then with a paring knife and spoon carefully carve out the center meat to form a bowl with walls and bottom ¼ inch thick, reserving the carved-out pulp. (The largest side of the slice should be the bowl's bottom. It's easiest to carve the bowl if you first insert the knife ¼ inch away from the edge all the way around to carve the walls.) Chop any large pieces of the reserved pulp. Peel the remaining end pieces of the eggplants (shape slightly if necessary) to form rounded lids no thicker than 1 to 1½ inches for the bowls. Set the bowls and lids aside.

Place the eggplant pulp in a 4-quart saucepan with *1 stick* of the butter, the 1 cup onions, the celery and bell peppers. Cook over high heat about 3 minutes, stirring occasionally. Add the first seasoning mix; stir well and continue cooking 5 minutes more, stirring occasionally and scraping pan bottom well. Add the shrimp or crawfish; cook about 2 minutes, stirring occasionally. Add *½ cup* of the stock (or oyster water) and cook 2 minutes more. Remove shrimp stuffing from heat and set aside.

In a 2-quart saucepan melt the remaining 1 stick butter over medium-low heat. Add the ½ cup finely chopped onions, the salt, white and red peppers, basil, nutmeg, lemon juice and garlic. Sauté about 4 minutes, stirring often. Stir in *⅓ cup* of the flour until well blended, then stir in the remaining 1 cup stock. Turn heat to high and bring to a boil, whisking frequently with a metal whisk. Continue cooking until mixture is gravy thick, about 1 minute, whisking constantly. Add the cream and return mixture to a rolling boil, whisking frequently. Reduce heat to a simmer and cook 3 to 5 minutes, stirring frequently so mixture doesn't stick. Stir in the oysters (drain them again if more oyster water has accumulated) and green onions; return heat to high and cook until oysters are reduced to about one-half in size, about 4 to 6 minutes, stirring frequently. Remove from heat.

Heat the serving plates in a 250° oven.

Place the remaining 1 cup flour, the bread crumbs and the milk in three separate pans (loaf, cake and pie pans work well). Add the egg(s) to the milk, blending well with a metal whisk. In a small bowl, thoroughly combine the second seasoning mix ingredients. Add *2 teaspoons* of the seasoning mix to the flour and *1 tablespoon* to the bread crumbs, combining each mixture well. Sprinkle the remaining seasoning mix on both sides of each eggplant bowl and lid.

Heat 1 inch oil in a large skillet or deep fryer to 350°. Dredge the eggplant bowls and lids well in the seasoned flour, shaking off excess, then coat with the milk mixture. Just before frying, dredge in the bread crumbs, shaking off excess. Fry in the hot oil until golden brown, about 1 to 2 minutes per side (adjust heat as necessary to maintain oil's temperature at about 350°). Do not crowd. Drain on paper towels and serve immediately.

To serve, spoon ¼ cup oyster sauce (without oysters) on each heated serving plate; place an eggplant bowl on top of the sauce, then spoon in about ¾ cup shrimp or crawfish stuffing; top with 2 tablespoons more sauce and an eggplant lid, and arrange 6 oysters on the plate. (Any leftover sauce is super over vegetables, pan-fried fish or veal.)

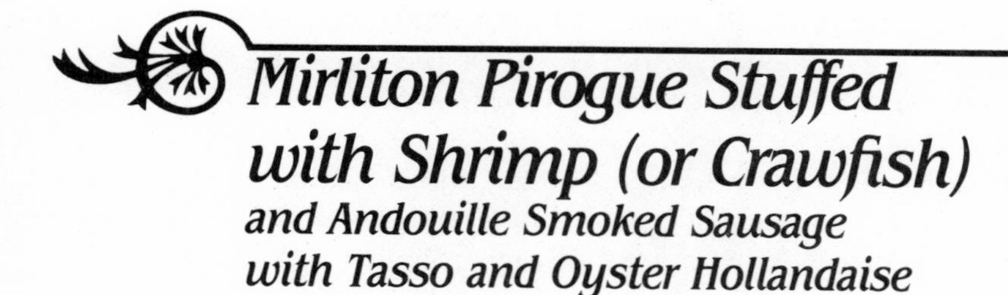

Mirliton Pirogue Stuffed with Shrimp (or Crawfish)

and Andouille Smoked Sausage with Tasso and Oyster Hollandaise

Color Picture 19

Makes 6 servings

The pirogues can be hollowed out ahead of time; cover well and refrigerate until ready to use.

3 large mirlitons (chayotes)
½ cup milk
1 egg, beaten
½ cup all-purpose flour
½ cup very fine dry bread crumbs

Seasoning mix:
1 tablespoon salt
1 teaspoon white pepper
1 teaspoon dry mustard
¾ teaspoon garlic powder
½ teaspoon onion powder
½ teaspoon ground red pepper (preferably cayenne)
½ teaspoon black pepper
½ teaspoon dried sweet basil leaves

Vegetable oil for deep frying
Tasso and Oyster Hollandaise Sauce (recipe follows)
3 tablespoons unsalted butter
1 cup chopped andouille smoked sausage (preferred) or any other good pure smoked pork sausage such as Polish sausage (kielbasa), about ¼ pound
1 pound large peeled shrimp or crawfish tails

Boil the mirlitons just until fork tender. Cool, then cut each in half lengthwise; peel and remove seed (eat or save to put in a salad). Carefully scoop pulp out with a spoon, leaving about a ¼-inch-thick shell. Coarsely chop the pulp and reserve for the stuffing.

In a pan (loaf, cake and pie pans work well) combine the milk and egg until well blended. Place the flour in a separate pan and the bread crumbs in another. Combine the seasoning mix ingredients in a small bowl; mix well. Add 2 *teaspoons* of the mix to the flour and 2 *teaspoons* to the bread crumbs, mixing each well. Season both sides of the mirliton halves by sprinkling with *2½ teaspoons* of the seasoning mix.

Heat 1 inch of oil in a large skillet (or use a deep fryer) to 350°. Meanwhile, dredge the mirlitons in the flour, shaking off excess; coat well with the egg wash, then, just before frying, dredge lightly in the bread crumbs. Fry the mirliton halves in the hot oil until golden brown, about 1 to 2 minutes per side. Drain on paper towels and keep warm with the serving plates in a 200° oven.

Make the Tasso and Oyster Hollandaise Sauce and set aside in a warm place. (Reserve 2 tablespoons of oyster liquor; see recipe.)

In a large skillet, melt the butter over high heat. Add the andouille and reserved mirliton pulp; sauté until browned, about 5 minutes, stirring occasionally and scraping the pan bottom well. Add the shrimp or crawfish and remaining seasoning mix. Continue cooking just until shrimp or crawfish are plump and cooked, about 3 minutes, stirring frequently. Pour in the reserved 2 tablespoons oyster liquor from the hollandaise and cook 1 minute more, stirring constantly. Serve immediately.

To serve, place one mirliton half on each warmed serving plate. With a slotted spoon place about ⅔ cup slightly drained shrimp mixture in it. Then arrange about 6 more shrimp (or several crawfish) on top, and pour a generous ⅓ cup hollandaise sauce over all. (The left-over hollandaise is great to dunk bread in with this meal.)

Tasso and Oyster Hollandaise Sauce

1 dozen medium to large oysters in their liquor (about 10 ounces)
1 pound unsalted butter
4 tablespoons margarine
4 egg yolks
2 teaspoons white wine
2 teaspoons lemon juice
½ teaspoon Tabasco sauce
½ teaspoon Worcestershire sauce
3 tablespoons finely chopped tasso (preferred) or other smoked ham (preferably Cure 81)

Place the oysters and their liquor in a small saucepan over high heat; cook until plump and edges curl, about 2 minutes, stirring once or twice. Remove from heat, drain oysters (reserve 2 tablespoons liquid to make the Shrimp and Andouille Stuffing), and cool. Then slice each oyster across into as many thin slices as possible.

Melt the butter and margarine in a 1-quart saucepan over low heat. Raise heat and bring to a rapid boil, then immediately remove from heat and cool 5 minutes. Skim froth from the top and discard. Pour butter into a large glass measuring cup and set aside.

Meanwhile, in a medium-size stainless steel mixing bowl or in the top of a double boiler, combine the remaining ingredients, except for the oysters. Mix together with a metal whisk until blended.

Place bowl over a pan of slowly simmering (not boiling) water. (Bowl must never touch the water.) Vigorously whisk the egg mixture, picking up the bowl frequently to let the steam escape; whip until the egg mixture is very light and creamy and has a sheen, about 5 minutes. (This amount of beating is important so that the cooked eggs will better be able to hold the butter.) Remove bowl from the pan of hot water. Gradually ladle about ¼ cup of the butter mixture (use the top butterfat, not the butter solids on the bottom) into the egg mixture while vigorously whipping the sauce; make sure the butter you add is well mixed into the sauce before adding more. Continue gradually adding the surface butterfat until you've added about 1 cup.

So that you can get to the butter solids, ladle out and reserve about ½ cup surface butterfat in a separate container. (The butter solids add flavor and also thin the sauce.) Gradually ladle all but ½ cup of the bottom solids into the sauce, whisking well. (Use any remaining bottom solids in another dish.) Then gradually whisk in enough of the reserved top butterfat to produce a fairly thick sauce. (The butterfat thickens the sauce, so you may not need to use it all.) Stir in the oysters. Keep the sauce in a warm place (such as on top of the stove) until ready to serve. Makes 3 cups.

BEEF, VEAL & LAMB

Louisiana Roast Beef

Makes 6 to 8 servings

¼ cup very finely chopped onions
¼ cup very finely chopped celery
¼ cup very finely chopped green bell peppers
2 tablespoons unsalted butter or margarine, melted, or
vegetable oil
1 teaspoon salt
1 teaspoon white pepper
¾ teaspoon black pepper
¾ teaspoon minced garlic
½ teaspoon dry mustard
½ teaspoon ground red pepper (preferably cayenne)
1 (3½- to 4-pound) boneless sirloin roast, top round roast,
or any good-quality beef roast with a layer of fat on top

In a small bowl combine the onions, celery, bell peppers, butter and seasonings, mixing well.

Place the roast in a large roasting pan, fat side up. With a large knife make 6 to 12 deep slits in the meat (to form pockets) down to a depth of about ½ inch from the bottom; do not cut all the way through. Fill the pockets to their depths with the vegetable mixture, reserving about 1 tablespoon of the vegetables to rub over the top of the roast. Bake uncovered at 300° until a meat thermometer reads 160° for medium doneness, about 3 hours. (For rarer roast, cook until thermometer reads 140°.) Serve immediately, topped with some of the pan drippings if you like.

Cajun Prime Rib

Makes 6 servings

This is so good it'll make your toes curl! Have the butcher crack the ribs when you buy the meat. Once the rib roast is prepared and cut into steaks, you can season them with this terrific seasoning mix, or not, as you prefer, and pan broil them or grill them indoors or out in your favorite way. Or "blacken" them, using the seasoning mix.

1 (4-bone) prime rib of beef roast, about 10½ pounds
About ¼ cup black pepper
About ¼ cup garlic powder
About ¼ cup salt
2 medium onions, thinly sliced

Seasoning mix (optional):
1 tablespoon plus 2 teaspoons salt
1 tablespoon plus 2 teaspoons white pepper
1 tablespoon plus 2 teaspoons whole fennel seeds
1 tablespoon plus ¾ teaspoon black pepper
2½ teaspoons dry mustard
2½ teaspoons ground red pepper (preferably cayenne)

Remove fat cap off top of meat (butcher can do this for you) and save. Place the roast, standing on the rib bones, in a very large roasting pan. Then with a knife make several dozen punctures through the silver skin so seasoning can permeate meat. Pour a very generous, even layer of black pepper over the top of the meat (the pepper should completely cover it); repeat with the garlic powder, then the salt, totally covering the preceding layer. Carefully arrange the onions in an even layer on top so as not to knock off the seasoning. Place the fat cap back on top. Refrigerate 24 hours.

Bake ribs in a 550° oven until the fat is dark brown and crispy on top, about 35 minutes. Remove from oven and cool slightly. Refrigerate until well chilled, about 3 hours. (This is done so the juices will solidify and the steaks can be cooked rare.)

Remove fat cap and discard. With the blade of a large knife, scrape off the onions and as much of the seasonings as possible and discard. Then with a long knife, slice between ribs into 6 steaks (4 will have bones); trim the cooked surface of meat from the 2 pieces that were on the outside of the roast. Season and cook in your favorite way for steaks.

To "blacken" the steaks: Combine the ingredients of the seasoning mix thoroughly in a small bowl; you will have about 8 tablespoons. Sprinkle the steaks generously and evenly on both sides with the mix, using about 4 teaspoons on each steak and pressing it in with your hands.

Heat a cast-iron skillet over very high heat until it is beyond the smoking stage and you see white ash in the skillet bottom—at least 10 minutes. (The skillet cannot be too hot for this method.) Place one steak in the hot skillet (cook only one steak at a time) and cook over very high heat until the underside starts to develop a heavy, black crust, about 2 to 3 minutes. Turn the steak over and cook until the underside is crusted like the first, about 2 to 3 minutes more. Repeat with remaining steaks. Serve each steak while piping hot. (**Note:** If you don't have a commercial hood vent over your stove, this dish may smoke you out of the kitchen. It's worth it! But you can also cook it outdoors on a gas grill; a charcoal fire doesn't get hot enough to "blacken" the steak properly.)

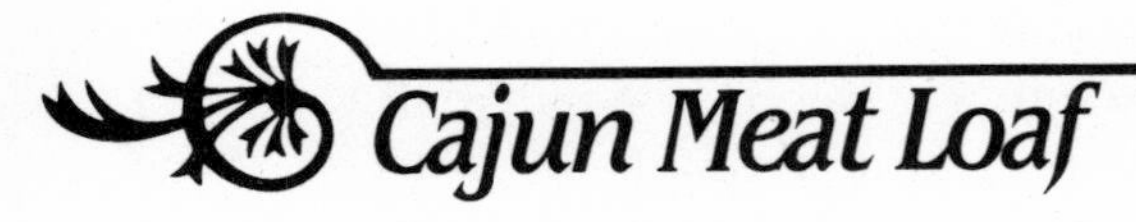

Cajun Meat Loaf

Makes 6 servings

This is best using both ground pork and ground beef, as the pork gives more flavor diversity. However, you can make it with ground beef only.

Seasoning mix:
2 whole bay leaves
1 tablespoon salt
1 teaspoon ground red pepper (preferably cayenne)

1 teaspoon black pepper
½ teaspoon white pepper
½ teaspoon ground cumin
½ teaspoon ground nutmeg

4 tablespoons unsalted butter
¾ cup finely chopped onions
½ cup finely chopped celery
½ cup finely chopped green bell peppers
¼ cup finely chopped green onions
2 teaspoons minced garlic
1 tablespoon Tabasco sauce
1 tablespoon Worcestershire sauce
½ cup evaporated milk
½ cup catsup
1½ pounds ground beef
½ pound ground pork
2 eggs, lightly beaten
1 cup very fine dry bread crumbs

Combine the seasoning mix ingredients in a small bowl and set aside.

Melt the butter in a 1-quart saucepan over medium heat. Add the onions, celery, bell peppers, green onions, garlic, Tabasco, Worcestershire and seasoning mix. Sauté until mixture starts sticking excessively, about 6 minutes, stirring occasionally and scraping the pan bottom well. Stir in the milk and catsup. Continue cooking for about 2 minutes, stirring occasionally. Remove from heat and allow mixture to cool to room temperature.

Place the ground beef and pork in an ungreased 13x9-inch baking pan. Add the eggs, the cooked vegetable mixture, removing the bay leaves, and the bread crumbs. Mix by hand until thoroughly combined. In the center of the pan, shape the mixture into a loaf that is about 1½ inches high, 6 inches wide and 12 inches long. Bake uncovered at 350° for 25 minutes, then raise heat to 400° and continue cooking until done, about 35 minutes longer. Serve immediately as is or with **Very Hot Cajun Sauce for Beef** (page 251).

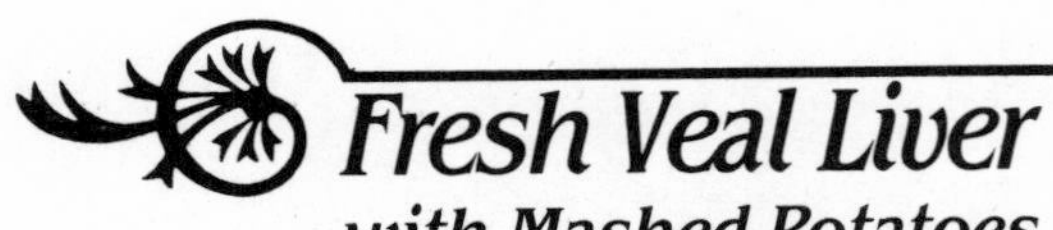

Fresh Veal Liver
with Mashed Potatoes, Smothered Onions and Bacon

Makes 6 servings

The liver is pan fried in this dish. See page 25 for more about pan frying.

18 slices bacon
2 pounds white potatoes, peeled and quartered
¾ cup evaporated milk
½ pound (2 sticks) unsalted butter
1 teaspoon salt
1 teaspoon white pepper

Seasoning mix:
1 tablespoon salt
1½ teaspoons sweet paprika
1 teaspoon onion powder
1 teaspoon garlic powder
1 teaspoon ground red pepper (preferably cayenne)
½ teaspoon white pepper
½ teaspoon dried thyme leaves
¼ teaspoon black pepper

1 cup raw wheat germ (see **Note**)
6 (6-ounce) slices fresh veal liver
Vegetable oil for frying
3 cups thinly sliced onions

Note: Raw wheat germ is available from health food and gourmet grocery stores.

Fry the bacon in a large heavy skillet until crisp. Drain on paper towels. Reserve the skillet with the bacon drippings.

Meanwhile, boil the potatoes until fork tender. Drain while still hot, reserving 1 cup water. Place the hot potatoes in a large bowl with the milk, butter, salt and white pepper. Stir with a wooden spoon until broken up, then beat with a metal whisk (or electric mixer with a paddle) until creamy and smooth. (If the potatoes are not velvety creamy, mix in up to 1 cup of the reserved water.) Set aside.

Heat the serving plates in a 250° oven.

Thoroughly combine the seasoning mix ingredients in a small bowl. In a pan (loaf, cake and pie pans work well), combine *2 teaspoons* of the mix with the wheat germ, mixing well; set aside. Sprinkle the liver on both sides with a total of *5 teaspoons* of the seasoning mix.

Pour off ¼ cup of the bacon drippings from the skillet and set aside. Add enough oil to the remaining drippings to have about ¼ inch in the skillet bottom. Heat the drippings to about 300°. Dredge liver in the seasoned wheat germ, shaking off excess. Fry the liver in the hot oil until browned, about 2 minutes per side. (Remove any burned wheat germ sediment as it accumulates in the pan.) Remove meat (undrained) to heated serving plates and set aside.

In a separate skillet heat the reserved bacon drippings over high heat until they begin to smoke. Add the onions and the remaining seasoning mix; stir well and sauté until caramelized (a rich dark color), about 5 minutes, stirring frequently. Remove from heat and serve immediately.

To serve, spoon about 2 tablespoons drained onions (use a slotted spoon) over each piece of liver and arrange 3 slices of bacon on top. Spoon a portion of mashed potatoes to the side of the liver.

Panéed Veal and Fettucini

Color Picture 18

Makes 6 servings

For more about pan frying, see page 25.

4 quarts hot water
2 tablespoons vegetable oil
1 tablespoon salt

¾ pound fresh fettucini, or ½ pound dry
½ pound (2 sticks) unsalted butter
2½ cups heavy cream
½ teaspoon ground red pepper (preferably cayenne), or less for the faint of heart
¾ cup plus 4 teaspoons, *in all*, finely grated Parmesan cheese (preferably imported)
1¾ cups very fine dry bread crumbs
1½ tablespoons minced fresh parsley
1½ tablespoons olive oil
¾ teaspoon white pepper
½ teaspoon onion powder
½ teaspoon garlic powder
3 eggs
6 (3½- to 4-ounce) slices of baby white veal, pounded thin
Vegetable oil for pan frying

Place the water, the 2 tablespoons oil and the salt in a large pot over high heat; cover and bring to a boil. When water reaches a rolling boil, add small amounts of fettucini at a time to the pot, breaking up oil patches as you drop it in. Return to boiling and cook uncovered to al dente stage (about 3 minutes if fresh pasta, 7 minutes if dry); do not overcook. During this cooking time, use a wooden or spaghetti spoon to lift fettucini out of the water by spoonfuls and shake strands back into the water. (It may be an old wives' tale, but this procedure seems to enhance the pasta's texture.) Then immediately drain in a colander and stop its cooking by running cold water over strands (if you used dry pasta, first rinse with hot water to wash off starch); after it has cooled thoroughly, about 2 to 3 minutes, pour a liberal amount of vegetable oil in your hands and toss fettucini. Set aside still in the colander.

Melt the butter in a large skillet over medium-low heat; add the cream and red pepper. Turn heat to medium-high. With a metal whisk whip the cream mixture constantly as it comes to a boil. Then reduce heat and simmer until the sauce has reduced some and thickened enough to coat a spoon well, about 7 to 8 minutes, whisking constantly. Remove from heat and gradually add *¾ cup* of the Parmesan, whisking until cheese is melted. Set aside.

Heat 6 large serving plates in a 250° oven.

In a shallow pan (cake and pie pans work well) combine the bread crumbs, parsley, olive oil, white pepper, onion and garlic; mix well. In a separate pan beat the eggs well, then beat in the remaining 4 teaspoons Parmesan. Soak the veal in the egg mixture for at least 5 minutes, being sure to coat it thoroughly. Meanwhile, heat ¼ inch oil to about 400° in a large skillet. Then just before frying, dredge veal in the bread crumbs, coating well and pressing the crumbs in with your hands; shake off any excess. Fry the veal in the hot oil until golden brown, about 1 minute per side. Do not crowd. (Change the oil midway through frying if the crumbs in the bottom start to burn.) Remove veal to a large platter and set aside.

Reheat the cheese sauce over medium-high heat, whisking frequently. (**Note:** If butter starts separating from the sauce, whisk in about 1 tablespoon cream or water.) Add the fettucini and toss until thoroughly coated and heated through, about 1 minute. Remove from heat and serve immediately.

To serve, place a piece of veal on each heated serving plate. Roll each portion of fettucini onto a large fork and lift onto the plate; top the fettucini with additional sauce from the skillet.

LAGNIAPPE

To test the doneness of fettucini, cut a strand in half near the end of the cooking time. When done, there should be only a speck of white in the center.

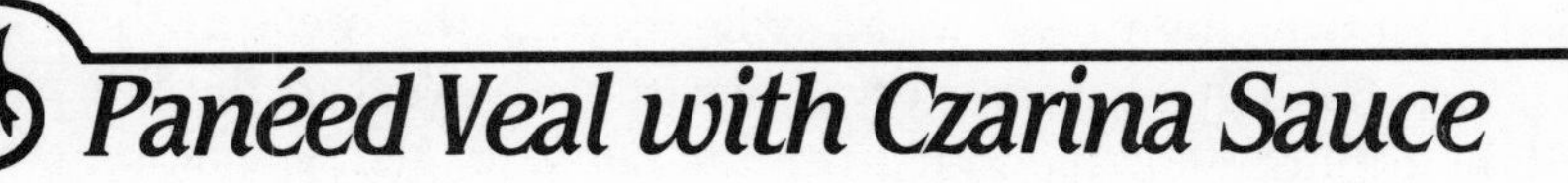

Panéed Veal with Czarina Sauce

Makes 6 servings

The veal in this dish is pan fried. *See page 25 for more about pan frying.*

Seasoning mix:
2¼ teaspoons salt
1¼ teaspoons sweet paprika

¾ teaspoon onion powder
½ teaspoon ground red pepper (preferably cayenne)
¼ teaspoon white pepper
¼ teaspoon garlic powder
¼ teaspoon dry mustard

6 (4-ounce) slices baby white veal, pounded until flat and even
¾ cup all-purpose flour
6 tablespoons unsalted butter, *in all*
4 tablespoons vegetable oil, *in all*
¾ cup julienned onions (see **NOTE**)
¾ cup julienned zucchini (see **NOTE**)
¾ cup julienned yellow squash (see **NOTE**)
1½ teaspoons lemon juice
1 cup heavy cream
¼ pound peeled crawfish tails or small shrimp
¼ cup finely grated Parmesan cheese (preferably imported)

NOTE: To julienne squashes, cut peelings ⅛ inch thick and cut these into strips ⅛ inch wide and 2 inches long; use only strips that have skin on one surface. Cut onions into similar strips.

In a small bowl combine the seasoning mix ingredients; mix well. Sprinkle each slice of veal with seasoning mix, using *¼ teaspoon* on each piece. In a pan (loaf, cake and pie pans work well) thoroughly mix *1 tablespoon* of the seasoning mix into the flour.

In a large skillet melt *2 tablespoons* of the butter with *2 tablespoons* of the oil over high heat. Meanwhile, dredge the meat in the seasoned flour, shaking off excess. Fry 3 pieces of the veal in the hot butter and oil until browned, about 1 minute per side, gently shaking the pan in a back-and-forth motion to keep the butter from burning. Remove meat from skillet to a platter (not on paper towels) and set aside. Drain and wipe skillet with a paper towel, then add *2 tablespoons* more *each* of butter and oil to the skillet and repeat with the remaining veal. Place the veal and serving plates in a 200° oven to keep warm.

Over high heat sauté the onions, zucchini and yellow squash in the butter-oil mixture left in skillet about 2 minutes, stirring frequently. Add the lemon juice, the remaining 2 tablespoons butter, the remaining seasoning mix and the cream. Bring to a simmer, stirring occasionally. Add the crawfish or shrimp and cook 1 minute, stirring once or twice. Then add the Parmesan and continue cooking just until the cheese is melted and the seafood cooked through, about 1 to 2 minutes. (If sauce starts to separate, add 1 or 2 tablespoons water and stir until sauce is smooth.) Remove from heat and serve immediately.

To serve, place each piece of veal on a heated serving plate and top with a portion of the sauce.

Cajun Shepherd's Pie

Color Picture 20

Makes 6 Cajun servings or 8 "no-fat-fad" servings

1½ pounds ground beef
½ pound ground pork
2 eggs, lightly beaten
½ cup very fine dry bread crumbs
¼ pound (1 stick) plus 3 tablespoons unsalted butter, *in all*
¾ cup finely chopped onions
¾ cup finely chopped celery
½ cup finely chopped green bell peppers
1 tablespoon plus 1 teaspoon minced garlic
1 tablespoon Worcestershire sauce
½ teaspoon Tabasco sauce

Meat seasoning mix:
2 teaspoons ground red pepper (preferably cayenne)
1½ teaspoons salt
1½ teaspoons black pepper
1¼ teaspoons white pepper
¾ teaspoon ground cumin
¾ teaspoon dried thyme leaves

¾ cup evaporated milk, *in all*
2 pounds white potatoes, peeled and quartered
1 teaspoon salt
1 teaspoon white pepper
1½ cups julienned carrots (see **Note**)
1 cup julienned onions (see **Note**)

Vegetable seasoning mix:
½ teaspoon salt
¼ teaspoon white pepper
¼ teaspoon onion powder
¼ teaspoon garlic powder
¼ teaspoon ground red pepper (preferably cayenne)

1½ cups julienned zucchini (see **Note**)
1 cup julienned yellow squash (see **Note**)
Very Hot Cajun Sauce for Beef (page 251)

Note: To julienne squashes, cut peelings ⅛ inch thick and cut these into strips ⅛ inch wide and 2 inches long; use only strips that have skin on one surface. Cut carrots and onions into similar strips.

In a 13x9-inch ungreased baking pan, combine the beef and pork. Mix in the eggs and bread crumbs by hand until thoroughly mixed. Set aside.

In a 1-quart saucepan, combine *3 tablespoons* of the butter, the onions, celery, bell peppers, garlic, Worcestershire, Tabasco and meat seasoning mix. Sauté over high heat about 5 minutes, stirring frequently and scraping the pan bottom well. Remove from heat and cool. Add the sautéed vegetable mixture and *¼ cup* of the milk to the meat and mix well by hand. Form into a 12x8-inch loaf and center in the pan. Bake at 450° until brown on top, about 30 minutes. Remove from oven; pour off drippings, reserving 2½ tablespoons. Set meat and drippings aside.

Meanwhile, boil the potatoes until fork tender; drain, reserving about 1 cup of the water. Place the potatoes, while still hot, in a large mixing bowl with the remaining 1 stick butter, ½ cup milk, the salt and white pepper. Stir with a wooden spoon until broken up, then beat with a metal whisk (or electric mixer with a paddle) until creamy and velvety smooth. (**Note:** Mix in some of the reserved potato water if potatoes are not creamy enough.)

In a large skillet (preferably nonstick) combine the reserved drippings with the carrots, onions and vegetable seasoning mix; sauté over high heat 1½ minutes, stirring frequently. Add the zucchini and yellow squash and continue sautéing until vegetables are noticeably brighter in color, about 3 to 4 minutes, stirring occasionally. Remove from heat.

Mound undrained vegetables on top of the meat loaf, away from the edges. Layer the mashed potatoes evenly over the top of the vegetables and top edges of the meat, using all the potatoes. Bake at 525° until brown on top, about 8 to 10 minutes. Serve immediately with about ½ cup Very Hot Cajun Sauce under each serving.

Paulette's Wonderful Meat Pie

Makes 6 main-dish or 12 appetizer servings

Dough:
¼ cup sugar
4 tablespoons unsalted butter, slightly softened
Heaping ¼ teaspoon salt
1 small egg, well beaten
2 tablespoons plus 2 teaspoons cold milk
1⅓ cups all-purpose flour

Filling:
¼ pound (1 stick) margarine
1 cup finely chopped onions
½ cup finely chopped celery
⅓ pound ground pork
2 teaspoons minced garlic
1 tablespoon chopped fresh thyme (all stems removed), or
¾ teaspoon dried thyme leaves
2 teaspoons ground red pepper (preferably cayenne)
1½ teaspoons black pepper
1¼ teaspoons salt
1¼ teaspoons sweet paprika

1 teaspoon dried sweet basil leaves
⅓ pound ground beef
1½ cups, packed, coarsely grated unpeeled red potatoes (about 6 ounces)
1 cup **Basic Beef** or **Pork Stock** (page 31)

Topping:

1 (8-ounce) package cream cheese, softened
¾ cup heavy cream
1 tablespoon very finely chopped fresh oregano, or ¾ teaspoon dried oregano leaves
1 tablespoon chopped fresh thyme (all stems removed), or ¾ teaspoon dried thyme leaves

To make the dough: Place the sugar, butter and salt in the bowl of an electric mixer or food processor. Beat on high speed just until the mixture is creamy, about 30 seconds. Add the egg and milk and beat until blended. Add the flour and beat just until blended (overmixing will produce a tough dough). With floured hands, mold the dough into a round, flat patty. Lightly dust the patty with flour and cover; let sit at least 1 hour before rolling out. (The dough will keep up to one week in the refrigerator. Let the dough come to room temperature before rolling out.)

To make the filling: Melt the margarine in a large skillet. Add the onions and celery and sauté over high heat until wilted, about 4 minutes, stirring occasionally. Reduce heat to medium and add the pork, garlic and seasonings. Cook about 4 minutes, stirring often, breaking up chunks of meat and scraping pan bottom well. (Lower the heat further if the onions begin to get dark brown.) Add the beef and mix thoroughly. Lower the heat and simmer about 5 minutes, stirring frequently and scraping pan bottom well. Stir in the potatoes and stock. Cook about 10 minutes over medium-low heat, stirring frequently. Using a strainer, drain the mixture very well and let cool at least 15 minutes before filling the pie dough. (If made ahead of time, refrigerate, reheat and drain when ready to assemble the pie.)

On a lightly floured surface, roll out the dough to fit an 8-inch round cake pan (1½ inches deep); the dough should be ¼ inch thick. Fit the dough into the greased and floured cake pan, pressing sides and bottom firmly to fit the pan. Trim the edges even with the pan top. Refrigerate 15 minutes.

Arrange pie weights or dried beans evenly on top of the dough. Bake at 350° for 20 minutes. Remove the weights and bake 15 minutes more, or just until the crust on bottom looks dry. Cool 5 minutes.

To make the topping: Beat the ingredients in a small bowl of an electric mixer until smooth and thoroughly blended.

Spoon the meat filling into the cake pan; spread the cheese topping over the filling, being careful not to get any filling into the topping. Bake at 350° until crust is golden brown, about 40 to 45 minutes. Cool about 10 minutes before serving.

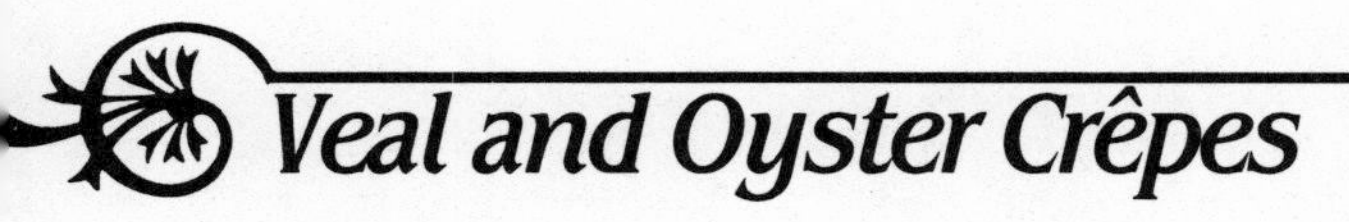

Veal and Oyster Crêpes

Makes 4 servings

8 **Crêpes** (recipe follows)
2 dozen small to medium oysters in their liquor, about ¾ pound
2 cups cold water

Seasoned flour mix:
½ cup all-purpose flour
1 teaspoon salt
½ teaspoon white pepper
¼ teaspoon ground red pepper (preferably cayenne)
¼ teaspoon onion powder
¼ teaspoon black pepper
¼ teaspoon dry mustard

Veal seasoning mix:
½ teaspoon salt
¼ teaspoon white pepper
¼ teaspoon ground red pepper (preferably cayenne)
¼ teaspoon onion powder
¼ teaspoon black pepper
¼ teaspoon dried sweet basil leaves
⅛ teaspoon garlic powder

1 pound boneless veal, cut into 1½x¼x¼-inch julienne strips
1 cup vegetable oil
4 tablespoons unsalted butter, *in all*
1 cup finely chopped green onions (tops only)
1 teaspoon minced garlic
1 cup heavy cream
½ teaspoon white pepper
¼ teaspoon ground red pepper (preferably cayenne)
¼ teaspoon dried sweet basil leaves
1 teaspoon Tabasco sauce

Make the crêpes up to 2 hours ahead.

Combine the oysters and cold water; stir and refrigerate at least 1 hour. Strain and refrigerate the oysters and oyster water until ready to use.

Combine the ingredients for the seasoned flour mix and the veal seasoning mix in separate bowls; mix well. Rub the veal seasoning mix into the meat with your hands until meat is evenly coated.

Heat the serving plates in a 250° oven.

In a large skillet heat the oil over high heat for 1 minute. Meanwhile, dredge the meat in the seasoned flour (reserve excess flour). Add the pieces of meat one at a time to the hot oil so pieces won't stick together and will brown well. Cook meat until medium brown on bottom sides before stirring; turn pieces of meat and cook until reddish brown on all sides.

Remove skillet from heat and pour off ¼ cup oil from the pan; discard. Add 2 *tablespoons* of the butter to the skillet. When melted, add the reserved flour, green onions and garlic; stir well. Add the remaining 2 tablespoons butter. Cook over high heat, stirring constantly, until butter is melted. Add *1½ cups* of the oyster water and cook 2 minutes, stirring occasionally. Add the cream and continue cooking 3 minutes, stirring frequently. Add the white and red peppers, basil and Tabasco. Continue cooking 3 minutes, stirring frequently. Stir in the drained oysters, then the remaining ½ cup oyster water. Cook 3 minutes, stirring occasionally. Remove from heat and serve immediately.

To serve, pour ¼ cup veal and oyster mixture over each open crêpe; fold crêpe in half. Put 2 crêpes on each heated plate and top with an additional ½ cup veal and oysters.

Crêpes

The batter may be made ahead of time and refrigerated. Let it return to room temperature before using.

¾ cup milk
1 large egg
1 tablespoon plus ½ teaspoon vegetable oil
¾ teaspoon sugar
⅛ teaspoon ground nutmeg
Pinch of salt
½ cup sifted all-purpose flour

In a small bowl combine the milk, egg, oil, sugar, nutmeg and salt; mix well with a metal whisk. Add the flour and whisk again just until blended and no lumps of flour remain; do not overbeat.

Very lightly oil an 8-inch slope-sided crêpe pan, then wipe it with a towel until the pan has only enough oil on it to be shiny. Heat the pan over medium heat about 2 minutes or until a drop of batter sizzles as soon as it's dropped in the pan. Then pick up the pan and pour 2 tablespoons batter into it, quickly tilting the pan so the batter thoroughly coats the bottom and slightly up the sides of the pan; make the crêpe as thin as possible. Cook the crêpe until the edges and bottom are golden brown, about 30 seconds to 1 minute; brown only one side of the crêpe. Remove the crêpe from the pan and place on a plate to cool, browned side up. Heat the pan about 15 seconds before cooking the next crêpe. Repeat with remaining batter, re-oiling pan if necessary. Cover crêpes with a damp cloth until ready to serve. They should be used within 2 hours. (You will have enough batter for about 10 crêpes.)

Veal with Oysters and Artichoke over Pasta

Makes 3 servings

The sauce for this dish is best if made only three servings at a time. If you want to make more than three servings, do so in separate batches but serve while piping hot.

1¼ cups cold water
9 oysters in their liquor, about 7 ounces
9 quarts water, *in all*
5 tablespoons olive or vegetable oil, *in all*
3½ tablespoons salt, *in all*
2½ teaspoons garlic powder
2 lemons, halved
1 large artichoke
½ pound fresh spaghetti, or ⅓ pound dry

Seasoned flour mix:
¼ cup all-purpose flour
1½ teaspoons salt
1¼ teaspoons white pepper
1 teaspoon onion powder
1 teaspoon ground red pepper (preferably cayenne)
½ teaspoon sweet paprika

½ pound (2 sticks) unsalted butter
½ pound boneless white veal, cut into 1½x¼x¼-inch julienne strips
½ cup finely chopped green onions
¾ cup heavy cream

Combine the 1¼ cups cold water with the oysters; refrigerate at least 1 hour. Strain and reserve oysters and oyster water in the refrigerator until ready to use.

In a large soup pot combine *6 quarts* of the water, *3 tablespoons* of the oil, *2 tablespoons* of the salt, the garlic powder and lemons. Cover and bring to a boil over high heat. Meanwhile, cut the stem off the artichoke (use a stainless steel knife so it doesn't discolor the artichoke). Trim the artichoke top down by about ½ inch. Add the artichoke (top down) and the stem to the boiling water; cover pan and boil just until leaves can be pulled off easily, about 25 minutes, stirring occasionally; drain. Cool artichoke slightly, then remove each leaf and scrape off the edible parts from the bottom of each with a spoon. Remove (and reserve) the innermost leaves covering the fuzzy choke. With a teaspoon, scoop out the choke from the center and discard, leaving the artichoke heart intact at the bottom. Cut the artichoke heart into thin slices. Chop edible parts from reserved innermost leaves. Trim the end of the stem and cut off and discard the stringy skin; then slice the tender center of the stem. The total of slices and trimmings should be about ⅔ cup. Set aside.

Place the remaining 3 quarts water, 2 tablespoons oil and 1½ tablespoons salt in a large pot over high heat; cover and bring to a boil. When water reaches a rolling boil, add small amounts of spaghetti at a time to the pot, breaking up oil patches as you drop spaghetti in. Return to boiling and cook uncovered to al dente stage (about 4 minutes if fresh, 7 minutes if dry); do not overcook. During this cooking time, use a wooden or spaghetti spoon to lift spaghetti out of the water by spoonfuls and shake strands back into the boiling water. (It may be an old wives' tale, but this procedure seems to enhance the spaghetti's texture.) Then immediately drain spaghetti into a colander; stop its cooking by running cold water over strands (if using dry spaghetti, first rinse with hot water to wash off starch). After the spaghetti has cooled thoroughly, about 2 to 3 minutes, pour a liberal amount of vegetable oil in your hands and toss spaghetti. Set aside still in the colander.

Heat 3 plates in a 250° oven.

Combine the seasoned flour ingredients in a medium-size bowl; mix well. Add the veal and toss until all pieces are well coated and as much flour as possible is absorbed. In a large skillet (preferably nonstick) melt *1 stick* of the butter over high heat. Add the veal pieces in a single layer (and any flour that wasn't absorbed by the meat) and sauté until golden brown and crispy on all sides, about 4 minutes. (It's important to cook the veal over *high* heat so the outside gets crispy without overcooking the inside.) Add the reserved artichoke, green onions and *4 tablespoons* more butter. Cook for about 2 minutes while shaking the pan fairly vigorously in a back-and-forth motion (versus stirring). Stir in *¼ cup* of the oyster water; cook and shake the pan 1 minute. Add the remaining 4 tablespoons butter, the remaining 1 cup oyster water and the cream. Continue cooking and shaking the pan about 1 minute more. Add the oysters and cook and shake the pan just until all butter is completely melted, about 2 minutes. Add the pasta and toss just until the pasta is coated and heated through, about 2 minutes. Serve immediately.

To serve, roll each portion of pasta on a large fork and place on a heated serving plate. Arrange oysters and some of the veal on top and spoon additional sauce remaining in the pan over all.

LAGNIAPPE

To test doneness of spaghetti, cut a strand in half near the end of cooking time. When done, there should be only a speck of white in the center, less than one-fourth the diameter of the strand.

Shaking the pan in a back-and-forth motion and the addition of oyster water and cream to the melting butter keep the sauce from separating and having an oily texture—stirring doesn't produce the same effect.

Cajun Meat Pies

Makes 8 individual pies for lunch or snacks

Take your choice of fillings: Andouille Smoked Sausage, Hot Meat, Creole, Hot and Sweet or Salty and Sweet.

Dough:

3 tablespoons unsalted butter, slightly softened
3 tablespoons sugar

2 eggs
½ teaspoon vanilla extract
5 tablespoons cold milk
About 2½ to 3½ cups all-purpose flour, *in all*

About 4 cups filling (recipes follow)
Vegetable oil for frying

Place the butter in the bowl of an electric mixer; with dough paddle, blend on high until creamy. Then blend in the following just until each is incorporated into the mixture: sugar, eggs (one at a time), vanilla and milk. Add *2½ cups* of the flour and mix on low speed until the flour won't fly out of the bowl when the speed is increased, about 5 to 10 seconds; then beat on high speed just until blended, about 5 seconds. Overbeating will produce a tough dough. (**Note:** If your mixer doesn't have a dough paddle, knead in the last remnants of flour by hand.) The dough should readily form a ball and hardly stick to the sides of the bowl; add more flour if necessary to achieve this consistency. Wrap in plastic wrap and refrigerate until ready to roll out (dough will keep several days).

Make the filling of your choice and set aside.

Flour a cutting board with about *2 tablespoons* of the remaining flour. Divide the dough into 6 equal pieces (you'll have enough scraps to make 2 more pies). Sprinkle a little flour over each piece of dough and form it into a ball. Roll out each portion with a floured rolling pin to a circle slightly larger than 7 inches in diameter, about ⅛ inch thick. (If the dough has been refrigerated several hours, it will tend to shrink after it's rolled. If this happens, roll it out as thinly as possible and wait 1 to 2 minutes before proceeding to the next step.) Place a 7-inch salad plate upside down on the dough and cut the dough around it. Use a long knife if needed to loosen the dough from the cutting board. Lightly rub the top of each circle with flour and fold in half. Reflour the board and rolling pin as needed.

If you made the filling several hours ahead of time, reheat it enough to redistribute the solidified fat.

Unfold each piece of dough and put ½ cup of filling to one side of the dough. Spread the filling over half the dough to within ½ inch of the edge. Fold the circle in half over the filling; seal the edges by pressing firmly with a fork, making a ½-inch decorative border. Trim the border neatly with a sharp knife to ¼ inch.

In a deep pan or deep fryer, heat at least 2 inches of oil to 350°. Fry the pies until they are a rich brown color, about 1½ to 2 minutes, holding them down under the surface of the oil with a fry basket or large metal spoon. Do not crowd. Drain on paper towels. Serve immediately.

Andouille Smoked Sausage Filling

¾ pound (3 sticks) unsalted butter
1 cup finely chopped onions
½ cup finely chopped celery
1 pound andouille smoked sausage (preferred) or any other good pure smoked pork sausage such as Polish sausage (kielbasa), diced into ¼-inch pieces
¾ cup all-purpose flour
About 3½ cups **Basic Beef Stock** (page 31)
2 teaspoons ground red pepper (preferably cayenne)
1 teaspoon dried thyme leaves

Melt the butter in a large skillet. Add the onions and celery. Sauté over medium-high heat for about 2 minutes. Add the andouille and brown 5 minutes, stirring occasionally. Add the flour and stir, scraping the pan bottom well. Stir in enough stock to make a thick creamy mixture, then add the red pepper and thyme. Continue cooking, stirring constantly, until very thick, about 6 to 7 minutes. Cool in the refrigerator at least 10 minutes before using. Makes about 5 cups or enough for 10 pies.

Hot Meat Filling

½ pound (2 sticks) margarine
1¼ cups finely chopped onions

1¼ cups finely chopped celery
¾ pound ground pork
1¼ tablespoons minced garlic
2½ teaspoons salt
2½ teaspoons ground red pepper (preferably cayenne)
2½ teaspoons sweet paprika
2 teaspoons black pepper
2 teaspoons dried sweet basil leaves
1½ teaspoons dried thyme leaves
¼ pound ground beef
2 cups coarsely grated red potatoes
1¼ cups **Basic Beef Stock** (page 31)
⅔ cup water

Melt the margarine in a large skillet. Add the onions and celery. Sauté over high heat until the vegetables wilt, about 3 to 4 minutes, stirring occasionally. Add the pork, garlic and seasonings and cook 10 minutes, stirring occasionally. Stir in the beef. Lower the heat and simmer until meat is well browned, about 8 minutes, stirring frequently and scraping pan bottom as needed. Turn heat to high and continue cooking until meat is crisp, about 5 minutes, stirring frequently. Then add the potatoes and stock; reduce heat to medium-low and continue cooking for 10 minutes, stirring occasionally. Add the water and cook about 2 minutes more, stirring often and scraping pan bottom well. Cool in the refrigerator at least 10 minutes before using. Makes about 5 cups or enough for 10 pies.

Creole Filling

4 tablespoons unsalted butter
1½ cups finely chopped onions
1 cup finely chopped green bell peppers
½ cup finely chopped celery
1 tablespoon minced garlic
¾ pound ground pork

¾ pound ground beef
3 bay leaves
2½ teaspoons ground red pepper (preferably cayenne)
1½ teaspoons salt
1½ teaspoons dried oregano leaves
1 teaspoon dried thyme leaves
1½ cups canned tomato sauce
1 cup water
1 cup finely chopped green onions

Melt the butter in a large skillet over high heat. Add the onions, bell peppers, celery and garlic and sauté about 2 minutes. Add the pork, but do not stir. Cover the pan and cook over high heat 5 minutes. Then stir the mixture, breaking up the meat chunks. Stir in the beef and continue cooking uncovered until meat is thoroughly browned, stirring occasionally. Add the seasonings and simmer uncovered about 3 minutes, stirring occasionally. Add the tomato sauce and continue cooking 5 minutes, stirring occasionally. Stir in the water and green onions. Reduce heat to low; cover and simmer 20 minutes. Remove cover and simmer 5 minutes more. Refrigerate for at least 10 minutes and remove bay leaves before using. Makes about 4½ cups or enough for 9 pies.

Hot and Sweet Filling

⅓ cup vegetable oil
½ pound ground pork
½ pound ground beef
¼ pound (1 stick) unsalted butter
1½ cups finely chopped onions
1½ cups finely chopped green bell peppers
¾ cup finely chopped celery
½ cup very finely chopped fresh cayenne peppers or
jalapeño peppers (see **NOTE**)

2 tablespoons minced garlic
3 bay leaves
1 tablespoon plus 1 teaspoon dried oregano leaves
1 tablespoon ground cumin
2 teaspoons salt
1 teaspoon ground red pepper (preferably cayenne)
1 teaspoon black pepper
½ teaspoon dried thyme leaves
1 cup **Basic Chicken Stock** (page 31), or water
Candied Sweet Potatoes (recipe follows)

Note: Fresh jalapeños are preferred; if you have to use pickled ones, rinse as much vinegar from them as possible.

Heat the oil in a large skillet over high heat; add the pork and cook about 2 minutes, stirring constantly and breaking up the meat chunks. Stir in the beef and cook until no pink color remains. Add the butter, onions, bell peppers, celery, cayenne peppers, garlic and seasonings. Stir until thoroughly mixed. Cook 5 minutes, stirring frequently to break up any remaining meat chunks and scraping pan bottom well. Add the stock and continue cooking about 5 minutes. Cover, reduce heat, and simmer 5 minutes. Remove cover and cook 5 minutes more, stirring often and continuing to scrape pan bottom well. Add the candied sweet potatoes with their juice. Stir well, breaking up potatoes into small bits. Cover and simmer 5 minutes. Remove from heat. Refrigerate at least 10 minutes and remove bay leaves before using. Makes about 4 cups or enough for 8 pies.

Candied Sweet Potatoes

2 medium-size sweet potatoes, peeled and cut into 1½- to
    2-inch chunks (see **Note**)
1 cup water
¼ cup sugar

¼ cup packed light brown sugar
4 tablespoons unsalted butter, *in all*
1½ teaspoons vanilla extract
Juice and grated rind from ⅛ lemon

In a 1-quart saucepan combine the sweet potatoes, water, sugars, *2 tablespoons* of the butter, the vanilla and lemon juice and rind. Cover and cook over medium heat for 30 minutes, stirring occasionally; uncover and cook until potatoes are fork tender, about 10 minutes. Add the remaining butter, stirring until completely melted. Cook uncovered until sauce is thick, about 2 minutes more. Makes about 1 cup.

NOTE: To use canned sweet potatoes, drain *1 (15-ounce) can sweet potatoes cut and packed in syrup*, reserving ½ cup syrup. In a 1-quart saucepan, place the reserved syrup, *⅓ cup sugar, 4 tablespoons unsalted butter*, the *juice and grated rind from ½ lemon* and *1 tablespoon vanilla extract*. Cook over high heat for about 2 minutes, whisking frequently with a metal whisk. Add *1½ cups* of the sweet potatoes (reserve the rest for another recipe); cover and reduce heat to very low. Simmer about 10 minutes; remove cover and cook until mixture is reduced to 1 cup, about 10 minutes more, stirring occasionally and taking care not to break up the potato pieces.

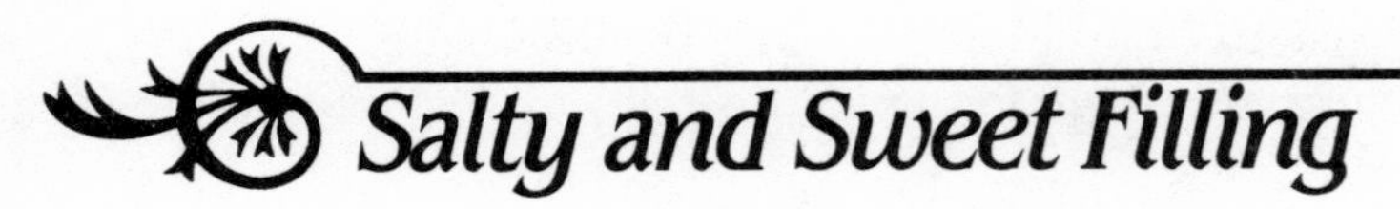

Salty and Sweet Filling

¼ cup vegetable oil
¾ pound ground pork
¾ pound ground beef
1½ cups finely chopped onions
1 cup finely chopped green bell peppers
½ cup finely chopped celery
1 tablespoon plus 1 teaspoon minced garlic
3 bay leaves
2½ teaspoons salt

2 teaspoons dried thyme leaves
1½ teaspoons dry mustard
1 teaspoon ground red pepper (preferably cayenne)
½ teaspoon ground cumin
½ teaspoon black pepper
1 cup **Basic Chicken Stock** (page 31), or water
4 tablespoons unsalted butter
Candied Sweet Potatoes, in their juice (preceding recipe)

In a large skillet heat the oil over high heat; add the pork and cook until no pink color remains, stirring constantly. Stir in the beef and continue cooking until no pink color remains. Add the onions, bell peppers, celery, garlic and seasonings. Cook 5 minutes, stirring constantly and breaking up any meat chunks. Add the stock and butter. Then cover, lower the heat to maintain a rapid simmer, and cook 5 minutes. Remove cover and cook 10 minutes, stirring often and scraping pan bottom well. Cover again and cook 10 minutes more. Then add the candied sweet potatoes with their juice, breaking them up into small bits and stirring them into the filling thoroughly. Remove from heat. Refrigerate at least 10 minutes and remove bay leaves before using. Makes about 4 cups or enough for 8 pies.

Lamb Curry

Makes 8 servings

This is a very flavorful (and hot) curry. Be brave!

Seasoning mix:
1½ teaspoons ground turmeric
1¼ teaspoons white pepper
1 teaspoon ground fenugreek (see **Note**), optional
1 teaspoon ground ginger
1 teaspoon ground red pepper (preferably cayenne)

¾ teaspoon ground coriander
½ teaspoon ground cumin
½ teaspoon black pepper
½ teaspoon dried sweet basil leaves

2 pounds boneless lamb
½ pound (2 sticks) unsalted butter, melted
4½ cups chopped onions, *in all*
¼ pound (1 stick) margarine, melted
½ cup, *in all*, minced jalapeño peppers (see **Note**)
2 tablespoons ground red pepper (preferably cayenne)
1 tablespoon ground ginger
1 teaspoon ground cumin
1 teaspoon ground coriander
1 cup chopped green bell peppers
¼ cup curry powder
½ pound (2 sticks) unsalted butter, softened
1 large overripe black-skinned banana, mashed
1 medium unpeeled apple, chopped
1 (15-ounce) can cream of coconut
1 cup coarsely chopped pecans, dry roasted
1 cup raisins
6 cups hot **Basic Cooked Rice** (page 224)

Note: Ground fenugreek is available in many gourmet and spice shops. Fresh jalapeños are preferred; if you have to use pickled ones, rinse as much vinegar from them as possible.

Combine the seasoning mix ingredients in a bowl; mix well. Remove most of the fat from the lamb and cut the lamb into 2-inch cubes. Toss the lamb with the seasoning mix and set aside.

In a 13x9-inch roasting pan, combine the 2 sticks melted butter, *2½ cups* of the onions, the margarine, *¼ cup* of the jalapeño peppers, the red pepper, ginger, cumin and coriander; mix well. Bake at 350° on the floor of the oven until the onions are dark brown but not burned, about 30 to 40 minutes. Remove from oven; stir in the remaining 2 cups onions, the bell peppers, the remaining ¼ cup jalapeño peppers, the curry powder and the softened butter, stirring until well combined and butter is broken up. Place on middle rack of oven and bake 20 minutes. Remove pan from oven; mix in the lamb, banana, apple, cream of coconut, pecans and raisins. Return to oven and bake 2 hours more, stirring every 30 minutes or so. Serve immediately.

To serve, spoon ¾ cup rice around the edges of each serving plate and mound about 1¼ cups lamb curry in the center.

POULTRY & RABBIT

Chicken Sauce Piquant

Makes 8 servings

Seasoning mix:
1 tablespoon plus 1 teaspoon salt
1 tablespoon black pepper
2 teaspoons onion powder
2 teaspoons garlic powder
2 teaspoons ground red pepper (preferably cayenne)
1 teaspoon white pepper
1 teaspoon dried thyme leaves

1 cup all-purpose flour
2 (2½- to 3-pound) fryers, each cut in 8 pieces
Vegetable oil for frying
1¾ cups chopped onions
1¾ cups chopped celery
1¾ cups chopped green bell peppers
1¾ cups peeled and chopped tomatoes
3 tablespoons finely chopped jalapeño peppers (see **Note**)
2 tablespoons minced garlic
1¾ cups canned tomato sauce
1 tablespoon plus 2 teaspoons Tabasco sauce
4 cups **Basic Chicken Stock** (page 31)
Hot **Basic Cooked Rice** (page 224), or noodles

Note: Fresh jalapeños are preferred; if you have to use pickled ones, rinse as much vinegar from them as possible.

Combine the seasoning mix ingredients in a small bowl, mixing well. In a paper or plastic bag, mix *1 tablespoon* of the seasoning mix into the flour. Remove excess fat from the chicken pieces and sprinkle the remaining mix evenly on the chicken pieces. Dredge the chicken in the seasoned flour until well coated.

In a large skillet heat ½ inch oil to 350°. Fry chicken (large pieces and skin side down first) until browned and crispy on both sides and meat is cooked, about 5 to 8 minutes per side. Do not crowd. (Lower heat if drippings start getting dark red-brown; don't let them burn.)

Drain on paper towels. Carefully pour the hot oil from the skillet into a glass measuring cup, leaving as much sediment in the pan as possible; then return ¼ cup hot oil to the skillet. Turn heat to high. Using a spoon, loosen any particles stuck to the pan bottom and then add the onions, celery and bell peppers; cook until sediment is well mixed into the vegetables, stirring constantly and scraping pan bottom well. Add the tomatoes, jalapeño peppers and garlic; stir well and cook about 2 minutes, stirring once or twice. Add the tomato sauce and cook about 3 minutes, stirring occasionally. Stir in the Tabasco and remove from heat.

Heat the serving plates in a 250° oven.

Meanwhile, place the chicken pieces and stock in a 5½-quart saucepan or large Dutch oven and bring to a boil. Cover, reduce heat to medium, and cook 5 minutes. Then stir *half* the tomato mixture into the stock; cover and simmer over low heat 5 minutes. Stir in the remaining tomato mixture, cover, and simmer 8 to 10 minutes more, stirring occasionally. Remove from heat and serve immediately over rice or noodles.

LAGNIAPPE

"Piquant" to a Cajun means "it's hot and 'hurts like a sticker in your tongue.'" If you want less "piquant," reduce the jalapeño peppers by half. Sauce Piquant is enjoyed with such gusto in Louisiana that the town of Raceland has a Sauce Piquant Festival every year dedicated to nothing but fish, meat, fowl and seafood made with variations of this sauce.

Rabbit Sauce Piquant

Makes 4 servings

If you have any of this left over (slim chance!), it's wonderful served over **Jambalaya** (pages 215–221).

Seasoning mix:
1 tablespoon plus 2 teaspoons salt
1¼ teaspoons dry mustard
1¼ teaspoons sweet paprika
1 teaspoon garlic powder
1 teaspoon black pepper
¾ teaspoon white pepper
¾ teaspoon onion powder
¾ teaspoon ground red pepper (preferably cayenne)
¼ teaspoon dried thyme leaves

1 (2- to 2½-pound) domestic rabbit
½ cup all-purpose flour
Vegetable oil for frying
2 cups chopped onions
2 cups chopped green bell peppers
1 cup chopped celery
¼ cup minced jalapeño peppers (see **NOTE**)
2½ cups peeled and chopped tomatoes
2 bay leaves
1 tablespoon Tabasco sauce
2 cups **Basic Rabbit** or **Chicken Stock** (page 31)
½ cup canned tomato sauce
1 teaspoon minced garlic
Hot **Basic Cooked Rice** (page 224) or noodles

NOTE: Fresh jalapeños are preferred; if you have to use pickled ones, rinse as much vinegar from them as possible.

In a small bowl combine the seasoning mix ingredients; mix well and set aside.

Cut the rabbit into 8 pieces (your butcher can do this for you): remove front and back legs; cut breast away from back; cut the back and the breast in half. Sprinkle about *2½ teaspoons* of the seasoning mix over both sides of the pieces of rabbit, rubbing it in with your hands.

Place the flour and *1 tablespoon* of the seasoning mix in a paper or plastic bag and shake until well mixed. Add the rabbit and shake to coat, shaking off excess flour.

Heat ¼ inch oil in a 4-quart saucepan to about 350° over high heat. Fry the rabbit in the hot oil until light golden brown, about 2 minutes per side (reduce heat if drippings start to get dark brown). Do not crowd. Drain rabbit on paper towels. Remove pan from heat and pour off all but ¼ cup oil into a glass measuring cup, leaving the sediment in the pan. Discard most of the oil from the measuring cup and pour the remaining sediment into the pan.

Add the onions, bell peppers, celery and jalapeño peppers; stir well. Turn heat to high and sauté about 3 minutes, stirring occasionally. Stir in the tomatoes, the remaining seasoning mix, the bay leaves and Tabasco. Continue cooking until the vegetables are tender but still brightly colored, about 5 minutes, stirring occasionally and scraping pan bottom well. Stir in the stock, tomato sauce and garlic. Continue cooking about 2 minutes. Add the rabbit to the pan, placing the meatiest pieces on the bottom. Stir, cover pan, reduce heat to very low, and simmer until tender, about 45 minutes, stirring occasionally so the mixture doesn't stick. Skim oil from the top and remove bay leaves. Serve immediately over rice or noodles.

LAGNIAPPE

"Piquant" to a Cajun means "it's hot and 'hurts like a sticker in your tongue.'" If you want less "piquant," reduce the jalapeño peppers by half. Sauce Piquant is enjoyed with such gusto in Louisiana that the town of Raceland has a Sauce Piquant Festival every year dedicated to nothing but fish, meat, fowl and seafood made with variations of this sauce.

Roasted Quail Stuffed with Crawfish Cornbread Dressing

Makes 4 servings

Seasoning mix:
2 whole bay leaves
1½ teaspoons salt
1½ teaspoons garlic powder
1 teaspoon white pepper
1 teaspoon ground red pepper (preferably cayenne)
½ teaspoon black pepper

7 tablespoons unsalted butter, *in all*
1½ cups very finely chopped onions
1½ cups very finely chopped celery
1½ cups very finely chopped green bell peppers
8 quail
1 cup **Crawfish Cornbread Dressing** (page 228), completely cooled
¼ cup all-purpose flour
3 cups, *in all*, **Basic Chicken Stock** (page 31)

Thoroughly combine the seasoning mix ingredients in a small bowl and set aside.

In a very large skillet melt *6 tablespoons* of the butter over high heat. Add the onions, celery and bell peppers and sauté about 1 minute, stirring occasionally. Add the seasoning mix and sauté about 3 minutes more, stirring once or twice. Move the vegetables to the outer edge of the skillet and place the quail breast side up in a single layer in the center of the pan; continue cooking until quail are browned on the bottom, about 5 minutes. Remove from heat. Stuff each quail with 2 tablespoons of the cornbread dressing and set aside.

Spoon the sautéed vegetables and any bottom sediment into an ungreased 13x9-inch baking pan, evenly covering the bottom. Place the quail on top, breast side up. Seal the pan with aluminum foil. Bake at 350° for 20 minutes. Remove foil and continue baking until done, about 40 minutes more. Remove quail and set aside. Transfer vegetables (discard bay leaves) and drippings to a food processor or blender and process until smooth, about 20 seconds.

Meanwhile, heat the serving plates in a 250° oven.

Place the puréed vegetables in a large skillet. Add the remaining 1 tablespoon butter and cook over high heat until butter is melted, stirring constantly. Add the flour and stir until smooth. Continue cooking for 1 minute, stirring constantly and scraping pan bottom well. Stir in ½ *cup* of the stock and cook about 3 minutes, allowing the mixture to form a film on the pan bottom each time before stirring. Stir in ½ *cup* more stock and stir well to dissolve browned mixture on pan bottom. Then add the remaining 2 cups stock and stir well. Bring mixture to a boil, whisking frequently with a metal whisk; continue cooking until mixture reaches a gravy consistency, about 4 minutes, whisking constantly. Remove from heat. Serve immediately.

To serve, place 2 quail on each heated serving plate and top with about ½ cup gravy.

Chicken Curry

Makes 6 servings

Seasoning mix:
2 tablespoons curry powder
1 teaspoon ground red pepper (preferably cayenne)
½ teaspoon ground cumin
½ teaspoon ground cinnamon
½ teaspoon ground turmeric
½ teaspoon black pepper
½ teaspoon dried sweet basil leaves
¼ teaspoon ground coriander

½ pound (2 sticks) unsalted butter
2 tablespoons chicken fat (preferred) or additional butter
3 cups chopped onions

5 tablespoons chopped jalapeño peppers (see **Note**)
2 cups unpeeled chopped apples, *in all*
1 cup sliced bananas
½ cup raisins
½ cup pecan halves or pieces, dry roasted
1 teaspoon salt
¾ teaspoon garlic powder
½ teaspoon ground red pepper (preferably cayenne)
½ teaspoon black pepper
½ teaspoon dried sweet basil leaves
¼ teaspoon white pepper
1 pound boneless chicken, cut into bite-size chunks, about
2 cups
1½ cups **Basic Chicken Stock** (page 31)
¾ cup canned cream of coconut
½ cup, lightly packed, coconut flakes
4½ cups hot **Basic Cooked Rice** (page 224)

Note: Fresh jalapeños are preferred; if you have to use pickled ones, rinse as much vinegar from them as possible.

Thoroughly combine the seasoning mix ingredients in a small bowl; set aside.

In a 4-quart saucepan combine the butter, chicken fat, onions, jalapeño peppers and the seasoning mix; cook over high heat until the butter melts, about 5 minutes, stirring frequently. Reduce heat to medium and simmer 20 minutes, stirring occasionally and scraping pan bottom as needed. Add *1 cup* of the apples, the bananas, raisins and pecans, stirring well. Simmer until mixture is fairly mushy, about 20 minutes, stirring frequently (add up to 4 tablespoons more butter or chicken fat if mixture seems too dry).

Combine the salt, garlic, red and black peppers, basil and white pepper; mix well and work into the chicken meat with your hands.

When the vegetable mixture finishes simmering, raise heat to high. Stir in the seasoned chicken and the remaining 1 cup apple; cook about 3 minutes, stirring frequently. Add the stock, cream of coconut and coconut flakes; stir, scraping pan bottom well. Reduce heat to low and simmer 15 minutes, stirring occasionally (lower heat further if mixture sticks to pan bottom). Serve immediately.

To serve, make a ring around each serving plate with ¾ cup rice; mound about ¾ cup curry in the center.

Smothered Rabbit

Makes 4 servings

Seasoning mix:
2¼ teaspoons salt
1½ teaspoons onion powder
1½ teaspoons sweet paprika
¾ teaspoon garlic powder
½ teaspoon white pepper
¼ teaspoon ground red pepper (preferably cayenne)
¼ teaspoon black pepper
¼ teaspoon dried sweet basil leaves
¼ teaspoon gumbo filé (filé powder), optional

1 (2- to 3-pound) domestic rabbit, cut in 8 pieces (page 30)
1 cup all-purpose flour
Vegetable oil for pan frying
1 cup finely chopped onions
½ cup finely chopped celery
6 cups **Basic Rabbit** or **Chicken Stock** (page 31)
Hot **Basic Cooked Rice** (page 224) or mashed potatoes

In a small bowl thoroughly combine the seasoning mix ingredients. Sprinkle 2 *teaspoons* of the mix on the rabbit pieces, patting it in with your hands. Combine 2½ *teaspoons* of the mix with the flour in a paper or plastic bag.

Heat about ¼ inch oil in a large heavy skillet to about 350°. Dredge the rabbit pieces in the seasoned flour, shaking off excess (reserve left-over flour). Cook in the hot oil until golden brown, about 2 minutes per side. Do not crowd. (Adjust heat as necessary to maintain oil's temperature at about 350°; if drippings start to burn, discard the oil and drippings and use fresh oil.) Drain rabbit on paper towels.

Combine the onions and celery in a small bowl and set aside.

Pour off all but ½ cup of the hot oil from the skillet, leaving as much sediment in the pan as possible. Return skillet to high heat and let remaining oil heat until it starts to smoke, about 2 minutes, scraping loose any sediment that may be stuck to pan bottom. With a long-handled metal whisk gradually whisk in the reserved flour until smooth. Continue cooking, whisking constantly, until the roux turns dark red-brown, about 2 to 3 minutes (being careful not to let it scorch or splash on your skin). Immediately stir in the reserved vegetable mixture and remove from heat. Continue stirring (change to a wooden spoon if necessary) until the roux stops darkening in color, about 3 minutes. Set aside.

✱ See page 26 for more about making roux.

In a 5½-quart saucepan or large Dutch oven, bring the stock to a boil. Add the roux to the stock by spoonfuls, whisking until roux dissolves between each addition. Stir in the remaining seasoning mix. Add the rabbit to the pot and cook about 5 minutes, stirring occasionally. Reduce heat to low and continue cooking until rabbit is tender and sauce is reduced to about 4 cups, about 50 to 60 minutes, stirring occasionally.

Serve immediately over rice or with mashed potatoes, allowing 2 pieces of rabbit and a generous portion of sauce for each person.

Roasted Goose with Smoked Ham Stuffing
and Spiced Fig Gravy

Makes 8 servings

The cornbread dressing and fig gravy can be made a day ahead—just reheat gravy before serving.

1 (9- to 11-pound) goose

First seasoning mix:
4 whole bay leaves
1½ teaspoons salt
1½ teaspoons white pepper
1½ teaspoons ground red pepper (preferably cayenne)
1½ teaspoons dried thyme leaves
¾ teaspoon onion powder
¾ teaspoon black pepper

½ pound smoked ham (preferably Cure 81), ground, about 2 cups
2 cups finely chopped onions
1½ cups finely chopped green bell peppers
1 cup finely chopped celery
1 cup, *in all*, **Basic Goose** or **Chicken Stock** (page 31)
4 cups finely crumbled **Cornbread Dressing** (page 227)

Second seasoning mix:
1 tablespoon salt
2 teaspoons sweet paprika
1 teaspoon garlic powder
1 teaspoon ground red pepper (preferably cayenne)
¾ teaspoon onion powder
¾ teaspoon ground sage
½ teaspoon white pepper
½ teaspoon black pepper
½ teaspoon dried thyme leaves
½ teaspoon gumbo filé (filé powder), optional

Spiced Fig Gravy for Fowl (page 257)

Remove all excess fat from the goose and tuck the wings backward underneath the back of the bird. Cook the fat (use enough to yield a little over ⅓ cup) in a small covered saucepan over low heat until completely rendered and browned; this gives the fat the sweetness of caramelization. Strain out ⅓ cup exactly.

Thoroughly combine the first seasoning mix ingredients in a small bowl and set aside.

In a large skillet melt the goose fat over high heat. Add the ham and fry about 2 minutes, stirring occasionally. Stir in the first seasoning mix and continue cooking until ham is browned, about 2 minutes, stirring often and scraping the pan bottom well. Stir in the onions, bell peppers and celery. Cook until vegetables are noticeably brighter in color and almost tender, about 7 to 9 minutes, stirring frequently and scraping pan bottom as needed. Add ½ *cup* of the stock; stir well to dissolve any mixture from the pan bottom and continue cooking until mixture sticks excessively, about 7 to 9 minutes, stirring and scraping frequently. Add the remaining ½ cup stock and cook and scrape about 1 minute. Stir in the Cornbread Dressing and continue cooking until mixture begins to stick excessively, about 3 minutes, stirring and scraping often. Remove from heat and set aside to cool. Makes about 5 cups stuffing.

Meanwhile, combine the second seasoning mix ingredients in a small bowl and mix well. Sprinkle the mix on the inside and outside of the goose, massaging it in with your hands and using all of the mix. Place the goose breast side up on a rack in a large roasting pan. Fill the goose with stuffing. Bake the goose at 250° until the drumsticks turn easily, about 5½ hours.

NOTE: Using a bulb baster, periodically syphon off excess fat as it accumulates beyond ½ inch and save for other cooking uses—it's great.

Serve immediately with a bowl of the Spiced Fig Gravy on the table.

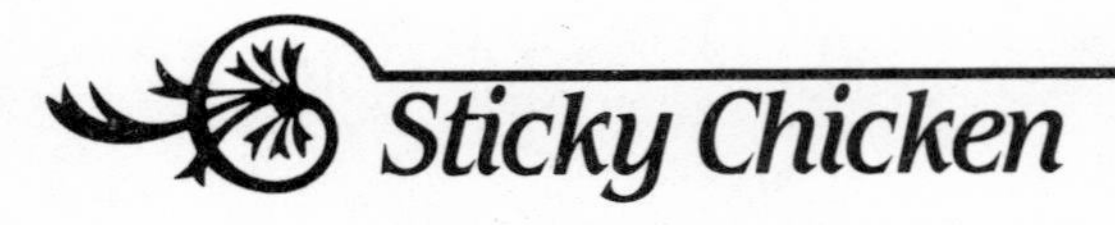

Sticky Chicken

Makes 6 to 8 servings

When I was a child, we raised lots of chickens. My mother devised this recipe to cook old roosters and hens. She would flour them lightly and cook them over very low heat. When they were done, the chicken actually did feel sticky. One of the memories that really stays with me is of my mother preparing this dish.

Seasoning mix:
1 tablespoon salt
1 teaspoon white pepper
1 teaspoon onion powder
1 teaspoon garlic powder
1 teaspoon ground red pepper (preferably cayenne)
½ teaspoon black pepper

1 (5- to 6-pound) stewing chicken, cut up
1½ cups all-purpose flour
Vegetable oil
3 cups chopped onions
1 cup chopped celery
6½ cups **Rich Chicken Stock** (page 32)
1 teaspoon salt
¾ teaspoon fresh sage, or ¼ teaspoon ground sage
½ teaspoon ground red pepper (preferably cayenne)
½ teaspoon black pepper
½ teaspoon dried thyme leaves
¼ teaspoon white pepper
¼ teaspoon dried sweet basil leaves
¼ teaspoon dried oregano leaves
Hot **Basic Cooked Rice** (page 224) or boiled potatoes

Combine seasoning mix ingredients. Generously sprinkle both sides of the chicken pieces with about *4 teaspoons* of the seasoning mix. Combine the remaining seasoning mix with the flour in a paper or plastic bag. Generously dust each chicken piece with the seasoned flour. Reserve leftover flour to make the roux.

In a large skillet heat 1 inch of oil to 230° to 250°. Cook the chicken pieces in the hot oil, maintaining the oil's temperature to a level just hot enough for the chicken to boil instead of fry. (This procedure tenderizes the chicken and brings the gelatin from within the bones to the surface.) Cook pieces of similar size together to ensure even cooking. Boil with skin side down about 20 minutes, then on the other side until tender, about 15 minutes more. Drain on paper towels.

Remove skillet from heat and let cool 15 minutes. Pour the oil into a large glass bowl, leaving the sediment in the pan. Pour ½ cup of the cooled oil back into the skillet and heat over high heat. Slowly whisk in

¾ cup of the reserved seasoned flour with a long-handled metal whisk; cook until the roux is smooth and medium colored, about 2 to 3 minutes, whisking constantly (be careful not to let it scorch or splash on your skin). Immediately stir in the onions and celery and continue cooking until onions are wilted, about 5 minutes, stirring constantly. Remove from heat.

✱ See page 26 for more about making roux.

In a 4-quart saucepan bring the stock to a boil. Add the roux mixture by spoonfuls to the boiling stock, blending well between each addition. Then add the boiled chicken pieces and the seasonings. Simmer uncovered over low heat for 1 hour (or longer if the chicken needs further tenderizing), stirring often. Serve immediately over rice or with boiled potatoes.

Chicken Tchoupitoulas

Makes 8 servings

Tchoupitoulas (pronounced in New Orleans "chop-a-TOO-lus") is the name of an Indian tribe in Louisiana. This dish is great to serve to a large number of people, since it is put together very easily if you do all but the final cooking ahead of time.

4 cups peeled and diced white potatoes

Seasoning mix:
2 teaspoons salt
1 teaspoon sweet paprika
¾ teaspoon ground red pepper (preferably cayenne)
½ teaspoon white pepper
½ teaspoon onion powder
½ teaspoon garlic powder
½ teaspoon dried sweet basil leaves

¼ teaspoon black pepper
¼ teaspoon dried thyme leaves
¼ teaspoon gumbo filé (filé powder), optional

8 chicken breasts, boned, with skin on
4 tablespoons unsalted butter
Vegetable oil for frying
Béarnaise Sauce (page 306)
2 cups diced tasso (preferred) or other smoked ham, preferably Cure 81 (see **Note**)
4 cups sliced mushrooms
1 cup chopped green onions

Note: If you use another smoked ham for the tasso, you will need to add *½ teaspoon white pepper, ½ teaspoon garlic powder, ½ teaspoon ground red pepper* (preferably cayenne), and *½ teaspoon black pepper.*

Boil the diced potatoes just until fork tender. Drain and set aside.

Combine the seasoning mix ingredients in a small bowl and mix thoroughly. Sprinkle chicken breasts on both sides generously with *4 teaspoons* of the mix, patting it in with your hands. Preheat a very large ovenproof skillet (preferably cast iron) for about 2 minutes over high heat. Place the chicken breasts skin side down in the skillet and place chunks of the butter on top. Bake uncovered at 350° on the floor of the oven for 35 minutes; turn meat over and continue baking until golden brown on both sides, about 10 minutes. Remove chicken and set aside. Pour the drippings into a glass measuring cup and reserve. Set skillet aside without wiping it.

Heat ½ inch oil in another large skillet until oil sizzles when a potato piece is put in, about 350°. Gently toss the potatoes with the remaining seasoning mix until evenly coated, keeping cubes intact. Fry potatoes in the hot oil until golden brown on all sides, about 12 to 15 minutes. Drain on paper towels.

Make the Béarnaise Sauce and set aside.

Warm the serving plates in a 250° oven.

In the skillet used to cook the chicken, cook the tasso or ham over high heat until well browned, about 3 to 4 minutes, stirring occasionally. Add the potatoes (and if you're using ham instead of tasso, add the additional *½ teaspoon each* of the white, red and black peppers and the garlic powder); sauté until potatoes are hot, about 1 to 2 minutes, stirring occasionally (add about half the reserved chicken drippings if pan is dry). Stir in the mushrooms and sauté for about 1 minute more (add about half of the remaining drippings if pan is dry again), stirring constantly. Then stir in the green onions and continue cooking and stirring about 1 minute. Remove from heat and serve immediately.

To serve, place ¾ cup drained potato mixture on each warmed serving plate. Arrange a chicken breast on top and spoon a generous ⅓ cup Béarnaise Sauce over all.

Creole Chicken and Dumplings

Makes 8 servings

Seasoning mix:
1 tablespoon salt
1½ teaspoons sweet paprika
1 teaspoon white pepper
1 teaspoon onion powder
1 teaspoon garlic powder
1 teaspoon ground red pepper (preferably cayenne)
1 teaspoon dried sweet basil leaves
½ teaspoon black pepper
½ teaspoon dried thyme leaves
½ teaspoon gumbo filé (filé powder), optional

2 (2½- to 3-pound) chicken fryers, each cut in 8 pieces
1 cup all-purpose flour
Vegetable oil for frying
Dumplings (recipe follows)
2 quarts **Basic Chicken Stock** (page 31)
3 cups chopped onions

3 cups chopped green bell peppers
2 cups heavy cream
2 tablespoons unsalted butter, melted

Combine the seasoning mix ingredients thoroughly in a small bowl. Sprinkle the chicken pieces on both sides with about *4 teaspoons* of the seasoning mix, patting it in with your hands. Combine *1 tablespoon* of the seasoning mix with the flour in a paper or plastic bag. Place chicken pieces in the bag and shake to coat. Reserve leftover flour to make the roux.

Heat 1 inch oil in a very large skillet over moderate heat to 230° to 250°. Cook the chicken in batches (large pieces and skin side down first) in the hot oil (adjust heat to maintain the oil's temperature). Cook until golden brown on both sides, about 30 minutes. Drain on paper towels.

Meanwhile, make the dumpling dough and set aside.

Combine the stock, onions, bell peppers, cream and the remaining seasoning mix in a 5½-quart saucepan or large Dutch oven. Bring the mixture to a boil; reduce heat and simmer until the bell peppers darken in color, about 5 minutes, stirring occasionally. Add the chicken pieces and continue simmering until chicken is tender, about 20 minutes, stirring occasionally.

Meanwhile, steam the dumplings by dropping the batter by teaspoonfuls onto a rack in a steamer and steaming until cooked through, about 5 to 7 minutes. (If you don't have a steamer, steam them in a colander over a small amount of water in a large saucepan; cover with a pan lid or aluminum foil.)

Heat the serving plates in a 250° oven.

To thicken the sauce, stir together a mixture of the melted butter and *2 tablespoons* of the remaining seasoned flour; stir in about ½ cup stock from the chicken pot and return this to the pot. Cover and simmer about 2 minutes. Add the dumplings and gently stir. Cook until dumplings are heated through, about 2 minutes. Adjust salt in sauce to taste and serve immediately.

To serve, place 2 pieces of chicken and about 5 dumplings on each heated serving plate. Top with about ½ cup of the sauce. (Any leftover sauce is great taken out on the back porch and eaten as soup.)

Dumplings

4 eggs
½ cup minced onions
2 teaspoons baking powder
1¼ teaspoons salt
1 teaspoon dry mustard
1 teaspoon ground red pepper (preferably cayenne)
¾ teaspoon dried thyme leaves
½ teaspoon ground nutmeg
½ teaspoon rubbed sage
½ cup milk
¼ pound (1 stick) unsalted butter, melted
2½ cups all-purpose flour

In a large mixing bowl combine the eggs and onions. Beat vigorously with a metal whisk until frothy, about 2 minutes. Add the baking powder (break up any lumps) and seasonings and whisk until blended. Stir in the milk and butter. Gradually add the flour; stir in the center at the beginning of each addition so it doesn't lump, then beat until smooth, adding about a third of the flour at a time. Cook as directed in preceding recipe. Makes about 4 dozen dumplings.

Chicken Big Mamou on Pasta

Makes 6 servings

6 quarts hot water
¼ cup vegetable oil
3 tablespoons salt
1½ pounds fresh spaghetti, or 1 pound dry

Seasoning mix:
2 teaspoons dried thyme leaves

1¼ teaspoons ground red pepper (preferably cayenne)
1 teaspoon white pepper
¾ teaspoon black pepper
½ teaspoon dried sweet basil leaves

1 pound plus 4 tablespoons unsalted butter, *in all*
1 cup very finely chopped onions
4 medium-size garlic cloves, peeled
2 teaspoons minced garlic
3¼ cups, *in all*, **Rich Chicken Stock** (page 32)
2 tablespoons Worcestershire sauce
1 tablespoon plus 1 teaspoon Tabasco sauce
2 (16-ounce) cans tomato sauce
2 tablespoons sugar
2 cups very finely chopped green onions, *in all*

Chicken seasoning mix:
1½ tablespoons salt
1½ teaspoons white pepper
1½ teaspoons garlic powder
1¼ teaspoons ground red pepper (preferably cayenne)
1 teaspoon black pepper
1 teaspoon ground cumin (optional)
½ teaspoon dried sweet basil leaves

2 pounds boneless chicken (light and dark meat), cut into ½-inch cubes

Place the hot water, oil and salt in a large pot over high heat; cover and bring to a boil. When water reaches a rolling boil, add small amounts of spaghetti at a time to the pot, breaking up oil patches as you drop spaghetti in. Return to boiling and cook to al dente stage (about 4 minutes if fresh, 7 minutes if dry); do not overcook. During this cooking time, use a wooden or spaghetti spoon to lift spaghetti out of the water by spoonfuls and shake strands back into the boiling water. (It may be an old wives' tale, but this procedure seems to enhance the spaghetti's texture.) Then immediately drain spaghetti into a colander; stop cooking process by running cold water over strands. (If you used dry spaghetti, first rinse with hot water to wash off starch.) After the pasta has cooled thoroughly, about 2 to 3 minutes, pour a liberal amount of vegetable oil in your hands and toss spaghetti. Set aside still in the colander.

Meanwhile, thoroughly combine the seasoning mix ingredients in a small bowl and set aside.

In a 4-quart saucepan, combine *1½ sticks* of the butter, the onions and garlic cloves; sauté over medium heat 5 minutes, stirring occasionally. Add the minced garlic and the seasoning mix; continue cooking over medium heat until onions are dark brown but not burned, about 8 to 10 minutes, stirring often. Add *2½ cups* of the stock, the Worcestershire and Tabasco; bring to a fast simmer and cook about 8 minutes, stirring often. Stir in the tomato sauce and bring mixture to a boil. Then stir in the sugar and *1 cup* of the green onions; gently simmer uncovered about 40 minutes, stirring occasionally.

Heat the serving plates in a 250° oven.

Combine the ingredients of the chicken seasoning mix in a small bowl; mix well. Sprinkle over the chicken, rubbing it in with your hands. In a large skillet melt *1½ sticks* of the butter over medium heat. Add the remaining 1 cup green onions and sauté over high heat about 3 minutes. Add the chicken and continue cooking 10 minutes, stirring frequently. When the tomato sauce has simmered about 40 minutes, stir in the chicken mixture and heat through.

To finish the dish, for each serving melt 2 tablespoons butter in a large skillet over medium heat. Add one-sixth of the cooked spaghetti (a bit less than a 2-cup measure); heat spaghetti 1 minute, stirring constantly. Add 1¼ cups chicken and sauce and 2 tablespoons of remaining stock; heat thoroughly, stirring frequently. Remove from heat. Roll spaghetti on a large fork and lift onto a heated serving plate. Repeat process for remaining servings.

LAGNIAPPE

To test doneness of spaghetti, cut a strand in half near the end of cooking time. When done, there should be only a speck of white in the center, less than one-fourth the diameter of the strand.

Eggplant Rabbit Rhode IV

Makes 6 servings

The pirogues can be hollowed out ahead of time; cover well and refrigerate until ready to use. You can use the rabbit bones and giblets (excluding the liver) to make the stock.

3 (1-pound) eggplants, peeled
6 slices bacon, coarsely chopped

Seasoning mix:
1 tablespoon plus 1 teaspoon salt
2½ teaspoons onion powder
2½ teaspoons sweet paprika
1¼ teaspoons garlic powder
1¼ teaspoons white pepper
1 teaspoon ground red pepper (preferably cayenne)
1 teaspoon dried sweet basil leaves
½ teaspoon black pepper
½ teaspoon gumbo filé (filé powder), optional

1½ cups all-purpose flour, *in all*
1 (2- to 3-pound) domestic rabbit, boned and cut into ¾-inch pieces (see page 30; the butcher can bone the rabbit, you can cut the ¾-inch pieces)
1½ cups finely chopped green bell peppers
1 cup finely chopped onions
1½ cups **Basic Rabbit** or **Chicken Stock** (page 31)
1½ cups heavy cream
Vegetable oil for frying
1¼ cups very fine dry bread crumbs
2 small eggs or 1 large egg, beaten
1 cup milk

Cut each eggplant in half lengthwise; cut a thin slice from the rounded side of each eggplant half so it will sit level. With a knife and spoon, carve out pulp from inside, leaving a ¼-inch-thick shell (use pulp in another recipe). Set aside. (If you're short of time, substitute a ½-inch-thick lengthwise slice of eggplant for each pirogue.)

In a heavy 4-quart saucepan fry the bacon until crisp. Remove from heat and transfer the bacon with a slotted spoon to drain on paper towels, leaving the drippings in the pan.

In a small bowl thoroughly combine the seasoning mix ingredients. In a medium-size bowl combine *1 tablespoon plus 1 teaspoon* of the mix with *¼ cup* of the flour. Dredge the rabbit pieces in the seasoned flour until well coated, shaking off any excess. Turn heat to medium-high under the bacon drippings and add the rabbit to the pan; cook until browned on all sides, about 2 to 3 minutes, stirring frequently and scraping the pan bottom well. Add the bell peppers, onions, bacon and *2½ teaspoons* of the seasoning mix; continue cooking until vegetables start getting tender, about 2 to 4 minutes, stirring and scraping pan bottom almost constantly. Stir in *¼ cup* of the flour, mixing well. Add the stock, stirring until all sediment from pan bottom is dissolved; cook 2 to 3 minutes, stirring frequently. Stir in the cream. Reduce heat to low and let mixture simmer about 10 minutes, stirring and scraping pan bottom often so it doesn't scorch.

Meanwhile, heat the serving plates in a 250° oven and fry the eggplant pirogues: In a large skillet or deep fryer, heat ¾ inch oil to 350°. While the oil heats, sprinkle *1 tablespoon* of the seasoning mix evenly on the eggplant pirogues. Place the remaining flour in a pan (loaf, cake and pie pans work well) and the bread crumbs in another. Add *2 teaspoons* of the seasoning mix to the flour and the remaining 1 tablespoon to the bread crumbs, mixing each well. In another pan combine the egg(s) and milk, blending well. Just before frying, dredge the pirogues in the seasoned flour, shaking off excess; coat thoroughly with the egg mixture, then dredge in the seasoned bread crumbs. Fry the pirogues in the hot oil until golden brown, about 1 to 2 minutes per side. Do not crowd. Adjust heat as necessary to maintain oil's temperature at about 350°. Drain on paper towels. Serve immediately.

To serve, place each pirogue on a heated serving plate and fill with about ¾ cup rabbit pieces and sauce.

Panéed Chicken and Fettucini

Makes 4 servings

It is important that the oil for frying the chicken be hot enough (at least 300°) to seal the meat in the bread crumbs without the oil penetrating the crumbs (see page 26).

3/8 pound (1½ sticks) unsalted butter
2 cups heavy cream
½ teaspoon ground red pepper (preferably cayenne)
½ cup plus ⅓ cup, *in all*, finely grated Parmesan cheese
(preferably imported)
4 quarts hot water
2 tablespoons vegetable oil
1 tablespoon salt
½ pound fresh fettucini, or 6 ounces dry
5 eggs

Seasoning mix:
¼ cup catsup
3 tablespoons Creole mustard (preferred) or brown
mustard
1 tablespoon white pepper
1 tablespoon ground red pepper (preferably cayenne)
2 teaspoons garlic powder
2 teaspoons sweet paprika
½ teaspoon dried thyme leaves
¼ teaspoon rubbed sage
¼ teaspoon dried sweet basil leaves

2 cups very fine dry bread crumbs, toasted
4 chicken-leg thigh pieces, skinned, boned and pounded
just until each fillet is flat and of uniform thickness
Vegetable oil for pan frying

Melt the butter in a large skillet over medium-low heat; add the cream and red pepper. Turn heat to medium-high. With a metal whisk whip the cream mixture constantly as it comes to a boil. Reduce heat and simmer until the sauce thickens enough to coat a spoon well, about 7 to 8 minutes, whisking constantly. Remove from heat and gradually add ½ *cup* of the Parmesan, whipping until cheese is melted; set this sauce aside.

Place the hot water, 2 tablespoons oil and salt in a large pot over high heat; cover and bring to a boil. When water reaches a rolling boil, add a handful of fettucini at a time to the pot, breaking up oil patches as you drop fettucini in. Return to boiling and cook to al dente stage (about 3 minutes if fresh, 7 minutes if dry); do not overcook. During this cooking time, use a wooden or spaghetti spoon to lift fettucini out of the water by spoonfuls and shake strands back into the boiling water. (It may be an old wives' tale, but this procedure seems to enhance the pasta's texture.) Then immediately drain fettucini into a colander; stop its cooking by running cold water over the fettucini. (If you used dry pasta, first rinse with hot water to wash off starch.) After the pasta has cooled thoroughly, about 2 to 3 minutes, pour a liberal amount of vegetable oil in your hands and toss the fettucini. Set aside still in the colander.

Combine the ingredients of the seasoning mix in a small bowl; mix well. Combine the eggs and the remaining ⅓ cup Parmesan in a pan (cake or pie pans work well); beat well. In a separate pan combine 2 *tablespoons* of the seasoning mix with the bread crumbs, mixing very well (a food processor or blender is easiest for this); set aside. Spread a thin layer of the remaining seasoning mix evenly on both sides of the chicken (use any remaining seasoning mix in another recipe). Then soak the chicken pieces in the egg mixture for 15 to 30 minutes.

Heat the serving plates in a 250° oven.

In a large skillet, heat about ¼ inch oil to at least 300°. Meanwhile, drain the excess egg mixture well from the chicken; dredge chicken pieces in the bread crumbs, pressing crumbs in with your fingertips. (There should be a thin, even layer of crumbs, with no clumps of crumbs in the meat creases.) Shake off excess crumbs and gently drop the chicken into the hot oil, skin side down first and flattening the meat as needed to make it fry evenly. Fry until golden brown on both sides, about 2 to 3 minutes per side. (Adjust heat as necessary to maintain the oil's temperature at least 300°.) Drain on paper towels.

Reheat the cheese sauce over medium-high heat, whisking frequently. (**Note:** If butter starts separating from the sauce, add about 1 tablespoon additional cream while reheating.) Add the fettucini and toss until thoroughly coated. Serve immediately.

To serve, place a piece of chicken on each heated serving plate. Roll each portion of fettucini onto a large fork and lift onto the plate; top the fettucini with additional sauce remaining in the pan.

LAGNIAPPE

To test doneness of fettucini, cut a strand in half near the end of the cooking time. When done, there should be only a speck of white in the center.

Panéed Rabbit and Fettucini

Makes 4 servings

The rabbit is pan fried for this dish. See page 25 for more about pan frying.

⅜ pound (1½ sticks) unsalted butter
2 cups heavy cream
½ teaspoon ground red pepper (preferably cayenne)
½ cup plus 6 tablespoons, *in all*, finely grated Parmesan cheese (preferably imported)
4 quarts hot water
2 tablespoons vegetable oil
1 tablespoon salt
½ pound fresh fettucini, or 6 ounces dry
6 eggs

Seasoning mix:
¼ cup catsup
3 tablespoons Creole mustard (preferred) or brown mustard

2 tablespoons sugar
1 tablespoon white pepper
1 tablespoon ground red pepper (preferably cayenne)
2 teaspoons garlic powder
2 teaspoons sweet paprika

3 cups very fine dry bread crumbs, toasted
4 rabbit back legs, boned and pounded (see page 30) just until each filet is flat and of uniform thickness
Vegetable oil for pan frying

Melt the butter in a large skillet over medium-low heat; when almost melted, add the cream and red pepper. Turn heat to medium-high and whisk mixture constantly with a metal whisk as it comes to a boil. Reduce heat and simmer until the sauce thickens enough to coat a spoon well, about 7 to 8 minutes, whisking constantly. Remove from heat and gradually add *½ cup* of the Parmesan, whipping it into the sauce until melted; set aside.

Combine the hot water, 2 tablespoons oil and salt in a large pot over high heat; cover and bring to a boil. When water reaches a rolling boil, add small amount of fettucini at a time to the pot, breaking up oil patches as you drop the strands in. Return to boiling and cook uncovered to al dente stage (about 3 minutes if fresh, 7 minutes if dry); do not overcook. During this cooking time, use a wooden or spaghetti spoon to lift the fettucini out of the water by spoonfuls and shake strands back into the boiling water. (It may be an old wives' tale, but this procedure seems to enhance the pasta's texture.) Then immediately drain fettucini into a colander; stop its cooking by running cold water over strands. (If you used dry pasta, first rinse with hot water to wash off starch.) After the pasta has cooled thoroughly, about 2 to 3 minutes, pour a liberal amount of vegetable oil in your hands and toss the fettucini. Set aside still in the colander.

Combine the eggs and the remaining 6 tablespoons Parmesan in a pan (cake and pie pans work well); beat well.

In a small bowl, thoroughly combine the seasoning mix ingredients. Combine *3 tablespoons* of the mix with the bread crumbs in a pan. Sprinkle the remaining seasoning mix evenly on both sides of the rabbit pieces. Then soak the rabbit in the egg mixture for 15 to 30 minutes.

Heat the serving plates in a 250° oven.

In a large skillet, heat ½ inch oil over high heat to at least 300°. Meanwhile, drain the excess egg mixture well from the rabbit; dredge rabbit pieces in the bread crumbs, pressing crumbs in with your fingertips. (There should be a thin, even layer of crumbs, with no clumps of crumbs in the meat creases.) Shake off excess crumbs and gently drop the rabbit into the hot oil, flattening the meat as needed to make it fry evenly. Fry until golden brown on both sides, about 5 to 6 minutes per side. Do not crowd. (Adjust heat as needed to maintain the oil's temperature.) Drain on paper towels.

Reheat the cheese sauce over medium-high heat, whisking frequently. (**NOTE:** If butter starts separating from the sauce, add about 1 tablespoon additional cream to the sauce while reheating.) Add the fettucini and toss until thoroughly coated. Serve immediately.

To serve, place a piece of rabbit on each heated serving plate. Roll each portion of fettucini onto a large fork and lift onto the plate; top the fettucini with additional sauce remaining in the pan.

LAGNIAPPE

To test doneness of fettucini, cut a strand in half near the end of the cooking time. When done, there should be only a speck of white in the center.

Chicken Etouffée

Makes 8 servings

This dish is excellent served with potato salad on the side.

2 (3-pound) chickens, each cut in 8 pieces
Salt
Garlic powder
Ground red pepper (preferably cayenne)
About 1¼ cups all-purpose flour
Vegetable oil for deep frying
½ cup finely chopped onions, *in all*
½ cup finely chopped celery, *in all*
½ cup finely chopped green bell peppers, *in all*
About 3½ cups, *in all*, **Chicken Stock** (recipe follows)

Seasoning mix:
1½ teaspoons salt
1½ teaspoons ground red pepper (preferably cayenne)
¾ teaspoon black pepper
½ teaspoon white pepper
½ teaspoon garlic powder

½ pound (2 sticks) unsalted butter, *in all*
¾ cup very finely chopped green onions
4 cups hot **Basic Cooked Rice** (page 224)

Remove excess fat from the chicken pieces. Rub a generous amount of salt, garlic powder and red pepper on both sides of each piece, making sure each is evenly covered. Let stand at room temperature for 30 minutes.

Meanwhile, in a paper or plastic bag combine the flour, ½ teaspoon salt, ½ teaspoon garlic powder and ½ teaspoon red pepper. Add the chicken pieces and shake until pieces are well coated. Reserve any excess flour.

In a large heavy skillet (preferably cast iron) heat 1½ inches of oil to 375°. Fry the chicken pieces until both sides are browned and the meat is cooked, about 5 to 8 minutes per side. Drain on paper towels and set aside. Carefully pour the hot oil into a large glass measuring cup, leaving as many of the browned particles in the skillet as possible. Scrape the skillet bottom with a metal whisk to loosen any stuck particles, then return ½ cup of the oil to the skillet.

Heat the oil in the skillet over high heat until it starts to smoke, about 5 minutes. (It may take longer if skillet is not cast iron.) Meanwhile, measure out ¾ cup flour (use the reserved flour from chicken coating and as much additional flour as needed to make ¾ cup). In a small bowl combine *¼ cup each* of the onions, celery and bell peppers.

When the oil is hot, remove the skillet from the heat and add the flour. Using a long-handled metal whisk, stir until all the flour is blended into the oil. Return the skillet to a medium-high heat and whisk constantly until the roux is dark red-brown to black, about 3 to 4 minutes (being careful not to let it scorch or splash on your skin). Immediately remove roux from heat and whisk in the vegetable mixture. Continue whisking until the roux stops turning darker, about 2 to 3 minutes. Set aside.

✱ See page 26 for more about making roux.

Bring *3½ cups* of the stock to a rolling boil in a 2-quart saucepan. Add the roux mixture by spoonfuls to the boiling stock, stirring until dissolved between each addition. Bring the mixture to a rolling boil again and simmer uncovered over low heat for 15 minutes, stirring fairly constantly. (The etouffée sauce should be the consistency of very thick gravy.) Set aside.

Combine the seasoning mix ingredients in a small bowl; mix well and set aside.

Melt *5 tablespoons* of the butter in a large skillet. Add the remaining ¼ cup each of onions, celery and bell peppers. Sauté over very low heat until the vegetables are completely wilted, about 10 to 12 minutes, stirring occasionally. Add the reserved etouffée sauce and the seasoning mix. Simmer 15 minutes longer, stirring frequently.

Heat the serving plates in a 250° oven.

Melt the remaining butter in a 4-quart saucepan over medium heat; add the green onions and sauté about 2 minutes. Add the chicken and etouffée sauce and bring to a boil over medium heat. Remove pan from heat and let sit 15 minutes. Skim off surface oil. Reheat the sauce just until well heated. You may need to thin the sauce with additional stock (preferred) or water. (The end result should be a thick brown gravy.) Serve immediately.

To serve, place ½ cup of rice and 2 pieces of chicken on each heated serving plate. Top rice with ⅓ cup sauce.

Chicken Stock for Etouffée

Giblets (excluding livers) from the chickens, optional
1 pound chicken back and/or necks
6 cups cold water
½ medium onion, unpeeled
2 cloves garlic, unpeeled and cut in thirds
1 celery stalk with top
2 bay leaves

Place the giblets, backs and/or necks and water in a 3-quart saucepan. Bring to a boil over high heat. Add the onions, garlic, celery and bay leaves, and simmer over very low heat for about 1 to 2 hours. Add water if needed to maintain about 5 cups of stock in the pan. Strain the liquid. Cool and refrigerate if not being used immediately. Makes about 5 cups.

Duck Etouffée

Makes 8 servings

The duck can be roasted and boned a day ahead and refrigerated until ready to make the etouffée. You can also make the stock ahead, but don't strain it.

2 (5- to 6-pound) domestic ducklings

First seasoning mix:
1 tablespoon salt
2 teaspoons sweet paprika
1 teaspoon garlic powder
1 teaspoon ground red pepper (preferably cayenne)
¾ teaspoon onion powder
¾ teaspoon ground sage
½ teaspoon white pepper
½ teaspoon black pepper
½ teaspoon dried thyme leaves
½ teaspoon gumbo filé (filé powder), optional

10 cups cold water
2 cups finely chopped onions, *in all*
1½ cups finely chopped celery, *in all*
1½ cups finely chopped green bell peppers, *in all*
2 bay leaves

Second seasoning mix:
1¼ teaspoons garlic powder
1¼ teaspoons ground red pepper (preferably cayenne)
1 teaspoon salt
1 teaspoon onion powder
¾ teaspoon white pepper
½ teaspoon black pepper

1 cup all-purpose flour
½ teaspoon minced garlic
⅓ cup finely chopped green onions
6 cups hot **Basic Cooked Rice** (page 224)
Potato Salad (page 237)

Remove visible fat from the ducks and fold the wings underneath the backs.

Combine the first seasoning mix ingredients in a small bowl; mix well. Sprinkle the seasoning mix on the inside and outside of the ducks and on the necks and giblets, massaging it in with your hands and using all of the mix. Place the necks and giblets inside the ducks and put the ducks on a rack in a large roasting pan, breast up. Bake at 250°

until drumsticks turn easily, about 5 to 5½ hours. Allow ducks to cool enough to handle; reserve 1 cup of the drippings. Remove the necks and giblets. Partially bone the ducks and cut each into 4 portions as follows: Slice each duck in half lengthwise; then carefully remove the wings, breastbone and backbone, leaving the skin attached to the meat; reserve the bones, wings, necks and giblets to make the stock; cut the 2 halves of boned meat in half (you will have breasts as one portion and legs and thighs as another portion). Refrigerate the meat while making the stock.

In a 4-quart saucepan cover the duck bones, wings and giblets (except the livers) with the cold water. Bring to a boil over high heat. Reduce heat and simmer about 1 hour, adding water if necessary to maintain about 7 cups of stock in the pan.

Combine *1 cup* of the onions, *1 cup* of the celery, *1 cup* of the bell peppers and the bay leaves in a medium-size bowl and set aside. In a small bowl combine the second seasoning mix ingredients; mix well and set aside.

If you've made the stock ahead of time, reheat it over high heat in a 4-quart saucepan until it reaches a boil.

Meanwhile, in a large heavy skillet, heat the reserved drippings over high heat until the drippings begin to smoke, about 5 minutes. Gradually add the flour, whisking with a long-handled metal whisk until smooth. Continue cooking, whisking constantly or quickly stirring with a wooden spoon, until the roux is dark red-brown to black, about 4 to 6 minutes (being careful not to scorch it or splash any on your skin). Immediately add the vegetable mixture and stir well. Then stir in the second seasoning mix. Remove roux from heat.

✱ See page 26 for more about making roux.

Add the roux by spoonfuls to the boiling stock, stirring until dissolved between each addition. Reduce heat to medium-low and cook about 30 minutes longer, stirring occasionally. Remove from heat and strain liquid into a 2-quart saucepan. (Discard the strained vegetables and bones.) Return liquid to high heat. Stir in the remaining 1 cup onions, ½ cup celery and ½ cup bell peppers and the garlic; bring to a boil. Reduce heat to a simmer and continue cooking until sauce reduces to 6 cups, about 15 minutes, stirring occasionally. Stir in the green onions and cook about 1 minute more. Remove from heat and skim any oil from the surface.

With a knife, scrape off as much unmelted fat as possible from under the skin of the duck pieces without completely detaching the skin. Place the duck in a 13x9-inch ungreased baking pan. Spoon the etouffée sauce over it. Bake at 350° until meat is heated through, about 30 minutes. Serve immediately on heated serving plates, allowing a generous ½ cup sauce over ¾ cup rice and a portion of duck. Serve with Potato Salad on the side.

Cheese and Hot Pepper Chicken

Makes 8 servings

Seasoning mix:
1 tablespoon salt
1 teaspoon onion powder
1 teaspoon garlic powder
1 teaspoon dry mustard
1 teaspoon ground red pepper (preferably cayenne)
½ teaspoon white pepper
½ teaspoon ground cumin
½ teaspoon black pepper
½ teaspoon dried thyme leaves
½ teaspoon dried oregano leaves
¼ teaspoon ground cinnamon

1¼ cups all-purpose flour
2 (2½- to 3-pound) chickens, cut in 16 pieces and at room temperature
Vegetable oil for frying
2⅔ cups chopped green bell peppers, *in all*
2 cups chopped onions
1 cup chopped green chilies, *in all*
2 bay leaves
2 teaspoons salt
2 teaspoons minced garlic

1½ teaspoons ground red pepper (preferably cayenne)
¾ teaspoon white pepper
¾ teaspoon black pepper
2 tablespoons finely chopped jalapeño peppers (see **NOTE**)
4 cups, *in all*, **Basic Chicken Stock** (page 31)
1½ cups heavy cream
1 cup dairy sour cream
1½ cups grated Monterey Jack cheese or other white nonprocessed cheese
1½ cups grated cheddar cheese
4 cups hot **Basic Cooked Rice** (page 224)

NOTE: Fresh jalapeños are preferred; if you have to use pickled ones, rinse as much vinegar from them as possible.

Thoroughly combine the seasoning mix ingredients in a small bowl, breaking up any mustard lumps. Combine *1 tablespoon* of the mix with the flour in a plastic or paper bag and set aside. Remove any excess fat from chicken pieces. Sprinkle the remaining seasoning mix evenly on the chicken, patting it in by hand. Dredge chicken in the seasoned flour. Reserve leftover flour.

Heat ½ inch of oil in a large skillet (I find this dish tastes significantly better if you *don't* use a nonstick type skillet) to 350°. Fry the chicken in batches, large pieces and skin side down first, just until light brown and crispy, about 2 to 4 minutes per side. (Lower heat if drippings in pan start to brown; you will use the drippings in the cream sauce, and you need them to remain light in color and taste so they won't dominate the cheese, peppers and cream flavors.) Drain on paper towels.

Carefully pour the hot oil into a glass measuring cup, leaving as much sediment as possible in the skillet; return ½ cup hot oil to the skillet. Add *2 cups* of the bell peppers, the onions and *⅔ cup* of the green chilies; turn heat to high and stir well to mix vegetables with the sediment on the pan bottom. Cook until onions start to brown, about 6 to 8 minutes, stirring occasionally. Add the bay leaves, salt, garlic and the red, white and black peppers; stir well. Then sprinkle 3 tablespoons of the reserved flour on the vegetable mixture and stir thoroughly. Stir in the jalapeño peppers and cook about 2 minutes, stirring occasionally (lower heat if sticking excessively). Stir in *1 cup* of the stock and scrape pan bottom well. Stir in 2 *cups* more stock and stir. Remove from heat.

Place the chicken in a 5½-quart saucepan or large Dutch oven. Add the vegetable mixture and the remaining 1 cup stock to the chicken; stir well. Bring to a boil and then simmer over low heat for 15 minutes, stirring occasionally and being careful not to let mixture scorch. Add the remaining ⅔ cup bell peppers, ⅓ cup green chilies, the cream and sour cream. Bring to a boil over medium heat, stirring fairly constantly. Then stir in the cheeses and cook just until cheese melts, stirring constantly. Serve immediately, allowing about ½ cup rice and 2 pieces of chicken per serving, topped with about ⅔ cup sauce. (Leftover sauce is wonderful over vegetables.)

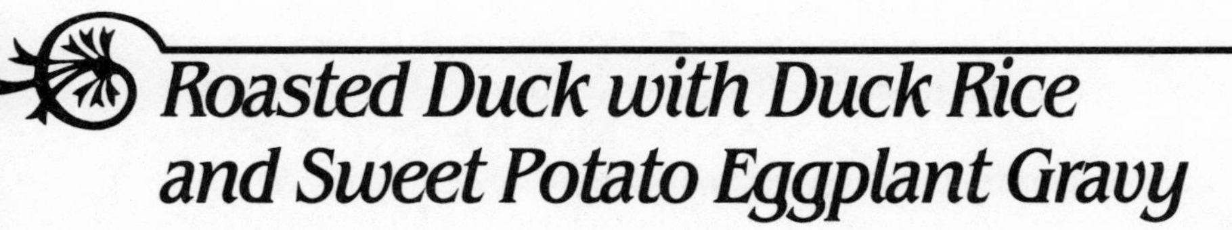

Roasted Duck with Duck Rice and Sweet Potato Eggplant Gravy

Makes 6 servings

3 (5- to 6-pound) domestic ducklings

Seasoning mix:
5 tablespoons salt
1 tablespoon plus 1 teaspoon onion powder
1 tablespoon plus 1 teaspoon garlic powder
1 tablespoon plus 1 teaspoon black pepper
1 tablespoon white pepper
1 tablespoon dried rosemary leaves, crushed
2 teaspoons rubbed sage
2 teaspoons ground red pepper (preferably cayenne)
1 teaspoon ground cumin

10½ cups **Duck Stock** (recipe follows)
Sweet Potato Eggplant Gravy (recipe follows)
Duck Rice (recipe follows)

Rinse the ducks and giblets well; drain well and place in a very large roasting pan.

In a small bowl combine the seasoning mix ingredients, mixing well. Sprinkle about *3 tablespoons* of the mix on the outside and inside of each duck, patting it in by hand; sprinkle the remaining seasoning mix on the giblets and necks and place inside ducks. Bake ducks at 250° until drumstick bones move easily, about 5 to 5½ hours.

Remove ducks from drippings and cool slightly; reserve drippings. Remove giblets and necks and set aside. Wipe off excess seasoning from the cooked ducks with a wet towel. Then split each duck in half lengthwise and carefully remove all bones except the large wing bones. (Reserve any meat scraps for the duck rice as you're boning the ducks and the bones and necks for the duck stock; chop and reserve the giblets for the duck rice.) Keeping each duck half intact, use a knife to scrape off any unmelted fat from under the skin without completely detaching the skin. Refrigerate meat while making the stock and save duck fat for making the gravy and duck rice.

Make the Duck Stock, the Sweet Potato Eggplant Gravy and the Duck Rice. (When you place the Duck Rice in the oven, also reheat the duck—skin up and in a single layer—in a baking pan until hot, about 45 minutes, depending on size.) Serve immediately.

To serve, for each person allow half a roasted duckling and a portion of rice, topping both with gravy.

Duck Stock

Bones and necks from the 3 roasted ducklings
3½ quarts cold water
2 onions, unpeeled and cut in quarters

Place all ingredients in a large pot. Bring to a rapid boil and then simmer uncovered at least 1½ hours. Add water as needed to maintain about 3 quarts of stock in the pot. Strain. Cool and refrigerate if not using immediately. Makes about 3 quarts.

Sweet Potato Eggplant Gravy

½ cup duck fat (from the reserved drippings and duck-skin fat)
4 cups peeled and chopped eggplant, *in all*
1½ cups chopped onions
1 cup peeled and finely chopped sweet potatoes
1 teaspoon minced garlic
3 bay leaves
1½ teaspoons salt, *in all*
1½ teaspoons white pepper, *in all*
1½ teaspoons, *in all*, ground red pepper (preferably cayenne)
1 teaspoon dry mustard
½ teaspoon dried thyme leaves
8 cups, *in all*, **Duck Stock** (preceding recipe)
½ cup, packed, dark brown sugar, *in all*
1 cup peeled sweet potatoes, cut into ½-inch dice
3 tablespoons Grand Marnier
½ cup finely chopped green onions

Melt the duck fat in a large skillet over medium-high heat. Add *3 cups* of the eggplant and sauté until eggplant starts to get soft, translucent and brown, about 5 minutes, stirring frequently. Add the onions and remaining 1 cup eggplant; cook until the onions start to brown, about 8 to 10 minutes, stirring occasionally. Add the finely chopped sweet potatoes; continue cooking and stirring for 4 minutes. Stir in the garlic and cook 3 minutes, stirring occasionally. Add the bay leaves, *1 teaspoon* of the salt, *1 teaspoon each* of the white and red peppers, the mustard and thyme; stir well, scraping pan bottom as needed.

Next, stir *1 cup* of the stock into the vegetables and cook 2 minutes, then add another *1 cup* stock; cook 5 minutes, stirring occasionally. Stir in *¼ cup* of the sugar and cook 2 minutes, stirring occasionally. Add another *1 cup* stock and cook 10 minutes, stirring occasionally. Add the remaining ¼ cup sugar and *1 cup* more stock; cook 10 minutes, stirring occasionally, then add another *1 cup* stock and cook 10 minutes more, stirring occasionally. Reduce heat to low and simmer 13 minutes. Stir in another *1 cup* stock and simmer for 3 minutes. Remove from heat and strain well, forcing as much liquid as possible through the strainer.

Place the strained gravy in a 2-quart saucepan. Add the diced sweet potatoes and *1 cup* stock; bring to a boil over high heat, then reduce heat and simmer 3 minutes, skimming off any froth from the surface. Stir in the Grand Marnier and continue simmering 7 minutes, stirring occasionally. Add the green onions, the remaining ½ teaspoon each of salt, white and red pepper and 1 cup more stock. Bring gravy to a boil and simmer until it reduces to about 3 cups, about 8 minutes, stirring occasionally. Makes 3 cups.

Duck Rice

½ cup chopped onions
1 tablespoon duck fat
1½ cups uncooked rice (preferably converted)
2½ cups **Duck Stock** (page 174)
Meat scraps from boning the roasted ducklings
Chopped roasted giblets from the roasted ducklings
¼ teaspoon salt
¼ cup very finely chopped green onions

In a large skillet sauté the onions in duck fat over medium heat until well browned but not burned, about 5 minutes, stirring often. Add the rice; cook 5 minutes over medium heat, stirring constantly. Add the stock, meat scraps, giblets and salt; stir well. Transfer the rice mixture to a baking pan; seal pan with aluminum foil and bake at 350° until all liquid is absorbed, about 45 minutes. Stir in the green onions. Makes about 6 cups.

Boneless Half-Chicken with Oyster Dressing and Gingersnap Gravy

Makes 6 servings

Prepare the half-chicken pieces for baking ahead of time up to the point of baking and use the leftover meat and bones to make the **Basic Chicken Stock** *(page 31) for the gravy.*

3 (3- to 3½-pound) chickens

Seasoning mix:
1 tablespoon salt
¾ teaspoon garlic powder
¾ teaspoon black pepper
½ teaspoon white pepper
½ teaspoon onion powder
½ teaspoon ground cumin
¼ teaspoon ground red pepper (preferably cayenne)
¼ teaspoon sweet paprika

½ cup finely chopped onions
¼ pound (1 stick) unsalted butter, cut into chunks
Oyster Dressing (recipe follows)
Gingersnap Gravy (recipe follows)

Cut the leg-thigh pieces from the chickens and bone along the length of the bones, leaving meat in one piece with the skin on. Bone the breasts lengthwise so that you get two breast pieces per chicken, also with the skin on.

Combine the seasoning mix ingredients in a small bowl; mix well and set aside.

To prepare each half-chicken, use one breast and one leg piece. In a roasting pan lay each leg (skin side up) on top of a breast (skin side up); tuck the edges of the leg meat and skin under the breast piece to form what will appear to be one piece of chicken. Generously season chicken "halves" on both sides with the seasoning mix, patting it in by hand. Plump up each piece so it is neatly formed and rounded with the skin side up. Sprinkle the onions and chunks of butter in the bottom of the roasting pan around the chicken. Refrigerate while making the stock. Then bake the chicken in a 425° oven until done, about 35 to 40 minutes. Set aside and keep warm. Reserve 1 cup of the pan drippings for the gravy.

Meanwhile, prepare the dressing. (If you don't have two ovens, bake the dressing at 350° as soon as you remove the chicken from the oven.) Then make the gravy and serve chicken immediately on heated serving plates. To serve, arrange one of the chicken halves and ½ cup oyster dressing on each plate; pour about ⅓ cup gravy over the top.

Oyster Dressing

About 20 small to medium oysters in their liquor, ½ pound
1 cup cold water
⅜ pound (1½ sticks) margarine, *in all*
1½ cups chopped onions, *in all*
1 cup chopped celery, *in all*
1 cup chopped green bell peppers, *in all*

Seasoning mix:
½ teaspoon salt
½ teaspoon garlic powder
½ teaspoon ground red pepper (preferably cayenne)
½ teaspoon sweet paprika
½ teaspoon black pepper
¼ teaspoon onion powder
¼ teaspoon dried oregano leaves
¼ teaspoon dried thyme leaves

1 teaspoon minced garlic
3 bay leaves
About 1 cup very fine dry bread crumbs
2 tablespoons unsalted butter, softened
¼ cup chopped green onions

Combine the oysters and water; stir and refrigerate at least 1 hour. Strain and reserve the oysters and oyster water; refrigerate until ready to use.

Melt *4 tablespoons* of the margarine in a large skillet over high heat. When margarine is almost melted, add *¾ cup* of the onions, *½ cup* of the celery and *½ cup* of the bell peppers. Sauté over high heat until onions are dark brown but not burned, about 8 minutes, stirring frequently.

Meanwhile, in a small bowl combine the seasoning mix ingredients; mix well. When the onions are browned, stir *2 teaspoons* of the seasoning mix and the garlic into the skillet. Reduce heat to medium and continue cooking for 5 minutes, stirring occasionally. Add the remaining ¾ cup onions, ½ cup celery, ½ cup bell peppers and 1 stick margarine and the bay leaves. Stir until margarine is melted. Continue cooking 10 minutes, stirring occasionally. Stir in the reserved oyster water and cook over high heat about 10 minutes, stirring occasionally. Stir in the remaining seasoning mix and enough bread crumbs to make a moist but not runny dressing; remove from heat. Stir in the drained oysters. Spoon dressing into an ungreased 8x8x2-inch baking pan and bake uncovered in a 350° oven for 30 minutes. Remove from oven, discard bay leaves, and stir in the butter and green onions. Makes about 3 cups.

Gingersnap Gravy

Seasoning mix:
1 teaspoon black pepper
½ teaspoon salt
½ teaspoon white pepper
½ teaspoon ground ginger
Scant ½ teaspoon dried thyme leaves
¼ teaspoon rubbed sage
¼ teaspoon ground red pepper (preferably cayenne)
⅛ teaspoon ground cumin

2 tablespoons chicken fat, pork lard or beef fat
2 tablespoons unsalted butter

¾ cup finely chopped onions
½ cup finely chopped celery
½ teaspoon minced garlic
6 cups **Basic Chicken Stock** (page 31)
1 cup pan drippings from roasted chicken (add stock if needed to make 1 cup)
8 gingersnap cookies
1 tablespoon light brown sugar, or to taste
1 teaspoon ground ginger, or to taste

Combine the seasoning mix ingredients in a small bowl and set aside.

Melt the fat and butter in a large skillet over medium heat. When almost melted, add the onions, celery and garlic; sauté 5 minutes, stirring occasionally. Stir in the seasoning mix and cook 5 minutes more, stirring occasionally. Add the stock and pan drippings; bring to a boil over high heat and boil rapidly until liquid reduces to about 1 quart, about 25 minutes. Then crumble the gingersnaps into the stock mixture and whisk with a metal whisk until they are dissolved. Continue cooking 10 minutes, whisking frequently and making sure the gingersnaps are thoroughly dissolved. During this time, taste the gravy; if the ginger flavor is not pronounced, add the 1 tablespoon brown sugar and the 1 teaspoon ginger or add both to taste. Strain the gravy. Makes 2½ to 3 cups.

PORK

Roasted Pork

Makes 6 servings

This dish will knock your socks off! It's wonderful with **Oyster Dressing** *(page 178), and the leftovers make terrific sandwiches.*

Seasoning mix:
2 teaspoons black pepper
1½ teaspoons salt
1 teaspoon white pepper
1 teaspoon ground red pepper (preferably cayenne)
1 teaspoon sweet paprika
1 teaspoon dried thyme leaves
½ teaspoon dry mustard

3 tablespoons unsalted butter
1 tablespoon pork lard or chicken fat (preferred) or vegetable oil
½ cup finely chopped onions
½ cup finely chopped celery
½ cup finely chopped green bell peppers
1 tablespoon minced garlic
1 (4-pound) boneless pork loin roast (have your butcher prepare)

Thoroughly combine the seasoning mix ingredients. Place all ingredients except the roast in a large skillet. Sauté about 4 minutes over high heat, stirring occasionally. Cool.

Meanwhile, place the roast in a baking pan, fat side up. Make several deep slits in the meat with a knife, to form pockets, being careful not to cut through to the bottom. Stuff the pockets with some of the vegetable mixture, then thoroughly rub vegetable mixture over the entire roast by hand. If any of the mixture is left, spread it evenly over the top and a little on the sides of the roast. Bake uncovered at 275° for 3 hours, then at 425° until dark brown on top and meat is white in the center, 10 to 15 minutes more.

Stuffed Pork Chops

Makes 6 servings

This dish is also good with **Oyster Dressing** *(page 178) substituted for the stuffing.*

2 unpeeled medium apples, coarsely chopped
7 tablespoons unsalted butter
3 tablespoons light brown sugar
1 teaspoon vanilla extract
½ teaspoon ground nutmeg

Seasoning mix:
1 tablespoon salt
1 teaspoon onion powder
1 teaspoon ground red pepper (preferably cayenne)
¾ teaspoon garlic powder
½ teaspoon white pepper
½ teaspoon dry mustard
½ teaspoon rubbed sage
½ teaspoon ground cumin
½ teaspoon black pepper
½ teaspoon dried thyme leaves

6 (1¾-inch-thick) pork chops
¾ pound ground pork
1 cup chopped onions
1 cup chopped green bell peppers
2 teaspoons minced garlic
1 (4-ounce) can diced green chilies and their juice
1 cup **Basic Pork** or **Chicken Stock** (page 31)
½ cup very fine dry bread crumbs
½ cup finely chopped green onions

In a food processor or blender, process the apples, *4 tablespoons* of the butter, the sugar, vanilla and nutmeg until smooth, about 3 to 4 minutes. Set aside.

In a small bowl thoroughly combine the seasoning mix ingredients; set aside.

Prepare the pork chops by cutting a large pocket (to the bone) into the larger side of each chop to hold the stuffing.

In a large skillet brown the ground pork in the remaining 3 tablespoons butter over high heat, about 3 minutes. Add the onions, bell peppers, garlic and 2 *tablespoons* of the seasoning mix, stirring well; cook about 5 minutes, stirring occasionally and scraping pan bottom well. Stir in the green chilies and continue cooking until mixture is well browned, about 6 to 8 minutes, stirring occasionally and scraping pan bottom as needed. Add the stock and cook 5 minutes, stirring frequently. Stir in the bread crumbs and cook about 3 minutes, then add the apple mixture and the green onions; cook about 2 minutes more, stirring constantly and scraping pan botttom as needed. Remove from heat.

Sprinkle the remaining seasoning mix evenly on both sides of the chops and inside the pockets, pressing it in by hand. Prop chops with pocket side up in an ungreased 13x9-inch baking pan. Spoon about ¼ cup stuffing into each pocket; reserve the remaining stuffing. Bake chops with pocket up at 400° until meat is done, about 1 hour 10 minutes. Place the remaining stuffing in a small pan in the oven for the last 20 minutes to reheat.

Serve immediately with each chop arranged on top of a portion of the remaining stuffing.

Pasta Chu Chu

Makes 2 servings

The sauce for Pasta Chu Chu (pronounced "shoe shoe") is best if made only two servings at a time. If you want to make more than two servings, do so in separate batches and serve each while piping hot.

2 quarts hot water
1 tablespoon salt
1 tablespoon vegetable oil
¼ pound fresh spaghetti, or about 3 ounces dry

Seasoning mix:
2 teaspoons salt
1 teaspoon white pepper
1 teaspoon garlic powder
1 teaspoon dry mustard
1 teaspoon sweet paprika
½ teaspoon ground red pepper (preferably cayenne)

7 tablespoons unsalted butter, *in all*
1 cup julienned pastrami (1½x¼x¼-inch strips)
⅔ cup julienned onions (see **NOTE**)
⅔ cup julienned carrots (see **NOTE**)
⅔ cup sliced mushrooms
⅔ cup julienned yellow squash (see **NOTE**)
⅔ cup julienned zucchini (see **NOTE**)
1 cup heavy cream

NOTE: To julienne squashes, cut peelings ⅛ inch thick and cut these into strips ⅛ inch wide and 2 inches long; use only strips that have skin on one surface. Cut onions and carrots into similar strips.

Place the hot water, salt and oil in a large pot over high heat; cover and bring to a boil. When water reaches a rolling boil, add small amounts of spaghetti at a time to the pot, breaking up oil patches as you drop spaghetti in. Return to boiling and cook uncovered to al dente stage (about 4 minutes if fresh, 7 minutes if dry); do not overcook. During this cooking time, use a wooden or spaghetti spoon to lift spaghetti out of the water by spoonfuls and shake strands back into the boiling water. (It may be an old wives' tale but this procedure seems to enhance the spaghetti's texture.) Then immediately drain spaghetti into a colander; stop cooking process by running cold water over strands. (If you used dry spaghetti, first rinse with hot water to wash off starch.) After the spaghetti has cooled thoroughly, about 2 to 3 minutes, pour a liberal amount of vegetable oil in your hands and toss spaghetti. Set aside still in the colander.

Heat the serving plates in a 250° oven.

Combine the seasoning mix ingredients thoroughly in a small bowl and set aside.

Melt *4 tablespoons* of the butter in a large skillet over high heat.

Add the pastrami and cook 1 minute, stirring frequently. Add the onions and carrots; stir and sauté until vegetables start to get tender, about 2 minutes. Add the mushrooms, squash, zucchini and *1½ teaspoons* of the seasoning mix; stir well. Stir in the cream. Add the remaining 3 tablespoons butter and cook, while constantly shaking the pan fairly briskly in a back-and-forth motion (versus stirring), until the butter melts and mixture starts to boil, about 3 to 4 minutes. Add the cooked spaghetti; cook just until spaghetti is heated through, about 1 minute, tossing constantly. Remove from heat and serve immediately.

To serve, roll half the spaghetti on a large fork and lift onto a heated serving plate. Spoon half of the sauce on top. (Use leftover seasoning mix in another recipe.)

LAGNIAPPE

To test doneness of spaghetti, cut a strand in half near the end of cooking time. When done, there should be only a speck of white in the center, less than one-fourth the diameter of the strand.

Shaking the pan in a back-and-forth motion and the addition of cream to the melting butter keep the sauce from separating and having an oily texture—stirring doesn't produce the same effect.

New Orleans Italian Sausage-Stuffed Eggplant with Red Gravy

Makes 6 servings

3 (12- to 14-ounce) eggplants, stems removed and halved lengthwise
8 cups, *in all*, **Basic Chicken Stock** (page 31)

First seasoning mix:
3 whole bay leaves
1½ teaspoons dried sweet basil leaves
1¼ teaspoons ground red pepper (preferably cayenne)
1 teaspoon white pepper
1 teaspoon black pepper
¾ teaspoon dried thyme leaves
⅛ teaspoon ground nutmeg

¼ pound (1 stick) margarine
2 cups chopped onions, *in all*
1½ cups chopped green bell peppers, *in all*
1 cup chopped celery, *in all*
1 pound sweet Italian sausage, casing removed, halved lengthwise
1 tablespoon plus 1½ teaspoons minced garlic, *in all*

Second seasoning mix:
1 teaspoon salt
½ teaspoon white pepper
½ teaspoon garlic powder
½ teaspoon ground red pepper (preferably cayenne)
½ teaspoon dried sweet basil leaves
½ teaspoon dried thyme leaves

2 tablespoons olive oil
2 tablespoons all-purpose flour
1 teaspoon Tabasco sauce
1½ cups canned tomato sauce
1 cup very fine dry bread crumbs

In a 5½-quart saucepan or large Dutch oven, combine the eggplants and the stock. Bring to a boil; continue boiling until eggplants are cooked, about 15 to 20 minutes, stirring occasionally to rotate eggplants in the pan. Drain (reserve 5 cups of the stock) and rinse with cold water just until cool enough to handle. With a spoon and a paring knife, carefully scrape the pulp out of the skins. Keep eggplant skins intact and leave about ½ inch pulp only at the stem end to help keep the skin in a boat shape; reserve skins and pulp.

Combine the first seasoning mix ingredients in a small bowl; mix well and set aside.

Meanwhile, in a 4-quart saucepan melt the margarine over high heat. Add *1 cup* of the onions, *1 cup* of the bell peppers and *½ cup* of the celery; sauté about 1 minute. Then add all except 3 inches (about 2 ounces) of the sausage and the first seasoning mix. Continue cooking for 5 minutes, breaking up the sausage so it looks like ground meat; stir often and scrape pan bottom as needed. Add *1 tablespoon* of the minced garlic; continue cooking until mixture is well browned and sticking excessively to the pan bottom, about 5 minutes, stirring almost constantly and scraping pan bottom as needed. Add *1 cup* of the reserved stock, stirring well until bottom sediment is dissolved. Continue cooking until mixture starts sticking excessively again, about 8 to 10 minutes, stirring frequently and scraping pan bottom as needed. Stir in *½ cup* more of the onions and the remaining ½ cup each of bell peppers and celery; cook about 2 minutes more, stirring and scraping almost constantly. Remove from heat. Add the reserved eggplant pulp to the sausage mixture. Chop up the eggplant pulp as you stir it into the sausage. Let pan sit a couple of minutes, then scrape any sediment from the pan bottom. Return the mixture to a low heat; cover and simmer 10 minutes, stirring frequently so mixture won't scorch. Add another *1 cup* stock and cook uncovered for 15 minutes, stirring often and scraping pan bottom well. Adjust salt to taste. Remove from heat.

Combine the second seasoning mix ingredients in a small bowl; mix well and set aside.

In a 2-quart saucepan, heat the olive oil over high heat until hot, about 2 minutes. With a metal whisk, mix in the flour until smooth, whisking constantly. Continue cooking, whisking constantly, until roux is medium brown, about 1 to 2 minutes, being careful not to let it scorch or splash on your skin.

✱ See page 26 for more about making roux.

Remove roux from heat; immediately add the remaining sausage, breaking it up into bits. Then stir in the remaining ½ cup onions; return to high heat and continue cooking about 1 minute, stirring constantly. Stir in the second seasoning mix, the remaining 1½ teaspoons minced garlic and the Tabasco. Stir in the tomato sauce; cook until thick and starting to stick, about 8 minutes, stirring almost constantly. Add the remaining 3 cups stock, stirring well. Cover and bring to a boil. Remove cover and reduce heat to maintain a simmer; cook until flavors marry and sauce reduces to 3 cups, about 45 minutes, stirring occasionally.

Meanwhile, transfer the eggplant mixture to an ungreased 13x9-inch baking pan. Stir in the bread crumbs, mixing well. Bake at 400° for 20 minutes; stir well and bake 20 minutes more. Serve immediately.

To serve, fill each eggplant skin with about ¾ cup of the stuffing. Place on a warmed serving plate (oval-shaped, if possible). Spoon ½ cup sauce on the plate, surrounding the eggplant with it.

Red Beans and Rice with Ham Hocks and Andouille Smoked Sausage

Makes 6 servings

It's a tradition in New Orleans to serve red beans and rice for lunch on Mondays.

1 pound dry red kidney beans
Water to cover the beans
6 large ham hocks (3½ to 4 pounds)
16 cups water, *in all*
2½ cups finely chopped celery
2 cups finely chopped onions
2 cups finely chopped green bell peppers
5 bay leaves
2 teaspoons white pepper
2 teaspoons dried thyme leaves
1½ teaspoons garlic powder
1½ teaspoons dried oregano leaves
1 teaspoon ground red pepper (preferably cayenne)
½ teaspoon black pepper
1 tablespoon Tabasco sauce

1 pound andouille smoked sausage (preferred) or any other good pure smoked pork sausage such as Polish sausage (kielbasa), cut diagonally into ¾-inch pieces
4½ cups hot **Basic Cooked Rice** (page 224)

Cover the beans with water 2 inches above beans. Let stand overnight. Drain just before using.

Place the ham hocks, *10 cups* of the water, the celery, onions, bell peppers, bay leaves and seasonings in a 5½-quart saucepan or large Dutch oven; stir well. Cover and bring to a boil over high heat. Reduce heat and simmer until meat is fork tender, about 1 hour, stirring occasionally. Remove ham hocks from pan and set aside.

Add the drained beans and *4 cups* of the water to the pan; bring to a boil, reduce heat, and simmer 30 minutes, stirring occasionally. Add the remaining 2 cups water and simmer 30 minutes, stirring often. Stir in the andouille and continue simmering until the beans start breaking up, about 35 minutes, scraping pan bottom fairly often. (If the beans start to scorch, do not stir. Immediately remove from heat and change to another pot without scraping any scorched beans into the mixture.) Add the ham hocks and cook and stir 10 minutes more. Serve immediately.

To serve, for each serving mound ¾ cup rice in the middle of a large heated serving plate. Place a ham hock on one end of the plate and about 2 pieces of andouille on the other end. Spoon a generous 1¼ cups of the red beans around the rice.

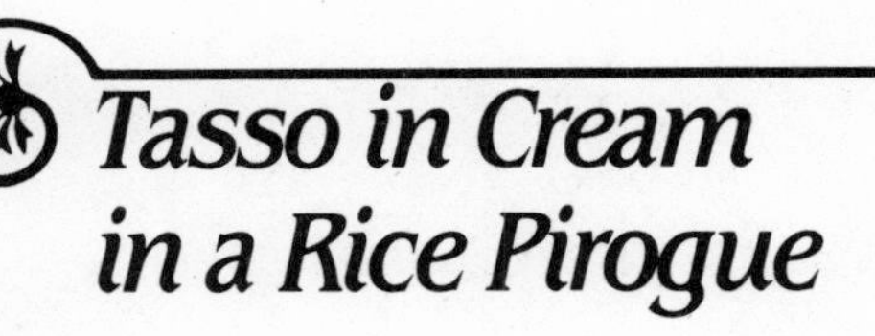

Tasso in Cream in a Rice Pirogue

Makes 6 servings

The pirogues can be made through the baking step a day ahead, tightly covered and refrigerated.

5 tablespoons unsalted butter
1 pound tasso (preferred) or other smoked ham (preferably Cure 81), or smoked goose or smoked turkey, cut into 1½x¼x¼-inch julienne strips (about 4 cups)
1⅔ cups julienned onions (see **Note**)
1¼ cups julienned zucchini (see **Note**)
1 cup julienned yellow squash (see **Note**)
¾ cup julienned carrots (see **Note**)
3 cups heavy cream
4 cups **Basic Cooked Rice** (page 224)
Rice Pirogues (recipe follows)
3 tablespoons finely grated Parmesan cheese (preferably imported)

Note: To julienne squashes, cut peelings ⅛ inch thick and cut these into strips ⅛ inch wide and 2 inches long; use only strips that have skin on one surface. Cut onions and carrots into similar strips.

Melt the butter over high heat in a large skillet. Add the tasso and cook over high heat for 5 minutes, stirring occasionally. Add the onions, zucchini, yellow squash and carrots and sauté 4 minutes, stirring occasionally. Add the cream and simmer for 2 minutes, stirring frequently. Add the rice and continue cooking and stirring for 5 minutes.

To serve, spoon about 1⅓ cups filling into each pirogue and sprinkle the top with Parmesan. Place an oar (see next recipe) on top and serve immediately.

15. *Barbecued Shrimp*

16. *Crab and Shrimp au Gratin in Eggplant Pirogue*

17. *Shrimp Creole*

18. *Panéed Veal and Fettucini*

19. *Mirliton Pirogue*
Stuffed with Shrimp and Andouille Smoked Sausage
with Tasso and Oyster Hollandaise

***20.** Cajun Shepherd's Pie*

21. *Rabbit Jambalaya*

22. Following page:
Seafood Filé Gumbo

Rice Pirogues

¼ pound (1 stick) unsalted butter
1 cup very finely chopped onions
3 eggs
2 tablespoons sugar
1 tablespoon baking powder
2 teaspoons vanilla extract
About 2¼ cups all-purpose flour, *in all*
2½ cups **Basic Cooked Rice** (see page 224)
1 teaspoon salt
Vegetable oil for deep frying

In a small skillet over high heat, melt the butter. Add the onions and sauté, stirring constantly, for about 3 minutes; set aside to cool.

In a medium-size bowl vigorously whip the eggs with a metal whisk until frothy and bubbles are reduced to the size of pinheads, about 2 minutes. Then whisk into the eggs, one at a time, the sugar, baking powder and vanilla. Using a spoon, thoroughly stir in *1½ cups* of the flour, then the rice, salt and the sautéed onions. Gradually stir in the remaining ¾ cup flour.

On a surface floured with about ⅓ cup flour, knead the rice dough until it is firm and no longer sticky, about 2 minutes (you may need more flour). Pinch off about one-sixth of the dough and roll it out with a floured rolling pin to a ⅛- to ¼-inch thickness. Place an oval casserole dish (about 5x9x1½ inches) face down over the dough. With a knife cut around the shape of the casserole, leaving an additional ¼-inch border. Lightly flour the inside of the casserole and the top of the dough. Fold the dough into quarters, then carefully place it in the casserole so that the corner of the fold is centered. Unfold the dough and line the casserole with it, pressing it firmly against the bottom and sides. Make sure the dough's thickness remains even and the dough comes up the sides and slightly over the casserole top. Prepare the other 5 pirogues in the same manner. With the remaining dough scraps, cut out 6 oars of the approximate size and shape shown at the end of the recipe. Bake the pirogues and oars on a cookie sheet in a 350° oven for 15 minutes.

Meanwhile, heat 1½ inches oil in a large skillet or deep fryer to 350°. Remove the baked pirogues from the casseroles and fry each in the hot oil until dark golden brown, about 4 to 5 minutes, turning occasionally. Do not crowd. Drain upside down on paper towels. Fry the oars in the same manner, allowing slightly less frying time.

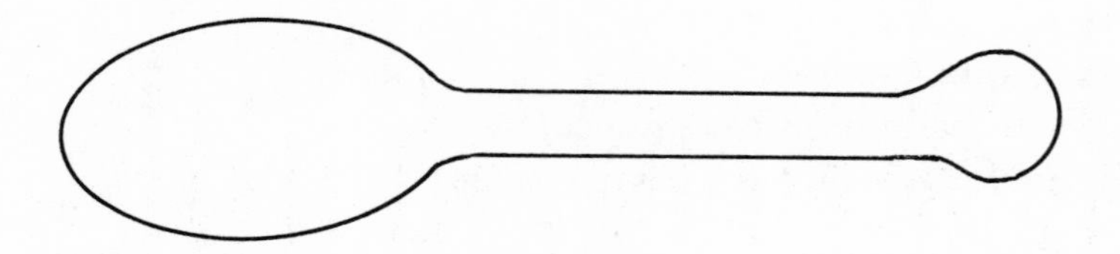

GUMBOS, SOUPS & STEWS

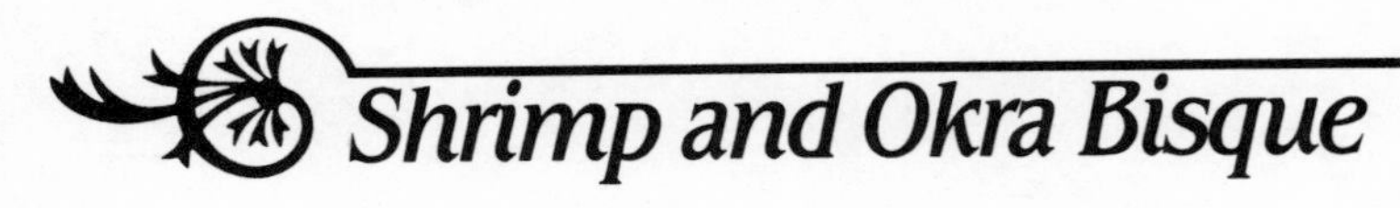

Shrimp and Okra Bisque

Makes 8 servings

Seasoning mix:
3 whole bay leaves
2 teaspoons salt
1½ teaspoons dry mustard
1¼ teaspoons white pepper
1 teaspoon ground red pepper (preferably cayenne)
1 teaspoon dried thyme leaves
½ teaspoon black pepper
½ teaspoon dried sweet basil leaves

¼ cup plus 2 tablespoons vegetable oil, *in all*
¾ pound okra, sliced ¼ inch thick (3 cups sliced), *in all*
¾ cup finely chopped onions
¾ cup finely chopped green bell peppers
½ cup finely chopped celery
4 tablespoons unsalted butter
2 teaspoons minced garlic
¼ cup all-purpose flour
5½ cups, *in all*, **Basic Seafood Stock** (page 32)
½ cup finely choppped green onions
3 dozen peeled medium shrimp, about ¾ pound

Combine the seasoning mix ingredients in a small bowl and set aside.

In a 4-quart saucepan, heat *¼ cup* of the oil over high heat for 1 minute. Stir in *2 cups* of the okra; cook until browned, about 6 minutes, stirring occasionally. Stir in the onions, bell peppers and celery and cook 1 minute. Add the butter and cook 1 minute; then stir in the garlic and cook 1 minute more. Add the seasoning mix and stir well; continue cooking over high heat for 3 minutes, stirring frequently and scraping pan bottom well. Add the remaining 2 tablespoons oil and the flour; stir and scrape the pan bottom well. Continue cooking until well browned, stirring frequently, about 2 minutes. Stir in *1½ cups* of the seafood stock and scrape the pan bottom well; then add 4 cups more stock and stir well. Bring to a boil, stirring often. Boil 2 minutes, then lower heat and simmer 5 minutes, stirring occasionally. Stir in the remaining 1 cup okra. Continue simmering 10 minutes, stirring occasionally. Add the green onions and simmer 3 minutes. Remove from heat. Add the shrimp, turn heat to medium, and simmer just until shrimp turn pink, about 1 minute. Serve immediately, allowing about ¾ cup for each serving.

Oyster Stew

Makes 4 main-course or 8 appetizer servings

1¼ cups cold water
3 dozen small to medium oysters in their liquor, about 18 ounces
¼ pound (1 stick) unsalted butter
1 cup finely chopped celery
½ teaspoon ground red pepper (preferably cayenne)
¼ teaspoon white pepper
¼ teaspoon salt
½ cup finely chopped green onions
2 cups heavy cream

Add the water to the oysters and refrigerate for at least 1 hour. Strain and reserve the oysters and oyster water; refrigerate until ready to use.

In a large skillet combine the butter, celery, peppers, salt and *¾ cup* of the oyster water; cook over high heat 3 minutes, shaking pan (versus stirring) almost constantly. Add the remaining ½ cup oyster water and continue cooking and shaking the pan 1 minute. Stir in the green onions. Gradually add the cream, whisking constantly. Bring the mixture to a boil, whisking almost constantly. Add the oysters and cook just until oysters curl, about 2 to 4 minutes, whisking constantly. Remove from heat and serve immediately, stirring well as you ladle out the portions.

For a main course, ladle 9 oysters, a little of the vegetables and 1 cup of the liquid into each serving bowl; for an appetizer, serve half that amount.

Oyster and Brie Soup

Makes 8 servings

Champagne is optional but delightful in this dish. Serve the same champagne with your dinner.

3 dozen small to medium oysters in their liquor, about 18 ounces
4 cups cold water
½ pound (2 sticks) unsalted butter
½ cup all-purpose flour
1 cup coarsely chopped onions
½ cup coarsely chopped celery
½ teaspoon white pepper
½ teaspoon ground red pepper (preferably cayenne)
1 pound fresh brie cheese, cut in small wedges, with rind on
2 cups heavy cream
½ cup champagne, optional

Combine oysters and water; stir and refrigerate at least 1 hour. Strain and reserve the oysters and oyster water; refrigerate until ready to use.

In a large skillet melt the butter over low heat. Add the flour and beat with a metal whisk until smooth. Add the onions and celery; sauté about 3 minutes, stirring occasionally. Stir in the peppers and sauté about 2 minutes more. Set aside.

In a 4-quart saucepan, bring the oyster water to a boil. Stir in the sautéed vegetable mixture until well mixed. Turn heat to high. Add cheese; cook until cheese starts to melt, about 2 minutes, stirring constantly. (Be careful not to let the cheese scorch.) Lower heat to a simmer and continue cooking for about 4 minutes, stirring constantly. Remove from heat, strain soup, and return to pot. Turn heat to high and cook about 1 minute, stirring constantly. Stir in the cream; cook until close to a boil, about 2 minutes. Stir in champagne, if desired. Turn off heat and add the oysters. Let pan sit about 3 minutes to plump the oysters. Serve immediately.

Egg and Dried Shrimp Gumbo

Makes 6 servings

My family had this at least once a month when I was growing up, and we loved it. It's great served with **Potato Salad** *(page 237) on the side.*

1 cup finely chopped onions
1 cup finely chopped green bell peppers
½ cup finely chopped celery

Seasoning mix:
3 whole bay leaves
1 teaspoon salt
1 teaspoon ground red pepper (preferably cayenne)
¾ teaspoon white pepper
½ teaspoon black pepper

⅔ cup vegetable oil
⅔ cup all-purpose flour
1 teaspoon Tabasco sauce
2 (1½-ounce) packages dried shrimp, or ¾ cup
7 cups **Basic Seafood Stock** (page 32)
1 teaspoon minced garlic
9 whole hard-boiled eggs, peeled (room temperature or warm)
1½ cups hot **Basic Cooked Rice** (page 224)

Combine the onions, bell peppers and celery in a medium-size bowl and set aside. In a small bowl combine the seasoning mix ingredients and set aside.

In a large heavy skillet heat the oil over high heat until it begins to smoke, about 4 minutes. Gradually add the flour, whisking constantly with a long-handled metal whisk until smooth. Continue cooking, whisking constantly, until the roux is dark red-brown to black, about 3 to 4 minutes, being careful not to let it scorch or splash on your skin. Immediately stir in the vegetable mixture and cook about 2 minutes, stirring constantly. Add the seasoning mix and Tabasco; cook for about 2 minutes, stirring almost constantly.

✱ See page 26 for more about making roux.

Stir in the shrimp, then cook about 2 minutes more, stirring occasionally. Remove from heat.

Meanwhile, place the stock and garlic in a 4-quart saucepan. Bring to a boil. Gradually add the shrimp mixture and stir until roux is dissolved between each addition. Return to a boil; reduce heat and simmer until shrimp are cooked and flavors married, about 20 minutes, stirring occasionally.

Add 6 of the whole hard-boiled eggs to the gumbo; cut the remaining 3 eggs in half and add. Turn heat to high and return mixture to a boil; then remove from heat and let sit 10 minutes. Skim oil from top and serve immediately.

To serve, place ¼ cup rice in each serving bowl; add 1 whole egg and 1 egg half to each. Spoon about 1 cup gumbo over the top. (**NOTE:** It's best if each person breaks up the eggs while eating the gumbo.)

Pork Backbone Stew

Makes 6 servings

Seasoning mix:
2½ tablespoons salt
1½ teaspoons ground red pepper (preferably cayenne)
1 teaspoon onion powder
1 teaspoon garlic powder
1 teaspoon ground cumin
½ teaspoon white pepper
½ teaspoon black pepper

About 6 pounds pork backbones (preferred) or pork neckbones (have your butcher cut into 2-inch squares)

2 cups all-purpose flour
2 cups pork lard or vegetable oil
2 cups finely chopped onions
2 cups finely chopped green bell peppers
1½ cups finely chopped celery
1 teaspoon white pepper
1 teaspoon ground red pepper (preferably cayenne)
1 teaspoon black pepper
8 cups **Basic Pork** or **Chicken Stock** (page 31)
3 cups hot **Basic Cooked Rice** (page 224), optional

Thoroughly combine the seasoning mix ingredients in a small bowl. Sprinkle the meat generously on both sides with some of the mix, rubbing it in by hand. In a pan (loaf, cake and pie pans work well) thoroughly combine the remaining mix with the flour. Dredge backbones in the flour, shaking off excess. Reserve ½ cup leftover flour for the roux.

Heat the pork lard in a large skillet over medium-high heat to 350°. Meanwhile, combine the onions, bell peppers, celery and peppers; set aside.

Brown the backbones well on both sides in the hot fat; drain on paper towels. Pour off all but about ½ cup fat from the skillet, leaving the sediment. Turn heat to high and heat just until fat begins to smoke. Slowly whisk in the reserved ½ cup flour with a long-handled metal whisk; cook, whisking constantly, until roux is dark red-brown to black, about 4 minutes, being careful not to let it scorch or splash on your skin. Immediately add the vegetable mixture; stir well until the vegetables have noticeably brightened in color, about 2 to 3 minutes. Remove from heat.

✱ See page 26 for more about making roux.

Heat the stock in a large soup pot to a rolling boil. Add the backbones and cook just until meat is tender. Then add the roux mixture by spoonfuls, stirring until well blended between each addition. Adjust heat to maintain a slow simmer; simmer uncovered until meat is falling off bones, about 1 hour, stirring occasionally. If the stew gets too thick, add more stock or water. Serve immediately in bowls as is, or over cooked rice.

Chicken and Andouille Smoked Sausage Gumbo

Makes 6 main-dish or 10 appetizer servings

1 (2- to 3-pound) chicken, cut up
Salt
Garlic powder
Ground red pepper (preferably cayenne)
1 cup finely chopped onions
1 cup finely chopped green bell peppers
¾ cup finely chopped celery
1¼ cups all-purpose flour
½ teaspoon salt
½ teaspoon garlic powder
½ teaspoon ground red pepper (preferably cayenne)
Vegetable oil for deep frying
About 7 cups **Basic Chicken Stock** (page 31)
½ pound andouille smoked sausage (preferred) or any other good pure smoked pork sausage such as Polish sausage (kielbasa), cut into ¼-inch cubes
1 teaspoon minced garlic
Hot **Basic Cooked Rice** (page 224)

Remove excess fat from the chicken pieces. Rub a generous amount of salt, garlic powder and red pepper on both sides of each piece, making sure each is evenly covered. Let stand at room temperature for 30 minutes.

Meanwhile, in a medium-size bowl combine the onions, bell peppers and celery; set aside.

Combine the flour, ½ teaspoon salt, ½ teaspoon garlic powder and ½ teaspoon red pepper in a paper or plastic bag. Add the chicken pieces and shake until chicken is well coated. Reserve ½ cup of the flour.

In a large heavy skillet heat 1½ inches of oil until very hot (375° to 400 °). Fry the chicken until crust is brown on both sides and meat is cooked, about 5 to 8 minutes per side; drain on paper towels. Carefully pour the hot oil into a glass measuring cup, leaving as many of the browned particles in the pan as possible. Scrape the pan bottom with a metal whisk to loosen any stuck particles, then return ½ cup of the hot oil to the pan.

Place pan over high heat. Using a long-handled metal whisk, gradually stir in the reserved ½ cup flour. Cook, whisking constantly, until roux is dark red-brown to black, about 3½ to 4 minutes, being careful not to let it scorch or splash on your skin. Remove from heat and immediately add the reserved vegetable mixture, stirring constantly until the roux stops getting darker. Return pan to low heat and cook until vegetables are soft, about 5 minutes, stirring constantly and scraping the pan bottom well.

✱ See page 26 for more about making roux.

Meanwhile, place the stock in a 5½-quart saucepan or large Dutch oven. Bring to a boil. Add roux mixture by spoonfuls to the boiling stock, stirring until dissolved between each addition. Return to a boil, stirring and scraping pan bottom often. Reduce heat to a simmer and stir in the andouille and minced garlic. Simmer uncovered for about 45 minutes, stirring often toward the end of cooking time.

While the gumbo is simmering, bone the cooked chicken and cut the meat into ½-inch dice. When the gumbo is cooked, stir in the chicken and adjust seasoning with salt and pepper. Serve immediately.

To serve as a main course, mound ⅓ cup cooked rice in the center of a soup bowl; ladle about 1¼ cups gumbo around the rice. For an appetizer, place 1 heaping teaspoon cooked rice in a cup and ladle about ¾ cup gumbo on top. This is super with **Potato Salad** (page 237) on the side.

Guinea Hen and Andouille Smoked Sausage Gumbo

Makes 6 main-dish or 12 appetizer servings

Guinea hens are similar to chickens. Make the **Guinea Hen Stock** *on page 31 ahead of time, using the hen backs, wing tips and giblets (excluding the livers). Strain, cool, and refrigerate until ready to use.*

Seasoning mix:
1½ tablespoons salt
2 teaspoons sweet paprika
1½ teaspoons white pepper
1½ teaspoons garlic powder
1 teaspoon onion powder
1 teaspoon ground red pepper (preferably cayenne)
¾ teaspoon dry mustard
¾ teaspoon black pepper
½ teaspoon ground cumin

2 (2½- to 3½-pound) guinea hens, each cut into 8 pieces (see **Note**)
About 1¼ cups all-purpose flour, *in all*
2 cups chopped onions, *in all*
2 cups chopped green bell peppers, *in all*
1½ cups chopped celery, *in all*
15 cups (3 quarts plus 3 cups, *in all*) **Basic Guinea Hen Stock** or **Basic Chicken Stock** (page 31)
Vegetable oil for frying
1 teaspoon minced garlic
3 bay leaves
½ pound andouille smoked sausage (preferred) or any other good pure smoked pork sausage such as Polish sausage (kielbasa), cut into 6 pieces (see **Note**)
1½ cups hot **Basic Cooked Rice** (page 224)

NOTE: If gumbo is to be served as an appetizer, bone the guinea hens and cut meat into bite-size pieces, and cut the sausage into 12 pieces.

In a small bowl combine the seasoning mix ingredients thoroughly; sprinkle *1 tablespoon* of the mix on both sides of the hen pieces, patting it in with your hands. In a paper or plastic bag, add *1 tablespoon* of the seasoning mix to *1 cup* of the flour, mixing well. Dredge the pieces in the flour, reserving the excess flour.

Combine ½ *cup each* of the onions, bell peppers and celery in a small bowl and set aside.

Place *8 cups* of the stock in a 5½-quart saucepan or large Dutch oven and bring to a simmer. Meanwhile, heat ½ inch oil in a large skillet to 350°. Fry the hen pieces in the hot oil (large pieces and skin side down first) until browned on each side, about 2 to 4 minutes per side. Do not crowd. (If the drippings start getting dark brown, reduce heat.) Drain on paper towels.

Pour the hot oil from the skillet, leaving ¼ cup oil (and as much sediment as possible) in the pan. (But if any sediment is burned, discard the oil and sediment and use fresh oil.) Whisk any sediment sticking to the bottom of the pan with a metal whisk. Turn heat to high and heat until oil begins to smoke. Meanwhile, measure out the reserved flour and enough additional flour to make ¼ cup. Using a long-handled metal whisk or wooden spoon, gradually stir the flour into the hot oil. Cook, whisking constantly or stirring briskly, until the roux is dark red-brown to black, about 2 to 4 minutes, being careful not to let it scorch or splash on your skin. Remove from heat and immediately stir in the reserved ½ cup each of onions, bell peppers and celery until well mixed. Continue stirring about 1 minute.

✸ See page 26 for more about making roux.

Add the roux by spoonfuls to the simmering stock, stirring between each addition until roux is dissolved. Stir in *1 tablespoon* of the seasoning mix. Turn heat to high and boil the stock mixture for about 35 minutes. Add *2 cups* of the stock, return to a boil, and boil about 30 minutes. Add the remaining 5 cups stock, return to a boil, and boil 5 minutes more. Remove from heat. Strain liquid (discard solids) and return liquid to saucepan. Turn heat to high. Add the pieces of fried hen, the remaining 1½ cups onions, 1½ cups bell peppers, 1 cup celery, the garlic, *1 teaspoon* of the seasoning mix (use any remaining mix in another recipe) and the bay leaves; mix well. Stir in the andouille and reduce heat to very low; simmer until hen is tender, about 2 hours, stirring occasionally so gumbo won't scorch. Skim off oil from the surface as mixture cooks. Serve immediately.

To serve for a main course, mound ¼ cup rice in the middle of each serving bowl. Spoon about 1 cup gumbo around the rice; arrange about 2 pieces of hen and a piece of andouille on top. For an appetizer, serve about half these amounts in a cup.

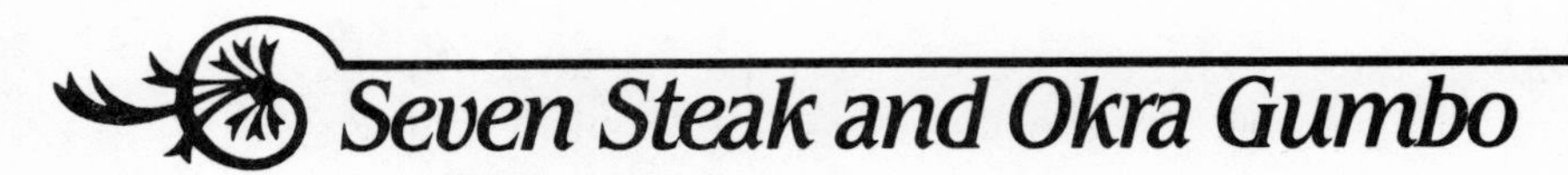

Seven Steak and Okra Gumbo

Makes 8 main-course servings

2½ pounds seven-steak or seven-bone steak or beef neck chops

Seasoning mix:
2 tablespoons salt
1 tablespoon sweet paprika
2 teaspoons white pepper
2 teaspoons onion powder
1½ teaspoons dried thyme leaves
1¼ teaspoons garlic powder
1 teaspoon dry mustard
1 teaspoon ground red pepper (preferably cayenne)
1 teaspoon dried sweet basil leaves
¾ teaspoon black pepper

½ cup pork lard, bacon fat, shortening or vegetable oil
½ cup all-purpose flour
2 pounds okra, sliced ¼ inch thick (8 cups sliced, *in all*)
3 cups chopped onions, *in all*
2 tablespoons unsalted butter
4 bay leaves
7½ cups, *in all*, **Basic Beef Stock** (page 31)
2 cups chopped celery
2 cups chopped green bell peppers

2 cups peeled and chopped tomatoes
2 tablespoons chopped jalapeño peppers, optional (see **Note**)
1 tablespoon minced garlic
¾ pound peeled medium shrimp, optional
3 cups hot **Basic Cooked Rice** (page 224)

Note: Fresh jalapeños are preferred; if you have to use pickled ones, rinse as much vinegar from them as possible.

Cut meat into 8 pieces of equal size. In a small bowl thoroughly combine the seasoning mix ingredients. Sprinkle meat with some of the mix, rubbing it into both sides of the meat by hand. Reserve leftover seasoning mix.

In a large, heavy skillet heat the pork lard. Meanwhile, combine *1½ teaspoons* of the seasoning mix with the flour in a pan (loaf, cake and pie pans work well); dredge meat in the seasoned flour. Brown meat on both sides in the hot fat. Remove from skillet and set aside.

Add *4 cups* of the okra to the skillet. Fry over high heat until many okra slices are dark brown, about 8 minutes, stirring occasionally. Add *1 cup* of the onions, the butter and *2 teaspoons* of the seasoning mix. Cook over high heat 4 minutes, stirring frequently. Add the bay leaves and *½ cup* of the stock; continue cooking 4 minutes, stirring often. Add *½ cup* more stock (along with frying, repeated additions of stock help break down the okra); cook 5 minutes, stirring occasionally and scraping pan bottom well if mixture starts to stick. Add *½ cup* more stock and continue cooking 3 minutes, stirring occasionally. Add the remaining 2 cups onions, the celery, bell peppers and the remaining seasoning mix; stir well. Cook 5 minutes, stirring occasionally. Stir in the tomatoes, jalapeño peppers (if desired) and garlic. Cook 5 minutes, stirring occasionally.

Transfer mixture to a gumbo or large soup pot. Add the remaining 6 cups stock and the meat. Cook covered over high heat for 10 minutes. Add the remaining 4 cups okra and lower heat to a simmer. Cook covered until meat is tender, about 20 minutes, being careful not to let gumbo scorch. Add shrimp (if desired), cover, and remove from heat; let sit 10 minutes. Serve immediately in bowls, allowing for each person about ⅓ cup rice, a portion of meat, and 1½ cups gumbo poured on top.

Cajun Seafood Gumbo with Andouille Smoked Sausage

Makes 10 main-dish or 20 appetizer servings

2 cups chopped onions
1½ cups chopped green bell peppers
1 cup chopped celery

Seasoning mix:
2 whole bay leaves
2 teaspoons salt
½ teaspoon white pepper
½ teaspoon ground red pepper (preferably cayenne)
½ teaspoon black pepper
½ teaspoon dried thyme leaves
¼ teaspoon dried oregano leaves

¾ cup vegetable oil
¾ cup all-purpose flour
1 tablespoon minced garlic
5½ cups **Basic Seafood Stock** (page 32)
1 pound andouille smoked sausage (preferred) or any other good pure smoked pork sausage such as Polish sausage (kielbasa), cut into ½-inch pieces
1 pound peeled medium shrimp
1 dozen medium to large oysters in their liquor, about 9 ounces
¾ pound crabmeat (picked over)
2½ cups hot **Basic Cooked Rice** (page 224)

Combine the onions, bell peppers and celery in a medium-size bowl and set aside. In a small bowl combine the seasoning mix ingredients; mix well and set aside.

Heat the oil in a large heavy skillet over high heat until it begins to smoke, about 5 minutes. Gradually add the flour, whisking constantly with a long-handled metal whisk. Continue cooking, whisking constantly, until roux is dark red-brown to black, about 2 to 4 minutes, being careful not to let it scorch or splash on your skin. Immediately add half the vegetables and stir well (switch to a spoon if necessary). Continue stirring and cooking about 1 minute. Then add the remaining vegetables and cook and stir about 2 minutes. Stir in the seasoning mix and continue cooking about 2 minutes, stirring frequently. Add the garlic; stir well, then cook and stir about 1 minute more. Remove from heat.

✱ See page 26 for more about making roux.

Meanwhile, place the stock in a 5½-quart saucepan or large Dutch oven. Bring to a boil. Add roux mixture by spoonfuls to the boiling stock, stirring until dissolved between each addition. Bring mixture to a boil. Add the andouille and return to a boil; continue boiling 15 minutes, stirring occasionally. Reduce heat and simmer 10 minutes more. Add the shrimp, undrained oysters and crabmeat. Return to a boil over high heat, stirring occasionally. Remove from heat and skim any oil from the surface. Serve immediately.

To serve as a main course, mound ¼ cup rice in the middle of each serving bowl. Spoon 1 cup gumbo over the top, making sure each person gets an assortment of the seafood and andouille. Serve half this amount in a cup as an appetizer.

Seafood Filé Gumbo

Color picture 22

Makes 4 main-dish or 8 appetizer servings

You can substitute pieces of fish for any or all of the seafood in this recipe. Be sure to use margarine instead of butter, because margarine is oilier and seems to conduct more heat. The extra heat, plus the additional oil, develops the gumbo filé to a more desirable taste, texture and color. Upon reaching a temperature above 140°, however, the oil separates out and rises to the surface. Some people prefer to skim the oil off before serving.

If the gumbo is made in advance, do not *add the seafood. When ready to serve, bring the gumbo to a rapid boil, lower the heat to a simmer, and add the seafood. Immediately cover the pot, turn off the heat, and let the pot stand covered 6 to 10 minutes.*

1 pound medium shrimp with heads and shells (see **Note**)
5 cups **Basic Seafood Stock** (page 32)

Seasoning mix:
1½ teaspoons ground red pepper (preferably cayenne)
1½ teaspoons sweet paprika
1 teaspoon salt
½ teaspoon white pepper
½ teaspoon black pepper
½ teaspoon dried thyme leaves
½ teaspoon dried oregano leaves
1 bay leaf, crumbled

¾ cup margarine (not butter)
2 cups chopped onions
2 cups chopped celery
2 cups chopped green bell peppers
3 tablespoons gumbo filé (filé powder)
1 tablespoon Tabasco sauce
1 teaspoon minced garlic
1¼ cups canned tomato sauce
1½ cups, packed, crabmeat (picked over), about ½ pound
1 dozen shucked oysters (about ½ pound), optional
1⅓ cups hot **Basic Cooked Rice** (page 224)

Note: If shrimp with heads and shells are not available, use ½ pound shrimp without heads but with shells and substitute other seafood ingredients for the shrimp heads in making the seafood stock.

Peel the shrimp, rinse and drain well, and use the heads and shells to make the seafood stock; refrigerate shrimp until ready to use.

Combine the seasoning mix ingredients in a small bowl and set aside.

In a 4-quart heavy soup pot, melt the margarine over medium heat. Add the onions, celery and bell peppers. Turn heat to high and stir in the gumbo filé, Tabasco, garlic and seasoning mix. Cook 6 minutes, stirring constantly. Reduce heat to medium and stir in the tomato sauce; continue cooking 5 minutes, stirring constantly. (During this time the mixture will begin sticking to the pan bottom. As it does so, continually scrape pan bottom well with a spoon. The scrapings not only add to the gumbo's flavor, but also decrease the gumbo filé's ability to thicken.) Add the stock and bring gumbo to a boil; reduce heat and simmer 45 to 60 minutes, stirring occasionally. Add the shrimp, crabmeat and oysters (if desired); cover and turn off the heat. Leave the pot covered just until the seafood is poached, about 6 to 10 minutes. Serve immediately.

For a main course, place about ⅓ cup of rice in each bowl and top with about 1 cup gumbo. For an appetizer, serve about half that amount.

Shrimp, Okra and Andouille Smoked Sausage Gumbo

Makes 9 main-dish or 18 appetizer servings

⅓ cup pork lard (preferred, chicken fat or vegetable oil)
2½ pounds okra, quartered lengthwise and sliced (8½ cups, *in all*)
1½ teaspoons white pepper, *in all*
1½ teaspoons ground red pepper (preferably cayenne), *in all*
1 teaspoon black pepper
2 cups finely chopped onions
10 cups (2 quarts plus 2 cups, *in all*) **Basic Seafood Stock** (page 32)
2 cups peeled and chopped tomatoes
2 teaspoons salt
1 teaspoon minced garlic
¾ teaspoon onion powder
½ teaspoon dried thyme leaves
¼ pound (1 stick) unsalted butter

1 pound andouille smoked sausage (preferred) or any other good pure smoked pork sausage such as Polish sausage (kielbasa), cut into ¼-inch slices
1 pound peeled medium shrimp
½ cup finely chopped green onions
2¼ cups hot **Basic Cooked Rice** (page 224)

In a 5½-quart saucepan or large Dutch oven (preferably cast iron), melt the fat over high heat until it begins to smoke, about 3 minutes. Add *6 cups* of the okra. Cook for about 3 minutes, stirring occasionally. Add *1 teaspoon* of the white pepper, *1 teaspoon* of the red pepper and the black pepper; stir well. Continue cooking until well browned, about 10 minutes, stirring frequently. Stir in the onions; cook for 5 minutes, stirring fairly often and scraping pan bottom as needed. Add *1 cup* of the stock; cook 5 minutes, stirring occasionally and scraping pan bottom well. Stir in the tomatoes and cook about 8 minutes, stirring and scraping frequently. Add another *2 cups* stock; cook for 5 minutes, stirring occasionally. Stir in the remaining ½ teaspoon white pepper, ½ teaspoon red pepper and the salt, garlic, onion powder and thyme. Add the butter and continue cooking over high heat, stirring until butter is melted and scraping the pan bottom well.

Add the remaining 7 cups stock, stirring well. Bring to a boil, stirring occasionally. Add the andouille and return to a boil; reduce heat and simmer about 45 minutes more, stirring occasionally. Add the remaining 2½ cups okra; simmer 10 minutes. Then add the shrimp and green onions. Return gumbo to a boil, then remove from heat. Skim any oil from the surface and serve immediately.

To serve, place a mounded ¼ cup rice in the center of each serving bowl; spoon 1½ cups gumbo around the rice. Serve half that amount for an appetizer.

Turtle Soup

Makes 8 to 10 main-course or 16 to 20 appetizer servings

This is a dish for a special occasion.

Seasoning mix:
5 whole bay leaves
1 tablespoon salt
2 teaspoons white pepper
1¾ teaspoons garlic powder
1¾ teaspoons ground red pepper (preferably cayenne)
1½ teaspoons onion powder
1½ teaspoons dried thyme leaves
1 teaspoon dry mustard
1 teaspoon black pepper
1 teaspoon dried sweet basil leaves
½ teaspoon ground cumin

3 pounds boneless fresh turtle meat (see **Note**)
4 tablespoons unsalted butter
4 tablespoons margarine
½ pound spinach, very finely chopped
2 cups very finely chopped onions
1 cup very finely chopped celery
3½ cups canned tomato sauce
⅔ cup all-purpose flour
1 teaspoon minced garlic
11 cups (2 quarts plus 3 cups, *in all*) **Rich Turtle** or **Beef Stock** (page 32)
1 cup, lightly packed, fresh parsley
¼ lemon, seeded
6 hard-boiled eggs, cut in quarters
⅓ cup sherry wine plus sherry to add at the table

Note: In Louisiana, fresh turtle meat is available in the better grocery stores and seafood markets. It's scarce, but before you give up looking for it, try Chinatown markets. It is also marketed frozen and the frozen is fine for turtle soup.

Combine the seasoning mix ingredients in a small bowl and set aside.

Finely chop the turtle meat in a food processor or with a knife.

In a 5½-quart saucepan or large Dutch oven melt the butter

and margarine over high heat. Add the turtle meat and cook until browned, about 6 to 8 minutes, stirring occasionally. Stir in the seasoning mix, spinach, onions and celery; cook for about 15 minutes, stirring occasionally. Stir in the tomato sauce and cook 10 minutes, stirring frequently toward the end of cooking time. Add the flour and garlic, stirring well; cook 5 minutes, stirring almost constantly and scraping the pan bottom well. Add 2 *cups* of the stock, stirring well to dissolve any mixture from the pan bottom. Then stir in 7 *cups* more stock, scraping pan bottom well. Bring soup to a boil, stirring occasionally and scraping pan bottom as needed. Continue boiling and stirring 5 minutes. Reduce heat to maintain a simmer and cook about 45 minutes, stirring fairly often and scraping pan bottom well. (While stirring and scraping the bottom, if the mixture sticking to the spoon looks scorched, quit stirring and pour the soup into a clean pot, leaving the scorched mixture behind.)

Meanwhile, in a food processor or blender, process the parsley and lemon until both are minced; add the eggs and process a few seconds, just until eggs are coarsely chopped.

When the soup has cooked 45 minutes, add the egg mixture to the soup, stirring well. Stir in the remaining 2 cups stock and the sherry. Cook 20 minutes more, stirring and scraping pan bottom occasionally. Remove from heat and discard bay leaves. Salt to taste and serve immediately.

To serve, allow about 1½ cups in each bowl for a main course, or ¾ cup as an appetizer. Pass additional sherry at the table (allow 1 to 3 teaspoons per 1½-cup serving).

JAMBALAYAS

Poorman's Jambalaya

Makes 4 main-course or 8 appetizer servings

Seasoning mix:
4 small whole bay leaves
1 teaspoon salt
1 teaspoon white pepper
1 teaspoon dry mustard
1 teaspoon ground red pepper (preferably cayenne)
1 teaspoon gumbo filé (filé powder), optional
½ teaspoon ground cumin
½ teaspoon black pepper
½ teaspoon dried thyme leaves

4 tablespoons margarine
6 ounces tasso (preferred) or other smoked ham (preferably Cure 81), diced, about 1½ cups
6 ounces andouille smoked sausage (preferred) or any other good pure smoked pork sausage such as Polish sausage (kielbasa), diced, about 1 heaping cup
1½ cups chopped onions
1½ cups chopped celery
1 cup chopped green bell peppers
1½ teaspoons minced garlic
2 cups uncooked rice (preferably converted)
4 cups **Basic Beef, Pork** or **Chicken Stock** (page 31)

Thoroughly combine the seasoning mix ingredients in a small bowl and set aside.

In a large heavy skillet (preferably cast iron) melt the margarine over high heat. Add the tasso and andouille; cook 5 minutes, stirring occasionally. Add the onions, celery, bell peppers, seasoning mix and garlic. Stir well and continue cooking until browned, about 10 to 12 minutes, stirring occasionally and scraping the pan bottom well. Stir in the rice and cook 5 minutes, stirring and scraping pan bottom occasionally. Add the stock, stirring well. Bring mixture to a boil; reduce heat and simmer until rice is tender but still a bit crunchy, about 20 minutes, stirring occasionally toward the end of cooking time. Meanwhile, heat the serving plates in a 250° oven. Remove bay leaves and serve immediately.

To serve as a main course, spoon 2 cups jambalaya onto each heated serving plate; for an appetizer, serve 1 cup.

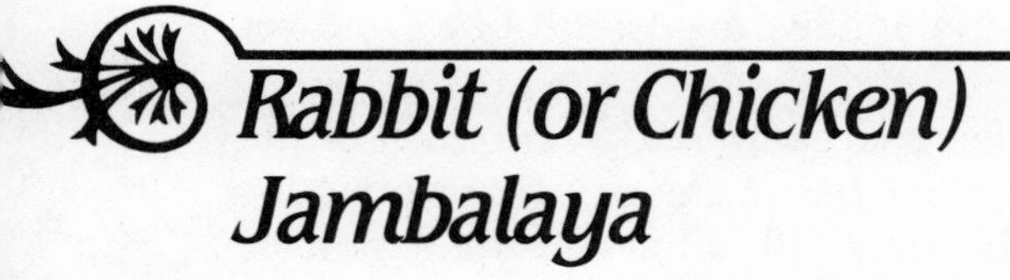

Rabbit (or Chicken) Jambalaya

Color picture 21

Makes 4 main-dish or 8 appetizer servings

This is delicious as is, or may be topped with **Creole Sauce** *(page 248).*

1 (about 3-pound) domestic rabbit or chicken, cut in pieces

Seasoning mix
2 whole bay leaves
1 teaspoon salt
1 teaspoon white pepper
1 teaspoon garlic powder
½ teaspoon ground red pepper (preferably cayenne)
¼ teaspoon black pepper
¼ teaspoon ground red sandalwood (see **Note**), optional

4 tablespoons margarine
1½ cups finely chopped onions, *in all*
1½ cups finely chopped celery, *in all*

1½ cups finely chopped green bell peppers, *in all*
½ teaspoon Tabasco sauce
1⅔ cups chopped tasso (preferred) or other smoked ham
(preferably Cure 81), about ½ pound
¾ cup canned tomato sauce
2 cups uncooked rice (preferably converted)
3 cups **Basic Rabbit** or **Chicken Stock** (page 31)

NOTE: Available at some gourmet spice shops.

Cut meat away from rabbit or chicken bones and chop into ¼-inch pieces; use scraps, bones and giblets (excluding the liver) to make the stock. Refrigerate meat until ready to use.

Combine the seasoning mix ingredients in a small bowl and set aside.

Melt the margarine in a 4-quart saucepan. Add ¾ *cup each* of the onions, celery and bell peppers; then stir in the seasoning mix, Tabasco and tasso. Cook over high heat until onions are dark brown, about 20 minutes, stirring constantly. Add the remaining ¾ cup each of onions, celery and bell peppers. Cook about 5 minutes, stirring occasionally. Add the tomato sauce and simmer about 5 minutes, stirring constantly. Add the rabbit and cook over high heat for 15 minutes, stirring occasionally. Stir in the rice, mixing well. Reduce heat and simmer for about 12 minutes. Add the stock. Bring the mixture to a boil; reduce heat and simmer covered over very low heat until rice is tender but still firm, about 15 minutes.

To serve, mold rice in an 8-ounce cup. Place 2 cups on each serving plate for a main course or 1 cup for an appetizer.

Chicken and Seafood Jambalaya

Makes 4 main-dish or 8 appetizer servings

This jambalaya may be eaten as is or topped with **Creole Sauce** *(page 248).*

Seasoning mix:
2 whole bay leaves
1½ teaspoons salt
1½ teaspoons ground red pepper (preferably cayenne)
1½ teaspoons dried oregano leaves
1¼ teaspoons white pepper
1 teaspoon black pepper
¾ teaspoon dried thyme leaves

2½ tablespoons chicken fat or pork lard or beef fat
⅔ cup chopped tasso (preferred) or other smoked ham (preferably Cure 81), about 3 ounces
½ cup chopped andouille smoked sausage (preferred) or any other good pure smoked pork sausage such as Polish sausage (kielbasa), about 3 ounces
1½ cups chopped onions
1 cup chopped celery
¾ cup chopped green bell peppers
½ cup chicken, cut into bite-size pieces, about 3 ounces
1½ teaspoons minced garlic
4 medium-size tomatoes, peeled and chopped, about 1 pound
¾ cup canned tomato sauce
2 cups **Basic Seafood Stock** (page 32)
½ cup chopped green onions
2 cups uncooked rice (preferably converted)
1½ dozen peeled medium shrimp, about ½ pound
1½ dozen oysters in their liquor (we use medium-size ones), about 10 ounces

Combine the seasoning mix ingredients in a small bowl and set aside.

In a 4-quart saucepan, melt the fat over medium heat. Add the tasso and andouille and sauté until crisp, about 5 to 8 minutes, stirring frequently. Add the onions, celery and bell peppers; sauté until tender but still firm, about 5 minutes, stirring occasionally and scraping pan bottom well. Add the chicken. Raise heat to high and cook 1 minute, stirring constantly. Reduce heat to medium. Add the seasoning mix and minced garlic; cook about 3 minutes, stirring constantly and scraping pan bottom as needed. Add the tomatoes and cook until chicken is tender, about 5 to 8 minutes, stirring frequently. Add the tomato sauce; cook 7 minutes, stirring fairly often. Stir in the stock and bring to a boil. Then stir in the green onions and cook about 2 minutes, stirring once or twice. Add the rice, shrimp and oysters; stir well and remove from heat. Transfer to an ungreased 8x8-inch baking pan. Cover pan snuggly with aluminum foil and bake at 350° until rice is tender but still a bit crunchy, about 20 to 30 minutes. Remove bay leaves and serve immediately.

To serve, mold rice in an 8-ounce cup. Place 2 cups on each serving plate for a main course or 1 cup for an appetizer.

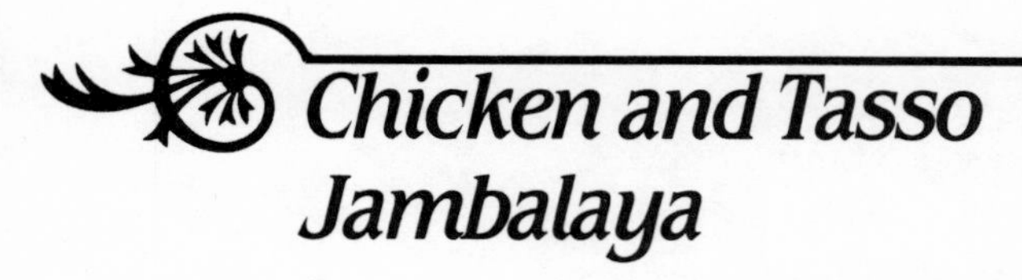

Chicken and Tasso Jambalaya

Makes 4 main-dish or 8 appetizer servings

This jambalaya is served as is or topped with **Creole Sauce** *(page 248)*

Seasoning mix:
2 whole bay leaves
2 teaspoons ground red pepper (preferably cayenne)
1½ teaspoons salt
1½ teaspoons white pepper
1 teaspoon dried thyme leaves
½ teaspoon black pepper
¼ teaspoon rubbed sage

2 tablespoons unsalted butter
½ pound chopped tasso (preferred) or other smoked ham (preferably Cure 81), about 2 cups

¾ pound boneless chicken, cut into bite-size pieces, about
2 cups
1 cup chopped onions, *in all*
1 cup chopped celery, *in all*
1 cup chopped green bell peppers, *in all*
1 tablespoon minced garlic
½ cup canned tomato sauce
1 cup peeled and chopped tomatoes
2½ cups **Basic Chicken Stock** (page 31)
1½ cups uncooked rice (preferably converted)

Combine the seasoning mix ingredients in a small bowl and set aside.

Melt the butter in a 2-quart saucepan over high heat. Add the tasso and cook until meat starts to brown, about 3 minutes, stirring frequently. Add the chicken and continue cooking until chicken is brown, about 3 to 5 minutes, stirring frequently and scraping the pan bottom well. Stir in the seasoning mix and ½ *cup each* of the onions, celery and bell peppers and the garlic. Cook until vegetables start to get tender, about 5 to 8 minutes, stirring fairly constantly and scraping pan bottom as needed. Stir in the tomato sauce and cook about 1 minute, stirring often. Stir in the remaining ½ cup each of the onions, celery and bell peppers and the tomatoes. Remove from heat. Stir in the stock and rice, mixing well. Transfer mixture to an ungreased 8x8-inch baking pan. Bake uncovered in a 350° oven until rice is tender but still a bit crunchy, about 1 hour. Remove from oven. Stir well and remove bay leaves. Let sit 5 minutes before serving.

To serve, mold rice in an 8-ounce cup and place 2 cups on each serving plate for a main course or 1 cup for an appetizer.

RICE, STUFFINGS & SIDE DISHES

Basic Cooked Rice

Makes 6 cups

If you make this ahead of time and store it, omit the bell peppers—they tend to sour quickly. Use chicken stock if you are serving the rice with a chicken dish, seafood stock with a seafood dish, beef with a beef dish. . . .

2 cups uncooked rice (preferably converted)
2½ cups **Basic Stock** (page 31)
1½ tablespoons very finely chopped onions
1½ tablespoons very finely chopped celery
1½ tablespoons very finely chopped green bell peppers
1½ tablespoons unsalted butter (preferred) or margarine, melted
½ teaspoon salt
⅛ teaspoon garlic powder
A pinch each of white pepper, ground red pepper (preferably cayenne) and black pepper

In a 5x9x2½-inch loaf pan, combine all ingredients; mix well. Seal pan snugly with aluminum foil. Bake at 350° until rice is tender, about 1 hour, 10 minutes. Serve immediately. However, you can count on the rice staying hot for 45 minutes and warm for 2 hours. To reheat left-over rice, either use a double boiler or warm the rice in a skillet with unsalted butter.

Dirty Rice

Makes 6 side-dish servings

Seasoning mix:
2 teaspoons ground red pepper (preferably cayenne)
1½ teaspoons salt

1½ teaspoons black pepper
1¼ teaspoons sweet paprika
1 teaspoon dry mustard
1 teaspoon ground cumin
½ teaspoon dried thyme leaves
½ teaspoon dried oregano leaves

2 tablespoons chicken fat or vegetable oil
½ pound chicken gizzards, ground
¼ pound ground pork
2 bay leaves
½ cup finely chopped onions
½ cup finely chopped celery
½ cup finely chopped green bell peppers
2 teaspoons minced garlic
2 tablespoons unsalted butter
2 cups **Basic Chicken** or **Pork Stock** (page 31)
⅓ pound chicken livers, ground
¾ cup uncooked rice (preferably converted)

Combine the seasoning mix ingredients in a small bowl and set aside.

Place the chicken fat, gizzards, pork and bay leaves in a large skillet over high heat; cook until meat is thoroughly browned, about 6 minutes, stirring occasionally. Stir in the seasoning mix, then add the onions, celery, bell peppers and garlic; stir thoroughly, scraping pan bottom well. Add the butter and stir until melted. Reduce heat to medium and cook about 8 minutes, stirring constantly and scraping pan bottom well (if you're not using a heavy-bottomed skillet, the mixture will probably stick a lot). Add the stock and stir until any mixture sticking to the pan bottom comes loose; cook about 8 minutes over high heat, stirring once. Then stir in the chicken livers and cook about 2 minutes. Add the rice and stir thoroughly; cover pan and turn heat to very low; cook 5 minutes. Remove from heat and leave covered until rice is tender, about 10 minutes. (The rice is finished this way so as not to overcook the livers and to preserve their delicate flavor.) Remove bay leaves and serve immediately.

Andouille Smoked Sausage Dressing

Makes 6 servings or about 5 cups

Use this dressing to stuff fowl, or serve it on the side.

4 tablespoons margarine
4 cups chopped onions, *in all*
2 cups chopped celery, *in all*
2 cups chopped green bell peppers, *in all*
1¼ pounds andouille smoked sausage (preferred) or any other good pure smoked pork sausage such as Polish sausage (kielbasa), ground, to yield 3 cups
4 tablespoons unsalted butter
2 tablespoons minced garlic
2 tablespoons Tabasco sauce
2 cups **Basic Chicken Stock** (page 31)
1½ cups very fine dry bread crumbs (preferably French bread)

Melt the margarine in a large skillet over high heat. Add *2 cups* of the onions, *1 cup* of the celery and *1 cup* of the bell peppers; sauté until onions are dark brown but not burned, about 10 to 12 minutes, stirring occasionally. Add the andouille and cook until meat is browned, about 5 minutes, stirring frequently. Add the remaining 2 cups onions, 1 cup celery and 1 cup bell peppers, the butter, garlic and Tabasco, stirring well. Reduce heat to medium and cook about 3 minutes, stirring occasionally. Stir in the stock and bring to a simmer; continue cooking until the oil rises to the top (until the water evaporates), about 10 minutes. Stir in the bread crumbs. Remove from heat. Transfer mixture to an ungreased 8x8-inch baking dish; bake uncovered in a 425° oven until browned on top, about 45 minutes, stirring and scraping pan bottom very well every 15 minutes.

Cornbread Dressing

Makes 8 servings or about 8 cups

Cajuns like their cornbreads and dressings sweet, so the crumbled cornbread we start with in this dish is sweet. If you prefer less sweet dressings, make your cornbread without sugar.

Seasoning mix:
2 teaspoons salt
1½ teaspoons white pepper
1 teaspoon ground red pepper (preferably cayenne)
1 teaspoon black pepper
1 teaspoon dried oregano leaves
½ teaspoon onion powder
½ teaspoon dried thyme leaves

¼ pound (1 stick) unsalted butter
4 tablespoons margarine
¾ cup finely chopped onions
¾ cup finely chopped green bell peppers
½ cup finely chopped celery
1 tablespoon minced garlic
2 bay leaves
¾ pound chicken giblets, boiled until tender, then ground (preferably), or finely chopped
1 cup **Basic Chicken Stock** (page 31)
1 tablespoon Tabasco sauce
5 cups finely crumbled **Cornbread** or **Cornbread Muffins** (page 41)
1 (13-ounce) can evaporated milk, or 1⅔ cups
3 eggs

Thoroughly combine the seasoning mix ingredients in a small bowl and set aside.

In a large skillet melt the butter and margarine with the onions, bell peppers, celery, garlic and bay leaves over high heat; sauté about 2 minutes, stirring occasionally. Add the seasoning mix and continue cooking until vegetables are barely wilted, about 5 minutes. Stir in the giblets, stock and Tabasco; cook 5 minutes, stirring frequently. Turn off heat. Add the cornbread, milk and eggs, stirring well. Spoon dressing into a greased 13x9-inch baking pan. Bake at 350° until browned on top, about 35 to 40 minutes.

Crawfish Cornbread Dressing

Makes about 4 cups

This is wonderful used as a stuffing for chicken or other fowl (e.g., **Roasted Quail,** *page 144).*

Seasoning mix:
2 whole bay leaves
1½ teaspoons sweet paprika
1 teaspoon salt
¾ teaspoon dried thyme leaves
½ teaspoon white pepper
½ teaspoon dry mustard
½ teaspoon ground red pepper (preferably cayenne)
¼ teaspoon black pepper

4 tablespoons unsalted butter (see **Note**)
1¾ cups finely chopped green bell peppers
1½ cups finely chopped celery
1 cup finely chopped onions
2 cups **Basic Seafood Stock** (page 32)
½ pound peeled crawfish tails (see **Note**)
3 cups finely crumbled **Cornbread** or **Cornbread Muffins** (page 41)

Note: If you buy crawfish and peel them yourself (or get a package of fat in the bag of peeled tails), substitute the crawfish fat for the butter.

Combine the seasoning mix ingredients in a small bowl; set aside.

In a large skillet melt the butter over high heat. Add the bell peppers, celery and onions and sauté about 2 minutes, stirring occasionally. Add the seasoning mix and sauté about 4 minutes more, stirring occasionally. Add the stock and bring to a boil. Add the crawfish and continue cooking about 10 minutes, stirring occasionally. Remove from heat, then with a slotted spoon lift out the crawfish and vegetables and place in a food processor or blender; process until smooth, about 15 to 30 seconds. Return mixture to skillet and place over high heat. Stir in the cornbread and continue cooking about 2 minutes, stirring occasionally. Remove from heat and use as desired. (**Note:** Let cool completely before using to stuff fowl.)

Rice, Apple and Raisin Dressing

Makes 8 to 10 servings or about 7 cups

Serve alongside **Oysters en Brochette** *(page 82) or roasted pork or veal, or use to stuff chicken, quail or squab.*

Seasoning mix:
2 teaspoons salt
1½ teaspoons white pepper
1 teaspoon garlic powder
1 teaspoon dry mustard
1 teaspoon ground red pepper (preferably cayenne)
½ teaspoon black pepper

¼ cup vegetable oil
1 cup chopped onions
1 cup chopped green bell peppers
½ cup pecan halves, dry roasted
½ cup raisins

4 tablespoons unsalted butter
1½ cups uncooked rice (preferably converted)
3 cups **Basic Pork, Beef** or **Chicken Stock** (page 31)
2 cups chopped unpeeled apples

Combine the seasoning mix ingredients in a small bowl and set aside.

In a 2-quart saucepan, heat the oil over high heat until very hot, about 2 minutes. Add the onions and bell peppers; sauté about 2 minutes, stirring occasionally. Add the pecans and continue cooking for about 3 minutes, stirring occasionally. Add the raisins and butter (these are added together so the raisins will absorb as much butter as possible). Stir until butter is melted, then cook until raisins are plump, about 4 minutes, stirring occasionally. Add the rice and seasoning mix and cook until rice starts looking frizzly (a bit like Rice Krispies), about 2 to 3 minutes, stirring almost constantly. Stir in the stock, scraping pan bottom well, then stir in the apples. Cover pan and bring to a boil; lower heat and simmer covered for 5 minutes. Remove from heat and let sit, covered, until rice is tender and stock is absorbed, about 30 minutes. (We cook the rice this slow way to let the flavors build to their maximum.) Serve immediately, allowing about ¾ cup per person.

Bienville Stuffing

Makes about 4 cups

This stuffing is excellent in many dishes such as **Fried Oysters Bayou Teche** *(page 85) or use it to stuff seafood such as trout. You can use leftover stuffing in* **Bienville Sauce** *(page 232) to serve over the stuffed seafood.*

Seasoning mix:
1½ teaspoons salt
1½ teaspoons sweet paprika
½ teaspoon white pepper
½ teaspoon ground red pepper (preferably cayenne)

- ¼ teaspoon black pepper
- ¼ teaspoon dried sweet basil leaves
- ¼ teaspoon dried thyme leaves
- ¼ teaspoon dried oregano leaves

⅓ pound bacon, cut into 1-inch pieces, about 1 cup
½ cup very finely chopped tasso (preferred) or other smoked ham (preferably Cure 81)
1 cup very finely chopped onions
1 cup very finely chopped celery
½ cup very finely chopped green bell peppers
2 cups thinly sliced mushrooms
½ pound peeled shrimp, cut into ¼-inch pieces
6 small to medium oysters in their liquor, about 3 ounces
1½ cups **Basic Seafood Stock** (page 32)
1 teaspoon minced garlic
¼ pound (1 stick) unsalted butter, melted
½ cup all-purpose flour
¼ cup heavy cream, plus additional cream if making the stuffing into a sauce
½ cup very finely chopped green onions, plus additional green onions if making the stuffing into a sauce

Combine the seasoning mix ingredients in a small bowl and set aside.

In a large skillet fry the bacon until crisp. Add the tasso to the bacon and sauté over low heat until the tasso is crisp, about 4 minutes, stirring occasionally. Drain off all but about 1 tablespoon drippings. Add the onions, celery and bell peppers. Sauté over medium heat about 7 minutes, stirring constantly. Add the mushrooms and continue cooking and stirring for about 3 minutes. Add the shrimp and oysters with their liquor and simmer about 2 minutes, stirring constantly. Stir in the stock, garlic and seasoning mix. Bring to a boil; reduce heat and simmer for about 6 minutes, stirring occasionally.

Meanwhile, in a small bowl combine the melted butter with the flour. After the shrimp and oyster mixture has simmered about 6 minutes, stir the butter mixture into it. Reduce heat to low and simmer about 7 minutes, stirring occasionally and scraping the pan bottom. Stir in the cream. Remove from heat and stir in the green onions. Let cool. Refrigerate until ready to use.

To make the Bienville Sauce, heat ½ cup stuffing over medium heat. Stir in *1 cup* cream and *3 tablespoons* green onions. Simmer over low heat, whisking constantly, until sauce is smooth and thickened, about 7 minutes. Makes about 1½ cups.

Candied Yams

Makes 10 to 12 side-dish servings

1 pound unsalted butter
2 pounds sweet potatoes, peeled and coarsely chopped
2 cups water
1 cup sugar
1 cup, packed, dark brown sugar
⅔ unpeeled orange, sliced and seeded (stem slice discarded)
⅔ unpeeled lemon, sliced and seeded (stem slice discarded)
2 sticks cinnamon
1 tablespoon vanilla extract
½ teaspoon ground mace

Heat the butter in a 4-quart saucepan over high heat; when about half melted, add the remaining ingredients. Stir, cover, and cook over high heat until mixture comes to a strong boil, about 10 minutes. Stir, then reduce heat and simmer covered for 20 minutes. Uncover and continue cooking until sweet potatoes are very tender, about 20 minutes, stirring occasionally. Remove from heat and discard cinnamon sticks. Serve immediately, undrained.

Brabant Potatoes

Makes 6 side-dish servings

Boiling the potatoes before frying them begins the starch breakdown, which helps tenderize the potatoes and leaves a surface starch; when fried, the outside becomes very crisp with a fluffy, tender and delicious inside.

2½ quarts water
2 tablespoons salt, *in all*
3 large (about 10 ounces each) white potatoes, unpeeled and scrubbed
¼ teaspoon white pepper
¼ teaspoon onion powder
¼ teaspoon garlic powder
¼ teaspoon black pepper
⅛ teaspoon ground cumin
⅛ teaspoon ground red pepper (preferably cayenne)
Vegetable oil for frying

Combine the 2½ quarts water with *1½ tablespoons* of the salt and bring to a rapid boil. Meanwhile, quarter the potatoes lengthwise, then cut into 1-inch cubes. Add potato cubes to the boiling water; cover and cook over high heat just until fork-tender, about 7 minutes. Drain immediately and rinse with cold water to cool.

In a small bowl combine the remaining 1½ teaspoons salt, the white pepper, onion, garlic, black pepper, cumin and red pepper; mix well. Sprinkle seasoning mixture evenly over potatoes while very gently tossing them, taking care not to break up chunks.

In a large, heavy skillet, heat 1 inch oil to 350°. Fry potatoes in several batches, one layer at a time (so all can catch pan-bottom heat), until golden brown on all sides, about 12 to 15 minutes, stirring occasionally. Drain on paper towels and serve immediately.

Corn Maque Choux

Makes 10 to 12 side-dish servings

My mother cooked a lot of sweet or semisweet dishes. One of these was Corn Maque Choux, which we ate with rice and gravy. Every Cajun family has its own recipe for Corn Maque Choux.

4 tablespoons unsalted butter
¼ cup vegetable oil
7 cups fresh corn cut off the cob (about seventeen 8-inch cobs), or frozen corn kernels
1 cup very finely chopped onions
¼ cup sugar
1 teaspoon white pepper
½ teaspoon salt
½ teaspoon ground red pepper (preferably cayenne)
2¼ cups, *in all*, **Basic Chicken, Beef** or **Pork Stock** (page 31)
4 tablespoons margarine
1 cup evaporated milk, *in all*
2 eggs

In a large skillet combine the butter and oil with the corn, onions, sugar, white pepper, salt and red pepper. Cook over high heat until corn is tender and starch starts to form a crust on the pan bottom, about 12 to 14 minutes, stirring occasionally, and stirring more as mixture starts sticking. Gradually stir in *1 cup* of the stock, scraping the pan bottom to remove crust as you stir. Continue cooking 5 minutes, stirring occasionally. Add the margarine, stir until melted, and cook about 5 minutes, stirring frequently and scraping pan bottom as needed. Reduce heat to low and cook about 10 minutes, stirring occasionally, then add *¼ cup* additional stock and cook about 15 minutes, stirring fairly frequently. Add the remaining 1 cup stock and cook about 10 minutes, stirring occasionally. Stir in *½ cup* of the milk and continue cooking until most of the liquid is absorbed, about 5 minutes, stirring occasionally. Remove from heat.

In a bowl combine the eggs and the remaining ½ cup milk; beat with a metal whisk until very frothy, about 1 minute. Add to the corn, stirring well. Serve immediately, allowing about ½ cup per person.

LAGNIAPPE

It's been my experience in dealing with starches and eggs in this type of recipe that you have to "cook the hell out of one" (starches) and leave the other alone. The heat from the corn is ample to do everything necessary to the eggs to give the dish a rich, frothy texture.

Cajun Stuffed Potatoes

Makes 6 servings

These are fantastic as a side dish with steak or roast, or as a main course for lunch.

6 firm potatoes, 3 to 4 inches in diameter (red potatoes preferred)
1 lemon wedge

Seasoning mix:
1 tablespoon sweet paprika
1 teaspoon ground red pepper (preferably cayenne)
½ teaspoon white pepper
½ teaspoon onion powder
½ teaspoon garlic powder
½ teaspoon black pepper

½ cup finely chopped bacon or ham
4 tablespoons unsalted butter
1 cup finely chopped onions
¾ cup finely chopped green bell peppers
About 3 cups, *in all*, **Basic Chicken Stock** (page 31)

Slice a thin piece from one end of each potato so it will stand upright; reserve the sliced-off pieces, unpeeled, for the stuffing. Rub the potato bottom with the lemon wedge to keep it from discoloring.

Using a teaspoon that won't bend easily, carve out the inside meat of each potato, leaving an opening about 1½ inches in diameter in the top. The potato meat should be removed in small, thin shavings until a shell ⅛ to ¼ inch-thick is left. Cover the hollowed-out potatoes with cold salted water until ready to stuff. Thinly slice any large pieces of shavings and the bottom slices; reserve for the stuffing.

Combine the seasoning mix ingredients in a small bowl; mix well and set aside.

In a large cast-iron or other heavy skillet, fry the bacon until crisp. (If you use ham, fry it in 1 tablespoon vegetable oil until well browned.) Add the potato shavings, butter, onions and seasoning mix to the bacon. Stir until ingredients are well combined. Spread the mixture evenly to cover the skillet bottom. Cook uncovered over high heat without stirring until a thin brown crust forms, about 4 to 5 minutes. Then stir, scraping skillet bottom well, and again spread mixture to cover skillet bottom. Cook until another crust forms, about 3 minutes; scrape again and repeat this procedure at least 2 more times until mixture is medium brown. Stir in the bell peppers and continue cooking until mixture starts getting dark brown and sticks excessively, stirring often and scraping skillet bottom well. Stir in *1 cup* of the stock and bring to a boil. Reduce heat to a simmer and cook until mixture is dark brown and slightly pasty with some lumps in it, about 5 minutes, stirring occasionally. Remove from heat.

Remove the carved potatoes from the salted water and drain well. Using a teaspoon and packing firmly, stuff each potato with the skillet mixture until mounded on top. (There may be some stuffing left over for you to eat right off while the potatoes are baking.)

Place the potatoes upright in a baking pan at least 2 inches deep and small enough to hold potatoes close together. Pour enough stock in the pan to have 1 inch of liquid. Cover the pan tightly with aluminum foil. Bake at 350° until potatoes are fork tender, about 1 hour. Serve immediately.

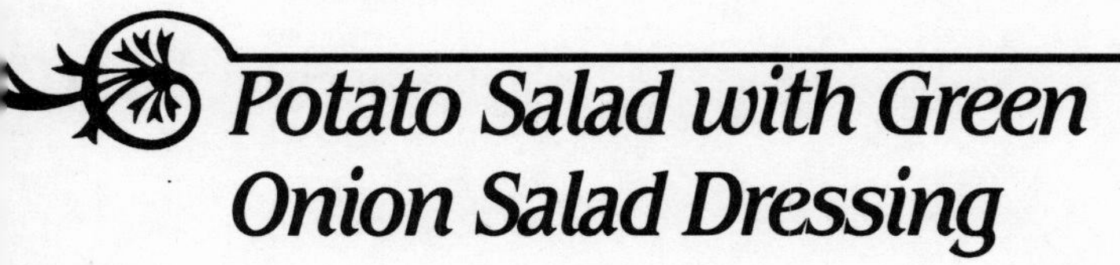

Potato Salad with Green Onion Salad Dressing

Makes 6 to 8 side-dish servings

4 medium-size white potatoes, cooked, peeled and coarsely chopped
6 hard-boiled eggs, finely chopped
¼ cup finely chopped onions
¼ cup finely chopped celery
¼ cup finely chopped green bell peppers
2 teaspoons ground red pepper (preferably cayenne)
2 teaspoons prepared mustard
1¼ teaspoons salt
¼ teaspoon white pepper
Green Onion Salad Dressing (page 273)

In a large bowl combine all the ingredients, mixing well. Refrigerate until ready to serve.

SAUCES & GRAVIES

Tartar Sauce

Makes about 2 cups

1½ tablespoons unsalted butter
½ cup finely chopped onions
1 medium apple, peeled and finely chopped
1¼ cups **Garlic Mayonnaise** (page 270)
¼ cup sweet pickle relish
2 teaspoons Tabasco sauce
1½ teaspoons white vinegar
1½ teaspoons lemon juice
½ teaspoon minced garlic

In a 1-quart saucepan melt the butter over high heat. Add the onions and sauté about 1 minute, stirring occasionally. Reduce heat to low and continue cooking until onions are lightly browned, about 2 minutes, stirring frequently. Stir in the apple; cook just until apples are tender, about 2 minutes, stirring occasionally. Remove from heat.

Transfer mixture to the medium bowl of an electric mixer. Add the remaining ingredients and beat on low speed until well blended. Refrigerate at least 2 hours before serving.

Cranberry Relish

Makes about 4 cups

1 (1-pound) package cranberries, rinsed and drained; discard wrinkled berries and stems
1½ cups sugar
2 tablespoons vanilla extract
Juice and pulp from ⅔ lemon, seeded
2 oranges, peeled, sliced and seeded

Place the cranberries, sugar and vanilla in a food processor; process a few seconds to reduce bulk. Add the lemon and process 5 seconds. Add oranges and process just until well mixed, about 5 seconds. Refrigerate at least 8 hours before serving.

Cranberry Sauce

Makes about 3½ cups

1 (1-pound) package cranberries, rinsed and drained;
discard wrinkled berries and stems
5 cups water
2 cups sugar
4 tablespoons unsalted butter
1 teaspoon salt
2 teaspoons vanilla extract
½ cup dairy sour cream

In a 4-quart saucepan, combine the cranberries, water and sugar. Bring to a boil over high heat, and continue boiling until thickened, about 30 to 35 minutes, stirring occasionally. Toward the end of the cooking time, use a potato masher to mash all berries. Reduce heat to low and add the butter and salt; simmer until butter melts, stirring occasionally. Remove from heat and stir in the vanilla. Cool to room temperature. Just before serving, fold in the sour cream and mix well. Serve immediately.

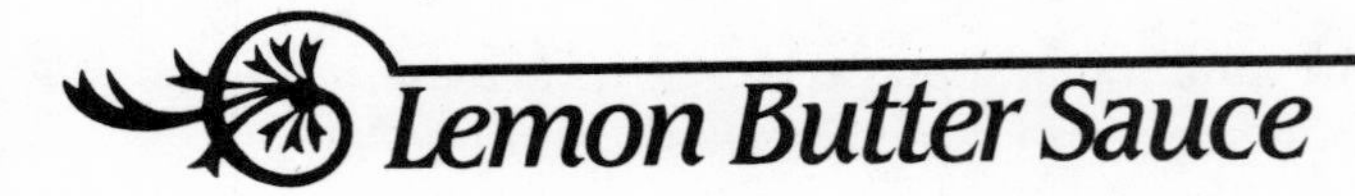

Lemon Butter Sauce

Makes 6 servings or about 1 cup

Serve this sauce over fish, veal, beef steaks or lamb chops.

½ pound (2 sticks) unsalted butter, very soft
½ lemon, peeled, seeded and very thinly sliced
⅛ teaspoon salt or to taste

In a 1-quart saucepan, melt half the butter with the lemon slices over medium-low heat, whisking constantly with a metal whisk. Add the remaining butter and the salt, whisking constantly until all the butter is melted. Turn heat to high and cook until mixture reaches a full boil, about 1 minute, whisking vigorously and constantly. Remove from heat and continue whisking about 30 seconds. Strain and serve immediately.

Browned Garlic Butter Sauce

Makes about ⅔ cup

This sauce is served over **Oysters en Brochette** *(page 82). It's also terrific over steak, lobster and grilled or blackened fish; or omit the garlic and serve it over vegetables. It's best to use salted butter to make this sauce because it will brown more easily.*

⅜ pound (1½ sticks) butter
2 teaspoons minced garlic
1 tablespoon plus 1 teaspoon minced fresh parsley

Melt the butter in a 1-quart saucepan over high heat until half melted, shaking the pan almost constantly. Add the garlic and continue cooking until butter is melted and foam on the surface is barely browned, about 2 to 3 minutes, shaking the pan occasionally. Stir in the parsley and cook until sauce is light brown and very foamy, about 1 to 2 minutes. Remove from heat and immediately drizzle over the food you're serving.

Meunière Sauce

Makes about 2 cups

1 cup **Basic Seafood Stock** (page 32)
¾ teaspoon minced garlic
¾ pound (3 sticks) unsalted butter, *in all*
2 tablespoons all-purpose flour
¼ cup Worcestershire sauce
¼ teaspoon salt

In a 2-quart saucepan combine the stock and garlic. Bring to a boil over high heat, then reduce heat and simmer 2 minutes. Remove from heat.

In a 1-quart saucepan melt *4 tablespoons* of the butter over high heat. Add the flour and whisk with a metal whisk until smooth, about 10 seconds. Remove from heat. Return stock mixture to a medium heat. Gradually add the butter mixture to the stock mixture, whisking constantly until smooth. Reduce heat to very low. Add the remaining 2½ sticks of butter, about a third at a time, whisking constantly each time until butter is melted. Gradually add the Worcestershire, whisking constantly, and add the salt. Continue cooking until sauce thickens slightly, about 5 minutes, whisking often. The sauce may be kept warm (or reheated) by setting the pan over another pan of hot (but not boiling) water.

New Orleans Bordelaise Sauce

Makes about ¼ cup

Use this sauce as a dip for boiled shrimp, crabs, crawfish or fried eggplant. You can double the recipe, stir in 2 tablespoons chopped fresh parsley *and drizzle the sauce over fish, chicken, pork chops, lamb or fried oysters.*

4 tablespoons unsalted butter
1 tablespoon minced garlic

In a 1-quart saucepan melt the butter over low heat; when almost melted add the garlic. Stir and simmer 1 to 2 minutes (if garlic starts to brown, remove from heat). Serve immediately.

New Orleans Italian Red Gravy

Makes about 6 cups

Serve this tomato gravy over pastas, chicken or fish.

½ cup olive oil
10 cloves garlic, sliced in half lengthwise
3 bay leaves
1 cup finely chopped onions
3 cups **Basic Chicken Stock** (page 31)
3 cups canned tomato sauce
1 tablespoon minced garlic

2 teaspoons salt
1 teaspoon ground red pepper (preferably cayenne)
1 teaspoon dried sweet basil leaves
1 teaspoon dried thyme leaves
½ teaspoon white pepper
½ teaspoon black pepper

Place the olive oil, garlic cloves and 2 of the bay leaves in a 2-quart saucepan over medium heat; brown garlic on both sides, about 2 to 3 minutes, stirring often. Remove garlic from pan. Add the onions to the pan and sauté until onion edges start to brown, about 6 to 8 minutes, stirring frequently. Add the remaining bay leaf and all other ingredients. Bring to a simmer; reduce heat if necessary to maintain a simmer, and cook about 20 minutes, stirring occasionally. Remove bay leaves before serving.

Giblet Gravy

Makes about 3 cups

Serve this over mashed potatoes, roasted chicken or turkey, or serve mixed with rice.

Seasoning mix:
1½ teaspoons salt
1 teaspoon ground red pepper (preferably cayenne)
1 teaspoon rubbed sage
1 teaspoon dried thyme leaves
½ teaspoon white pepper
½ teaspoon dried oregano leaves
¼ teaspoon black pepper

3 tablespoons unsalted butter
¼ pound chicken gizzards, ground
½ cup chopped onions

½ cup chopped celery
½ cup chopped green bell peppers
2 teaspoons minced garlic
¼ cup all-purpose flour
3⅓ cups **Basic Chicken Stock** (page 31)
½ pound chicken livers, ground

Combine the seasoning mix ingredients in a small bowl and set aside.

Melt the butter in a large skillet over high heat. Add the gizzards, onions, celery and bell peppers; sauté until gizzards are browned, about 5 minutes, stirring occasionally. Reduce heat to medium and add the garlic, seasoning mix and flour; cook until flour is a rich brown color, about 3 minutes, stirring frequently and scraping pan bottom well. Add the stock; bring to a boil over high heat and simmer about 5 minutes, stirring occasionally. Stir in the livers and continue simmering until gravy has reduced to about 3 cups, about 10 minutes, stirring occasionally.

Oyster Sauce for Beef

Makes 6 servings or about 3 cups

This sauce is wonderful over prime ribs, broiled filets or pan-fried veal tournedos.

½ cup cold water
2 dozen medium to large oysters in their liquor, about 1 pound
1½ cups **Rich Beef Stock** (page 32)
5 cups heavy cream (see **Note**)

Combine the water and oysters. Stir and refrigerate at least 1 hour. Strain oysters and reserve oysters and oyster water; refrigerate until ready to use.

In a large skillet (preferably nonstick) heat oysters in *½ cup* of the oyster water over high heat until oysters are plump and edges are curled, about 3 to 5 minutes, stirring occasionally. Remove pan from heat and spoon oysters into a bowl, leaving the liquid in the pan; set oysters aside.

Return pan to high heat. Add the stock; bring to a boil and then simmer until mixture reduces to ¼ cup, about 15 minutes, stirring occasionally. Add the cream, whisking with a metal whisk until well blended; bring mixture to a boil, stirring occasionally. Reduce heat to maintain a rapidly bubbling foam and continue cooking until mixture is very thick, about 30 minutes, stirring fairly often (especially toward end of cooking time). Add the oysters, stirring well; cook until oysters are heated through, about 1 to 2 minutes. Remove from heat and serve immediately, allowing about ½ cup per serving.

NOTE: If sauce separates at end of cooking time, gradually add up to about 1 cup additional cream (or seafood stock, oyster juice or water) and cook and stir until sauce is creamy again.

Barbecue Sauce

Makes about 5 cups

This sauce is super used to barbecue chicken, pork or ribs.

Seasoning mix:
1½ teaspoons black pepper
1 teaspoon salt
1 teaspoon onion powder
1 teaspoon garlic powder
½ teaspoon white pepper
½ teaspoon ground red pepper (preferably cayenne)

½ pound sliced bacon, minced
1½ cups chopped onions
2 cups **Basic Pork, Beef** or **Chicken Stock** (page 31)
1½ cups bottled chili sauce
1 cup honey

¾ cup coarsely chopped pecans, dry roasted
5 tablespoons orange juice (also slice and save rind and pulp from ½ the squeezed orange)
2 tablespoons lemon juice (also slice and save rind and pulp from ¼ the squeezed lemon)
2 teaspoons minced garlic
1 teaspoon Tabasco sauce
4 tablespoons unsalted butter

Combine the seasoning mix ingredients in a small bowl and set aside.

In a 2-quart saucepan fry the bacon over high heat until crisp. Stir in the onions, cover pan, and continue cooking until onions are dark brown but not burned, about 8 to 10 minutes, stirring occasionally. Stir in the seasoning mix and cook about 1 minute. Add the stock, chili sauce, honey, pecans, orange juice, lemon juice, orange and lemon rinds and pulp, garlic and Tabasco, stirring well. Reduce heat to low; continue cooking about 10 minutes, stirring frequently. Remove orange and lemon rinds. Continue cooking and stirring about 15 minutes more to let the flavors marry. Add the butter and stir until melted. Remove from heat. Let cool about 30 minutes, then pour into a food processor or blender and process just until pecans and bacon are finely chopped, about 10 to 20 seconds.

Creole Sauce

Makes about 2½ cups

This sauce is terrific served with chicken, rabbit, shrimp, oysters or egg dishes, such as omelets, or served over **Jambalayas** *(see pages 215 to 221).*

Seasoning mix:
2 whole bay leaves
¾ teaspoon dried oregano leaves
½ teaspoon salt

½ teaspoon white pepper
½ teaspoon ground red pepper (preferably cayenne)
½ teaspoon sweet paprika
½ teaspoon black pepper
½ teaspoon dried thyme leaves
½ teaspoon dried sweet basil leaves

4 tablespoons unsalted butter
1 cup peeled and chopped tomatoes
¾ cup chopped onions
¾ cup chopped celery
¾ cup chopped green bell peppers
1½ teaspoons minced garlic
1¼ cups **Basic Chicken Stock** (page 31)
1 cup canned tomato sauce
1 teaspoon sugar
½ teaspoon Tabasco sauce

Thoroughly combine the seasoning mix ingredients in a small bowl and set aside.

Melt the butter in a large skillet over medium heat. Stir in the tomatoes, onions, celery and bell peppers; then add the garlic and seasoning mix, stirring thoroughly. Sauté until onions are transparent, about 5 minutes, stirring occasionally. Stir in the stock, tomato sauce, sugar and Tabasco; bring to a boil. Reduce heat to maintain a simmer and cook until vegetables are tender and flavors are married, about 20 minutes, stirring occasionally. Remove bay leaves before serving.

Andouille Smoked Sausage Sauce

Makes about 3 cups

This sauce is a component of **Eggs Basin Street** *(page 303); it can also be used over* **Red Beans and Rice** *(page 190), pasta, omelets and other egg dishes, or in sausage poboys. In addition, it can be folded into rice and used as a dressing, or folded into bread crumbs and used as a stuffing.*

6 ounces andouille smoked sausage (preferred) or any other good pure smoked pork sausage such as Polish sausage (kielbasa), ground (1½ cups)
1 tablespoon vegetable oil
¾ cup chopped onions
¾ cup chopped celery
¾ cup chopped green bell peppers
1½ tablespoons all-purpose flour
1 bay leaf
¼ teaspoon dry mustard
⅛ teaspoon salt
⅛ teaspoon white pepper
⅛ teaspoon ground red pepper (preferably cayenne)
2 cups hot **Basic Beef** or **Pork Stock** (page 31)

In a large skillet cook the andouille and oil over high heat about 2 minutes, stirring frequently. Reduce heat to medium and continue cooking until andouille starts to brown, about 3 minutes, stirring frequently and scraping pan bottom well. Add the onions, celery and bell peppers; continue cooking until vegetables are tender but still firm, about 7 minutes, stirring frequently. Turn heat to high (this moves the oil to bottom of mixture). Add the flour and seasonings; cook until mixture sticks almost to the point of scorching, about 2 minutes, stirring constantly and scraping pan bottom well.

Add the stock, stirring well. Bring to a simmer, then reduce heat to very low and continue simmering about 5 minutes. Remove bay leaf and serve.

Very Hot Cajun Sauce for Beef

Makes 3½ cups or about 6 servings

This sauce is excellent with **Cajun Meat Loaf** *(page 112), roast beef sandwiches, hamburgers, pot roast and* **Cajun Shepherd's Pie** *(page 119).*

¾ cup chopped onions
½ cup chopped green bell peppers
¼ cup chopped celery
¼ cup vegetable oil
¼ cup plus 1 tablespoon all-purpose flour
¾ teaspoon ground red pepper (preferably cayenne)
½ teaspoon white pepper
½ teaspoon black pepper
2 bay leaves
¼ cup minced jalapeño peppers (see **Note**)
1 teaspoon minced garlic
3 cups **Basic Beef Stock** (page 31)

Note: Fresh jalapeños are preferred; if you have to use pickled ones, rinse as much vinegar from them as possible.

Combine the onions, bell peppers and celery in a small bowl and set aside while you start the roux. (**Note:** Unlike the roux in most other recipes in this book, the roux we use here is light brown. Therefore, instead of heating the oil to the smoking stage, we heat it to only 250°; this prevents the roux from getting too brown.)

✸ See page 26 for more about making roux.

In a heavy 2-quart saucepan heat the oil over medium-low heat to about 250°. With a metal whisk, whisk in the flour a little at a time until smooth. Continue cooking, whisking constantly, until roux is light brown, about 2 to 3 minutes. Be careful not to let the roux scorch or splash on your skin. Remove from heat and with a spoon immediately stir in the vegetable mixture and the red, white and black peppers; return pan to high heat and cook about 2 minutes, stirring constantly. Add the bay leaves, jalapeño peppers and garlic, stirring well. Continue cooking about 2 minutes, stirring constantly. (We're cooking the seasonings and vegetables in the light roux and the mixture should, therefore, be pasty.) Remove from heat.

In a separate 2-quart saucepan, bring the stock to a boil. Add the roux mixture by spoonfuls to the boiling stock, stirring until dissolved between each addition. Bring mixture to a boil, then reduce heat to a simmer and cook until the sauce reduces to 3½ cups, about 15 minutes. Skim any oil from the top and serve immediately.

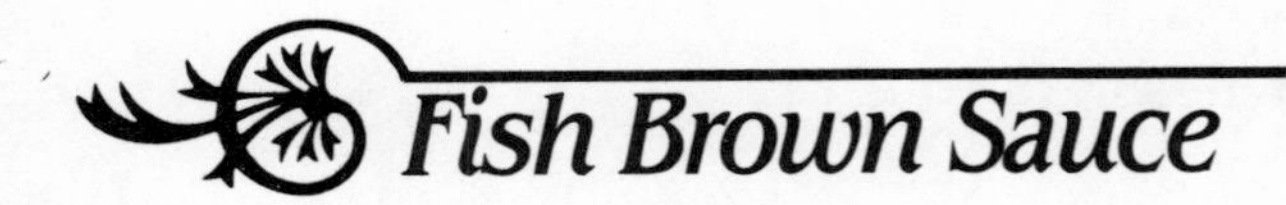

Fish Brown Sauce

Makes 6 servings or about 1½ cups

Serve this delicious sauce over broiled, fried or baked fish fillets or broiled, fried or baked oysters.

Seasoning mix:
1 whole bay leaf
½ teaspoon salt
½ teaspoon garlic powder
¼ teaspoon white pepper
¼ teaspoon dried oregano leaves

¼ teaspoon dried thyme leaves
⅛ teaspoon ground red pepper (preferably cayenne)

2 tablespoons vegetable oil
3 tablespoons all-purpose flour, *in all*
¼ cup finely chopped onions
4 teaspoons canned tomato sauce
1 teaspoon Worcestershire sauce
2 cups hot **Basic Seafood Stock** (page 32)
2 tablespoons burgundy wine, *in all*
2 tablespoons unsalted butter, softened

Combine the seasoning mix ingredients in a small bowl and set aside.

Heat the oil in a heavy 1-quart saucepan over high heat just until the oil starts to smoke, about 1 to 2 minutes. With a metal whisk, mix in *2 tablespoons* of the flour, whisking constantly and scraping pan bottom well, until the roux is dark red-brown to black, about 2 minutes, being careful not to let it scorch or splash on your skin. (Remove from heat momentarily if it is browning too fast for you to control, continuing to stir constantly.) Immediately whisk in the onions; reduce heat to low and continue stirring and cooking about 1 minute. Add the tomato sauce and stir and cook 1 minute. Then stir in the seasoning mix and the Worcestershire (the mixture should now be thick and dark red-brown); cook 2 to 3 minutes, stirring constantly. Add the stock; turn heat to high and bring to a boil, stirring often. Reduce heat to maintain a simmer and cook about 6 to 8 minutes, stirring often. Stir in *1 tablespoon* of the burgundy and remove from heat.

✱ See page 26 for more about making roux.

In a small bowl mix the butter and remaining 1 tablespoon flour until creamy. Return sauce to low heat; gradually add the butter mixture to the sauce, whisking until well blended each time. Return sauce to a simmer and simmer 10 minutes, stirring often. Add the remaining 1 tablespoon burgundy. Remove from heat and discard bay leaf. Serve immediately.

Shrimp and Crab Butter Cream Sauce

Makes about 5 cups

This sauce is served over **Stuffed Mirliton** *(page 72). It's also great over stuffed fish, vegetables, pasta and omelets.*

½ pound (2 sticks) unsalted butter, *in all*
¼ cup finely chopped onions
3 tablespoons all-purpose flour
1½ cups **Basic Seafood Stock** (page 32)
1 cup heavy cream
½ teaspoon salt
½ teaspoon ground red pepper (preferably cayenne)
2 dozen peeled medium shrimp, about ¾ pound
1 cup, packed, lump crabmeat (picked over), about ½ pound

In a heavy 1-quart saucepan melt *1 stick* of the butter with the onions over medium heat; sauté about 1 minute. Add the flour and blend with a metal whisk until smooth. Reduce heat to low and continue cooking and whisking constantly for 1 minute. (If mixture starts to brown, remove from heat.)

Meanwhile, bring the stock to a boil in a 2-quart saucepan. Add the butter-flour mixture and the remaining 1 stick butter. Cook over high heat until the butter melts, whisking constantly. Gradually add the cream, whisking constantly, then mix in the salt and red pepper. Lower heat to medium and stir in the shrimp and crabmeat. Continue cooking just until shrimp are pink and plump, about 1 to 2 minutes, stirring occasionally. Remove from heat.

Spiced Peach Gravy for Fowl

Makes about 3½ cups

4 cups peeled and chopped peaches, about 4 large peaches
1½ cups sugar
1 cup water
4 tablespoons unsalted butter
1 cup finely chopped onions
¾ cup finely chopped green bell peppers
½ cup finely chopped celery
2 bay leaves
½ teaspoon salt
½ teaspoon white pepper
½ teaspoon ground red pepper (preferably cayenne)
½ teaspoon rubbed sage
3 cups **Basic Chicken Stock** (page 31)
3 peeled peaches, sliced in thin wedges

In a 2-quart saucepan combine the chopped peaches, sugar and water. Bring mixture to a boil over high heat; reduce heat to a simmer and continue cooking until mixture caramelizes (turns dark brown and is very thick), about 45 minutes, stirring occasionally and more often toward the end of cooking.

Meanwhile, in a 1-quart saucepan, combine the butter, onions, bell peppers, celery and seasonings; sauté over medium heat until vegetables are tender, about 10 minutes, stirring frequently and scraping pan bottom well. Add the stock, stirring well to dissolve any sediment on bottom of pan. Bring to a boil, then reduce heat to a simmer and cook 20 minutes, stirring occasionally. When the peach mixture has caramelized, stir the stock mixture into it and cook over medium heat for about 10 minutes, stirring occasionally. Remove from heat and discard bay leaves.

Strain the contents of the skillet and reserve the liquid in the skillet. Purée the strained solids in a food processor or blender until smooth, about 30 seconds, pushing the sides down once with a rubber spatula. Cook the reserved liquid over high heat 5 minutes to reduce. Add *1 cup* of the purée, stirring well; cook about 5 minutes, stirring frequently. (You will have a little leftover purée to snack on while cooking.) Stir in the peach wedges; cook until softened, about 5 minutes, stirring often. Remove from heat and serve immediately with roasted, broiled or fried chicken or other fowl.

Spiced Pear Gravy for Fowl

Makes about 2½ cups

1 cup sugar
4 cups peeled and chopped pears, about 3 large pears
2 cups water, *in all*
¼ cup drippings from roasted fowl, or 4 tablespoons unsalted butter
½ cup finely chopped onions
½ cup finely chopped celery
½ cup finely chopped green bell peppers
½ teaspoon salt
½ teaspoon white pepper
½ teaspoon ground red pepper (preferably cayenne)
1¾ cups hot **Basic Chicken Stock** (page 31)
1 peeled and cored pear, sliced

Combine the sugar and the chopped pears in a large skillet (not cast iron), stirring until sugar is dissolved. Cook over high heat about 1 minute, stirring once or twice. Stir in *1 cup* of the water and continue cooking until mixture caramelizes (turns dark brown and very syrupy), about 20 to 25 minutes, stirring occasionally and scraping pan bottom well. Remove from heat and stir in the remaining 1 cup water. Set aside.

Place the ¼ cup drippings from the fowl (or melt the butter) in a

1-quart saucepan. Add the onions, celery, bell peppers and seasonings; sauté over high heat until vegetables start to get tender, about 3 minutes, stirring occasionally and scraping pan bottom well. Remove from heat. Stir the vegetable mixture into the caramelized pears, then add the stock. Turn heat to high and cook 15 minutes, stirring occasionally. Remove from heat.

Strain the contents of the skillet and reserve the liquid in the skillet. Purée the strained solids in a food processor or blender until smooth, about 30 seconds, pushing the sides down once with a rubber spatula. Add the purée to the strained liquid, stirring well. Turn heat to high and cook 2 minutes, stirring frequently. Stir in the sliced pear; reduce heat and simmer until pear slices are cooked, about 5 to 7 minutes. Remove from heat and serve immediately alongside roasted chicken or other fowl.

Spiced Fig Gravy for Fowl

Makes about 4 cups

2 (17-ounce) jars whole figs in heavy syrup
1 cup sugar
¼ cup drippings from roasted fowl, or 4 tablespoons unsalted butter
1¼ cups finely chopped onions, *in all*
1 cup finely chopped celery, *in all*
½ cup finely chopped green bell peppers
½ teaspoon salt
½ teaspoon white pepper
½ teaspoon ground red pepper (preferably cayenne)
½ teaspoon dried thyme leaves
4½ cups, *in all*, hot **Basic Goose** or **Chicken Stock** (page 31)
½ orange, seeded and thinly sliced

Drain the syrup from the figs and reserve both.

In a large skillet (not cast iron) combine the fig syrup and sugar, mixing well. Cook over high heat until mixture caramelizes (turns dark brown and very syrupy), about 18 to 20 minutes, stirring occasionally. Set aside.

Place the ¼ cup drippings (or melt the butter) in a 1-quart saucepan. Add *¾ cup* of the onions, *½ cup* of the celery, the bell peppers and seasonings; sauté over high heat until vegetables start to wilt, about 3 minutes, stirring occasionally. Stir the vegetable mixture into the caramelized fig sauce and add *2 cups* of the stock, stirring well. Turn heat to high and cook 15 minutes, stirring occasionally. Add the orange slices and continue cooking about 5 minutes, stirring occasionally. Add *1 cup* more stock and the remaining ½ cup each of onions and celery; cook about 10 minutes more, stirring occasionally. Remove from heat.

Strain the contents of the skillet and reserve the liquid in the skillet. Purée the strained solids in a food processor or blender until smooth, about 30 seconds, pushing the sides down once with a rubber spatula. Add the puréed mixture to the strained liquid, stirring well. Turn heat to high and cook until mixture starts to thicken, about 5 minutes, stirring frequently. Stir in the figs (drain them again if necessary) and simmer about 3 minutes, stirring occasionally and being careful not to break up the figs. Stir in the remaining 1½ cups stock; bring to a boil, reduce heat, and simmer until mixture is a sauce, about 18 minutes more, stirring occasionally. Remove from heat and serve immediately alongside roasted chicken or other fowl. This sauce also accompanies **Roasted Goose with Smoked Ham Stuffing** (page 148).

Hollandaise Sauce

Makes about 2⅔ cups

I'm not a chemist, so when I describe the principles of making hollandaise sauce, they are based on my experience of what happens right in the bowl in which you make the sauce: We beat the egg yolks over heat long enough to fill them with lots of air bubbles—but we are careful to control the heat so the yolks don't harden. (In order for the butter to enter, fill and expand the bubbles in the yolks, they have to be in a liquid state.)

Once we start adding the melted butter, we don't apply any heat again because that would cause the oil to expand too much and break the air bubbles, resulting in a separated sauce. For the same reason, we don't reheat the sauce once it is completed. But we don't let the sauce get too cool, either, because the oil will congeal and contract and cause the bubbles to burst. The ideal is to keep the sauce as close to body temperature as possible.

I particularly recommend using unsalted butter in making this fine sauce (and all its variations) because the unsalted is generally a better product.

1 pound unsalted butter
4 tablespoons margarine
4 egg yolks
2 teaspoons white wine
2 teaspoons lemon juice
½ teaspoon Tabasco sauce
½ teaspoon Worcestershire sauce

Melt the butter and margarine in a 1-quart saucepan over low heat. Raise heat and bring to a rapid boil. Remove from heat and cool 5 minutes. Skim foam from the top and discard. Pour butter into a large glass measuring cup and set aside.

Meanwhile, in a medium-size stainless steel mixing bowl or in the top of a double boiler, combine all the remaining ingredients. Mix together with a metal whisk until blended.

Place bowl over a pan of slowly simmering (not boiling) water. (Bowl must never touch the water.) Vigorously whisk the egg mixture, picking up the bowl frequently to let the steam escape; whip until the egg mixture is very light and creamy and has a sheen, about 6 to 8 minutes. (This amount of beating is important so that the cooked eggs will better be able to hold the butter.) Remove bowl from the pan of hot water. Gradually ladle about ¼ cup of the butter mixture (use the top butterfat, not the butter solids on the bottom) into the egg mixture while vigorously whipping the sauce; make sure the butter you add is well mixed into the sauce before adding more. Continue gradually adding the surface butterfat until you've added about 1 cup.

So that you can get to the butter solids, ladle out and reserve about ½ cup surface butterfat into a separate container. (The butter solids add flavor and also thin the sauce.) Gradually ladle all but ⅓ cup of the bottom solids into the sauce, whisking well. (Use any remaining bottom solids in another dish.) Then gradually whisk in enough of the reserved top butterfat to produce a fairly thick sauce. (The butterfat thickens the sauce, so you may not need to use it all.) Serve immediately (or as soon as possible, keeping the sauce in a warm place, such as on top of the stove, until ready to serve).

Herbal Hollandaise

Makes about 2 cups

Use only fresh herbs for this wonderful sauce.

1 pound unsalted butter
4 tablespoons margarine
4 egg yolks
2 teaspoons white wine
2 teaspoons lemon juice
1 tablespoon finely chopped fresh oregano leaves
1½ teaspoons finely chopped fresh thyme leaves
1 teaspoon finely chopped fresh basil leaves
½ teaspoon Tabasco sauce
½ teaspoon Worcestershire sauce

Follow exactly the same directions as given for **Hollandaise Sauce** (preceding recipe), combining the fresh herbs with the yolks along with the other remaining ingredients.

New Orleans Béarnaise Sauce

Makes about 2⅔ cups

3 tablespoons white wine
1 teaspoon dried tarragon leaves
½ teaspoon very finely chopped fresh parsley, optional
Warm **Hollandaise Sauce** (page 258)

In a small saucepan combine the wine, tarragon and, if desired, parsley. Cook over high heat until most of the liquid is evaporated, about 2 minutes, stirring occasionally. Stir into the hollandaise. Serve immediately.

Choron Sauce

Makes about 3 cups

¾ cup peeled and finely chopped tomatoes
Warm **Hollandaise Sauce** (page 258)

In a 1-quart saucepan cook the tomatoes over medium heat until tender and very little liquid remains, about 8 to 10 minutes, stirring frequently. Stir tomatoes into the hollandaise. Serve immediately.

Asparagus Hollandaise

Makes about 2½ cups

Serve this hollandaise over asparagus, steak or lobster.

3 dozen thin asparagus spears (large end about the diameter of a pencil)
1 pound unsalted butter, *in all*
¼ cup water
4 tablespoons margarine
4 egg yolks
2 teaspoons white wine
2 teaspoons lemon juice
½ teaspoon Tabasco sauce
½ teaspoon Worcestershire sauce

Cut ½ inch off the tips of the asparagus and set aside. Finely chop enough off of the remaining top ends of spears to yield ½ cup. (Use remainder of spears in another recipe.) Place the ½ cup chopped asparagus and *1 tablespoon* of the butter in a 1-quart saucepan; sauté over high heat for 2 minutes, stirring occasionally. Add the water and continue cooking until very tender, about 3 minutes, stirring occasionally. If necessary, add another ¼ cup water and continue cooking until most of the water is evaporated. Place the undrained chopped asparagus in a food processor or blender and purée until smooth, about 15 seconds, pushing down the sides with a rubber spatula. Set aside.

Melt the remaining butter and the margarine in a 1-quart saucepan over low heat. Raise heat and bring to a rapid boil. Remove from heat and cool 5 minutes. Skim froth from top and discard. Pour into a large glass measuring cup and set aside.

Meanwhile, in a medium-size stainless steel mixing bowl or in the top of a double boiler, combine the puréed asparagus, reserved asparagus tips and all remaining ingredients. Mix together with a metal whisk until blended. Place bowl over a pan of slowly simmering (not boiling) water. (Bowl must never touch water.) Vigorously whisk the egg mixture, picking up the bowl frequently to let the steam escape; whip until the egg mixture is very light and creamy and has a sheen, about 7 to 9 minutes. (This amount of beating is longer than for plain hollandaise and is important so that the cooked eggs will better be able to hold the butter.) Remove bowl from the pan of hot water. Gradually ladle about ¼ cup of the butter mixture (use the top butterfat, not the butter solids on the bottom) into the egg mixture while vigorously whipping the sauce; make sure the butter you add is well mixed into the sauce before adding more. Continue gradually adding the surface butterfat until you've added about 1 cup.

So that you can get to the butter solids, ladle out and reserve about ½ cup surface butterfat into a separate container. (The butter solids add flavor and also thin the sauce.) Gradually ladle all but ½ cup of the bottom solids into the sauce, whisking well. (Use any remaining bottom solids in another dish.) Then gradually whisk in enough of the reserved top butterfat to produce a fairly thick sauce. (The butterfat thickens the sauce, so you may not need to use it all.) Serve immediately (or as soon as possible, keeping the sauce in a warm place, such as on top of the stove, until ready to serve).

Vegetable Mousseline

Makes about 3½ cups

This variation on hollandaise sauce is great over pan-fried fish.

1 pound unsalted butter, *in all*
4 tablespoons margarine
4 egg yolks
2 teaspoons white wine
2 teaspoons lemon juice
½ teaspoon Tabasco sauce
½ teaspoon Worcestershire sauce
1 cup julienned carrots (see **Note**)
1 cup julienned onions (see **Note**)
½ teaspoon salt

½ teaspoon ground red pepper (preferably cayenne)
¼ teaspoon white pepper
1 cup julienned yellow squash (see **NOTE**)
1 cup julienned zucchini (see **NOTE**)
1½ cups **Basic Seafood Stock** (page 32)
½ cup heavy cream

NOTE: To julienne squashes, cut peelings ⅛ inch thick and cut these into strips ⅛ inch wide and 2 inches long; use only strips that have skin on one surface. Cut carrots and onions into similar strips.

Melt *all but 1 tablespoon* of the butter with the margarine in a 1-quart saucepan over low heat. Raise heat and bring to a rapid boil. Remove from heat and cool 5 minutes. Skim froth from the top and discard. Pour into a large glass measuring cup and set aside.

Meanwhile, in a medium-size stainless steel mixing bowl or in the top of a double boiler, combine the egg yolks, wine, lemon juice, Tabasco and Worcestershire. Mix together with a metal whisk until blended.

Place bowl over a small pan of slowly simmering (not boiling) water. (Bowl must never touch the water.) Vigorously whisk the egg mixture, picking up the bowl frequently to let the steam escape; whip until the egg mixture is very light and creamy and has a sheen, about 6 to 8 minutes. (This amount of beating is important so that the cooked eggs will better be able to hold the butter.) Remove bowl from the pan of hot water. Gradually ladle about ¼ cup of the butter mixture (use the top butterfat, which thickens the sauce, not the butter solids on the bottom) into the egg mixture while vigorously whipping the sauce; make sure the butter you add is well mixed into the sauce before adding more. Continue gradually adding enough of the surface butterfat to produce a thick sauce; you will probably need to add all but about ⅔ cup. (Use remaining butter mixture in another dish.) Set aside in a warm place.

In a 2-quart saucepan melt the remaining 1 tablespoon butter over medium-low heat. Add the carrots; sauté about 2 minutes, stirring occasionally. Stir in the onions and cook 1 minute. Add the salt and ground peppers and cook and stir 1 minute. Stir in the yellow squash and zucchini and cook about 1 minute, stirring often. Turn heat to high and add the stock; cook 1 minute. Remove from heat. Strain the stock, setting the vegetables aside. Return stock to pan, bring to a boil, and then simmer about 15 minutes to reduce liquid to about 1 tablespoon. Set aside.

Strain the reserved vegetables again to remove any excess water that may have accumulated; stir them into the hollandaise sauce.

In a chilled medium-size bowl, whip the cream with a metal whisk until stiff peaks form, about 3 minutes; do *not* overbeat. Fold the whipped cream into the hollandaise until smooth. Add *1 teaspoon* of the reduced stock, stirring well. Serve immediately (or as soon as possible, keeping the sauce in a warm place until ready to serve).

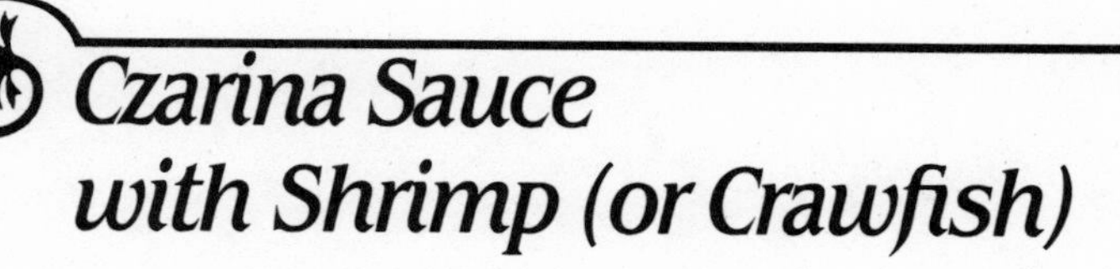

Czarina Sauce with Shrimp (or Crawfish)

Makes 6 to 8 servings

Serve this sauce over pasta, fish, veal or rice. If serving over veal or fish, allow in the sauce about 3 medium to large shrimp or a scant ¼ cup crawfish tails per person. If serving over pasta or rice, allow about 10 to 12 medium to large shrimp or a scant 1 cup crawfish tails per person.

5 tablespoons unsalted butter, *in all*
1 cup julienned onions (see **Note**)
1 cup julienned yellow squash (see **Note**)
1 cup julienned zucchini (see **Note**)
1 teaspoon ground red pepper (preferably cayenne)
½ teaspoon white pepper
1 tablespoon lemon juice
Peeled shrimp or crawfish tails (see above)
2 cups heavy cream
½ cup finely grated Parmesan cheese (preferably imported)
½ teaspoon salt

Note: To julienne squashes, cut peelings ⅛ inch thick and cut these into strips ⅛ inch wide and 2 inches long; use only strips that have skin on one surface. Cut onions into similar strips.

Melt *4 tablespoons* of the butter in a 2-quart saucepan (preferably nonstick) over high heat. Add the onions, squash and zucchini and sauté until vegetables start to get tender, about 2 minutes, stirring occasionally. Add the peppers and continue cooking about 1 minute. Add the lemon juice and shrimp or crawfish and cook until the seafood turns pink, about 1 minute. Stir in the cream, the remaining 1 tablespoon butter and the Parmesan. Cook until heated through, stirring constantly. Remove from heat and stir in the salt. Serve immediately, allowing about ½ cup sauce per serving including the seafood.

SALAD DRESSINGS

Homemade Mayonnaise

Makes about 2 cups

1 large egg, or 1 small egg plus 1 egg yolk
1½ cups vegetable oil
1 tablespoon cider vinegar
1 teaspoon Tabasco sauce, optional
½ teaspoon salt
½ teaspoon white pepper

Place the egg (or egg and egg yolk) in a food processor or blender; blend about 30 seconds. With the machine on, slowly add the oil in a thin, steady stream. When the mixture becomes thick and creamy, add the vinegar and blend about 30 seconds. Add the Tabasco (if you want a Louisiana touch), salt and white pepper, and process until mixture is well blended, about 1 minute, pushing the sides down once or twice with a rubber spatula. Refrigerate for at least 30 minutes before serving.

NOTE: *The following recipes for flavored mayonnaises are unconventional and not the way things were done in the past. There are endless uses for them—from a lowly sandwich or tuna salad to the finest seafood. I think they're superb on sandwiches; we use them on our po boy sandwiches made with French bread and various fillings. Unusual combinations we've found to be terrific are Oyster Mayonnaise on roast beef, Garlic Mayonnaise on oyster or shrimp po boys, Beef Mayonnaise on ham sandwiches or po boys, and Shrimp Mayonnaise on cold roast lamb sandwiches. They make great dips and are special for all kinds of salads that call for mayonnaise dressings.*

Beef Mayonnaise

Makes about 2½ cups

2 cups **Basic Beef Stock** (page 31)
2 tablespoons unsalted butter
3 tablespoons finely chopped onions
3 tablespoons finely chopped celery
2 teaspoons minced garlic
1 bay leaf
1 teaspoon white pepper
1 teaspoon dry mustard
1 teaspoon ground red pepper (preferably cayenne)
2 teaspoons sugar
1 teaspoon salt
1 egg
2 cups vegetable oil, *in all*

Reduce the stock in a saucepan over high heat to ¼ cup. Set aside.

In a 1-quart saucepan melt the butter over high heat. Add the onions, celery, garlic and bay leaf; sauté for about 1 minute, stirring frequently. Stir in the white pepper, mustard and red pepper; cook and stir about 1 minute. Reduce heat to medium-low and add the sugar and salt. Continue cooking about 2 minutes; stirring often. Cool 10 minutes and remove bay leaf.

In a food processor or blender, beat the egg about 30 seconds. Add the vegetable mixture and blend about 15 seconds. With the machine running, gradually add *1⅓ cups* of the oil in a thin, steady stream, then in the same manner add the stock, then the remaining ⅔ cup oil. Blend about 30 seconds more, pushing sides down with a rubber spatula. Refrigerate for at least 30 minutes before serving.

Garlic Mayonnaise

Makes about 2½ cups

2½ tablespoons minced garlic
2 tablespoons unsalted butter
2 tablespoons very finely chopped onions
1 tablespoon lemon juice
½ teaspoon salt
½ teaspoon Tabasco sauce (optional)
¼ teaspoon white pepper
¼ teaspoon ground red pepper (preferably cayenne)
1 egg plus 1 egg yolk
2 cups vegetable oil

In a 1-quart saucepan combine the garlic, butter, onions, lemon juice, salt, Tabasco, and white and red peppers. Sauté over medium-low heat for about 4 minutes, stirring occasionally. Remove from heat and let cool for 15 minutes.

In a food processor or blender, beat the egg and egg yolk for 30 seconds. Then beat in the sautéed mixture for about 15 seconds. With the machine still running, slowly add the oil in a thin, steady stream; process until thick and creamy, about 15 seconds more, pushing the sides down once with a rubber spatula. Refrigerate for at least 30 minutes before serving.

Oyster Mayonnaise

Makes about 1½ cups

Seasoning mix:

1 small whole bay leaf
½ teaspoon salt
½ teaspoon dry mustard

½ teaspoon ground red pepper (preferably cayenne)
¼ teaspoon white pepper
¼ teaspoon dried sweet basil leaves
⅛ teaspoon dried thyme leaves
Pinch of dried oregano leaves

1 tablespoon unsalted butter
2½ tablespoons finely chopped onions
1 tablespoon finely chopped celery
3 shucked oysters (we use medium-size ones)
1 small egg
1¼ cups vegetable oil
1 tablespoon white vinegar
½ teaspoon Tabasco sauce, optional

Combine the seasoning mix ingredients in a small bowl and set aside.

Melt the butter in a 1-quart saucepan over medium heat. Add the onions and celery; sauté for about 1 minute, stirring almost constantly. Turn heat to low and add the seasoning mix and oysters; cook for about 5 minutes more, stirring constantly and scraping pan bottom as needed. Remove from heat, discard bay leaf, and let cool 15 minutes.

Place mixture in a food processor or blender with the egg; blend 30 seconds. With the machine still running, slowly add the oil in a thin, steady stream. Add the vinegar and, if desired, the Tabasco; blend until mixture is smooth, about 1 minute, pushing the sides down at least once with a rubber spatula. Refrigerate for at least 30 minutes before serving.

Shrimp Mayonnaise

Makes about 2 cups

Seasoning mix:
1 small whole bay leaf
½ teaspoon salt
½ teaspoon dry mustard
½ teaspoon ground red pepper (preferably cayenne)
¼ teaspoon white pepper
¼ teaspoon dried sweet basil leaves
⅛ teaspoon dried thyme leaves
Pinch of dried oregano leaves

2 tablespoons unsalted butter
3 tablespoons finely chopped onions
1 tablespoon finely chopped celery
3 peeled large shrimp
1 egg
1¼ cups vegetable oil
2 teaspoons lemon juice
2 teaspoons white vinegar

Combine the seasoning mix ingredients in a small bowl and set aside.

Melt the butter in a 1-quart saucepan over medium heat. Add the onions and celery; sauté for about 1 minute, stirring almost constantly. Turn heat to low and add the seasoning mix and shrimp. Continue cooking for 5 minutes, stirring frequently and scraping pan bottom as needed. Remove from heat, discard bay leaf, and let cool 15 minutes.

In a food processor or blender, process the egg for about 30 seconds. Add the shrimp mixture and process a few seconds more. With the machine still running, gradually add the oil in a thin, steady stream, then the lemon juice and vinegar, pushing down the sides once with a rubber spatula. Refrigerate for at least 30 minutes before serving.

Green Onion Salad Dressing

Makes about 1½ cups

This is very good for **Potato Salad,** *page 237.*

1 egg plus 1 egg yolk
1⅛ cups vegetable oil
Scant ½ cup finely chopped green onions
1½ tablespoons Creole mustard (preferred) or brown mustard
1 tablespoon white vinegar
¼ teaspoon salt
⅛ teaspoon white pepper

Blend the egg and egg yolk in a food processor or blender until frothy, about 2 minutes. With the machine on, gradually add the oil in a thin stream. When the mixture is thick and creamy, add the remaining ingredients and blend thoroughly. Refrigerate until ready to use.

Hot Pepper Vinegar

Makes about 1½ cups

1 cup plus 2 tablespoons water
6 tablespoons white vinegar
¼ teaspoon ground red pepper (preferably cayenne)
⅛ teaspoon salt
4 jalapeño peppers, quartered

In a 2-quart saucepan combine the water, vinegar and seasonings; bring to a boil over high heat. Add the jalapeños and remove from heat. Cool and refrigerate, covered, overnight. Strain before using.

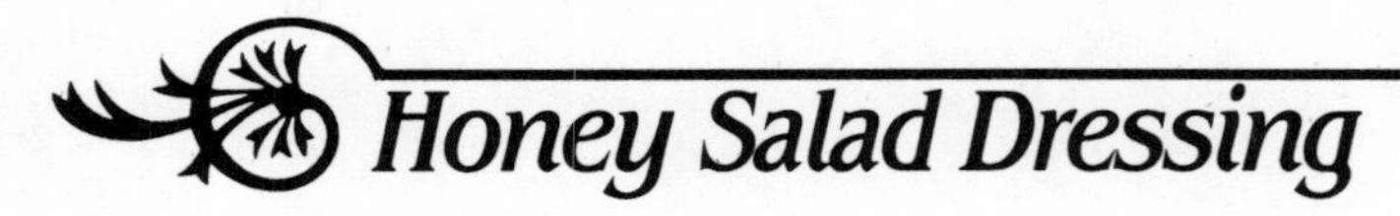

Honey Salad Dressing

Makes about 3½ cups

Serve this unusual and scrumptious dressing over your favorite lettuce or fruit salad. Make the Hot Pepper Vinegar a day ahead.

1¼ cups chopped pecans, dry roasted until dark in color
1 cup honey
½ cup sesame seeds, toasted
½ cup coarsely chopped onions
1 egg
Hot Pepper Vinegar (preceding recipe)

In a food processor or blender, combine the pecans, honey, sesame seeds, onions and egg; process a few seconds until smooth. Pour into a jar and stir in the vinegar until well blended. Refrigerate until ready to use.

Hard-Boiled Egg and Hot Pepper Vinegar Dressing

Makes about 3 cups

Make the Hot Pepper Vinegar a day ahead. This dressing is awesome over green salads, avocado, chilled fish or chicken, or in potato salad.

4 hard-boiled eggs
1 cup coarsely chopped onions
½ cup coarsely chopped green bell peppers
1 tablespoon minced garlic

2 teaspoons salt
1 teaspoon dry mustard
Hot Pepper Vinegar (page 273)

In a food processor or blender, combine all ingredients except the vinegar; process a few seconds until eggs are broken up. Add the vinegar and continue processing until all ingredients are very finely minced, about 1 to 2 minutes. Refrigerate until ready to use.

Blue Cheese Salad Dressing

Makes about 1 quart

1 egg
½ cup chopped onions
1 teaspoon minced garlic
2 cups vegetable oil
½ cup buttermilk
2 teaspoons white pepper
1 teaspoon salt
½ teaspoon ground red pepper (preferably cayenne)
½ pound blue cheese, coarsely crumbled

In a food processor or blender, combine the egg, onions and garlic; process a few seconds until well mixed. With the machine still running, add the oil in a thin, steady stream; then add the buttermilk and seasonings and process a few seconds more until well mixed, pushing the sides down once with a rubber spatula. Transfer mixture to a large bowl and add the cheese; mix with a metal whisk to break up any large lumps, but leave the cheese somewhat lumpy. Refrigerate until ready to use.

Thousand Island Dressing

Makes about 3 cups

1 raw egg
¼ cup coarsely chopped onions
1 cup vegetable oil
1 cup peeled and chopped tomatoes
2 hard-boiled eggs
1 teaspoon salt
1 teaspoon white pepper
½ teaspoon ground red pepper (preferably cayenne)
½ cup sweet relish

In a food processor or blender, process the raw egg and onions 5 to 10 seconds. With the machine still running, add the oil in a thin, steady stream; then add the tomatoes, hard-boiled eggs and seasonings and process a few seconds until smooth, pushing the sides down once with a rubber spatula. Transfer mixture to a bowl and stir in the relish. Refrigerate until ready to use.

Ol' Myra's Salad Dressing

Makes about 1⅓ cups

3 anchovies
1 raw egg
2 hard-boiled egg yolks
2 tablespoons cider vinegar
1 teaspoon dry mustard
1 teaspoon coarsely ground black pepper

1 teaspoon minced garlic
½ teaspoon white pepper
½ teaspoon ground red pepper (preferably cayenne)
1 cup olive oil

In a food processor or blender, process all but the olive oil a few seconds until smooth. With the machine running, add the olive oil in a thin, steady stream and continue processing a few seconds more until smooth, pushing the sides down once with a rubber spatula. Refrigerate until ready to use.

APPETIZERS

Rabbit Tenderloin with Mustard Sauce

Color Picture 24

Makes 6 appetizer servings

6 (2- to 3-ounce) boneless domestic rabbit tenderloins (have your butcher prepare; page 30)

Seasoning mix:
1 teaspoon salt
¾ teaspoon garlic powder
½ teaspoon onion powder
¼ teaspoon ground red pepper (preferably cayenne)
¼ teaspoon black pepper
¼ teaspoon dried sweet basil leaves
⅛ teaspoon white pepper
⅛ teaspoon ground coriander

½ cup all-purpose flour
Vegetable oil for deep frying
Unsalted butter for frying
Mustard Sauce (recipe follows)

Peel any silver skin from the rabbit and discard. Combine the ingredients of the seasoning mix, mixing well; sprinkle the rabbit lightly and evenly with about 1½ teaspoons of the mix and combine the remaining seasoning with the flour in a medium-size bowl or a plastic bag.

Pour ¼ inch of oil in a large skillet and heat to about 350°. Add about one-third that amount of butter, being careful, as the butter will sizzle briefly. Meanwhile, coat the rabbit with the seasoned flour, shaking off excess. Immediately add the rabbit to the skillet and fry until golden brown, about 1½ minutes per side. Drain on paper towels. Serve immediately.

To serve, cut each tenderloin diagonally into slices ¼ inch thick and arrange in a crescent around the edge of a salad plate. Pour about 2 tablespoons of Mustard Sauce in the center of each plate.

Mustard Sauce

½ cup heavy cream
½ cup dairy sour cream
6 tablespoons Creole mustard (preferred) or brown mustard
2 teaspoons Worcestershire sauce
1½ teaspoons prepared mustard
½ teaspoon salt
¼ teaspoon black pepper
⅛ teaspoon white pepper
⅛ teaspoon ground red pepper (preferably cayenne)
⅛ teaspoon dried sweet basil leaves

Combine all the ingredients in a 1-quart saucepan over medium-low heat. Simmer and stir until thickened, about 15 to 20 minutes, stirring constantly. Cool to room temperature. Makes about 1 cup.

Cajun Popcorn with Sherry Wine Sauce

Makes 12 appetizer servings

It's very important to cook this as quickly as possible and not below 350°, so the seafood will be crisp but not overcooked.

2 eggs, well beaten
1¼ cups milk
½ cup corn flour (see **Note**)
½ cup all-purpose flour
1 teaspoon sugar
1 teaspoon salt

½ teaspoon onion powder
½ teaspoon garlic powder
½ teaspoon white pepper
½ teaspoon ground red pepper (preferably cayenne)
¼ teaspoon dried thyme leaves
⅛ teaspoon dried sweet basil leaves
⅛ teaspoon black pepper
2 pounds peeled crawfish tails, small shrimp or lump
    crabmeat (picked over)
Vegetable oil for deep frying
Sherry Wine Sauce (recipe follows)

Note: Corn flour is available at many health food stores and is recommended. If not available, substitute all-purpose flour.

Combine the eggs and milk in a small bowl, blending well.

In a large bowl combine the flours, sugar and seasonings, mixing well. Add half the egg mixture and whisk until well blended, then thoroughly blend in the remaining egg mixture. Let sit 1 hour at room temperature (to let the flour expand).

Heat 1 inch oil in a large skillet or deep fryer to 370°. Coat the seafood with the batter and fry in batches in the hot oil until golden brown on both sides, about 2 minutes total, turning once or twice while cooking. Do not crowd. (Adjust heat to maintain oil's temperature as close to 370° as possible.) Drain on paper towels. Serve immediately with Sherry Wine Sauce on the side.

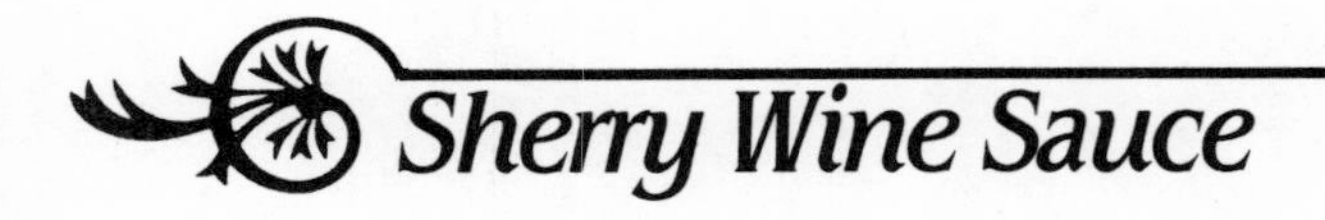

Sherry Wine Sauce

1 egg yolk
¼ cup catsup
3 tablespoons finely chopped green onions
2 tablespoons dry sherry
1 teaspoon Creole mustard (preferred) or brown mustard

¼ teaspoon salt
¼ teaspoon white pepper
¼ teaspoon Tabasco sauce
½ cup vegetable oil

Place all ingredients except the oil in a food processor or blender; process about 30 seconds. With the machine still running, add the oil in a thin, steady stream; continue processing until smooth, about 1 minute, pushing the sides down once with a rubber spatula. Makes about 1 cup.

Coconut Beer Shrimp with Sweet and Tangy Dipping Sauce

Makes 6 main-dish or 12 appetizer servings

Seasoning mix:
1 tablespoon ground red pepper (preferably cayenne)
2¼ teaspoons salt
1½ teaspoons sweet paprika
1½ teaspoons black pepper
1¼ teaspoons garlic powder
¾ teaspoon onion powder
¾ teaspoon dried thyme leaves
¾ teaspoon dried oregano leaves

2 eggs
1¾ cups all-purpose flour, *in all*
¾ cup fresh beer
1 tablespoon baking powder
4 dozen medium shrimp, peeled (but with tails on) and deveined, about 2 pounds

3 cups grated coconut, about 6 ounces
Vegetable oil for deep frying
Sweet and Tangy Dipping Sauce (recipe follows)

Thoroughly combine the seasoning mix ingredients in a small bowl. In a separate bowl combine 2 *teaspoons* of the mix with the eggs, *1¼ cups* of the flour, the beer and baking powder; mix well, breaking up any lumps.

In a small bowl combine the remaining ½ cup flour with *1½ teaspoons* of the seasoning mix; set aside. Place the coconut in a separate bowl.

Sprinkle both sides of the shrimp with the remaining seasoning mix. Then, holding the shrimp by the tail, dredge each in the flour mixture, shaking off excess, then dip in batter (except for tail), allowing excess to drip off, and then coat generously with grated coconut and place on a baking sheet.

Heat oil in a deep fryer to 350°. Drop shrimp, one at a time, into the hot oil and fry until golden brown, about 30 seconds to 1 minute per side. Do not crowd. (You may want to cut the first shrimp in half after frying to best estimate frying time; the batter should be cooked through but the shrimp not overcooked.) Drain on paper towels. Serve immediately with Sweet and Tangy Dipping Sauce.

To serve as a main dish, put about ⅓ cup sauce in each of 6 small bowls and place each on a serving plate; surround each bowl with about 8 shrimp. For an appetizer, serve 4 shrimp per person with about 3 tablespoons sauce on the side.

Sweet and Tangy Dipping Sauce

1 (18-ounce) jar orange marmalade, or 1⅔ cups
5 tablespoons Creole mustard (preferred) or brown mustard
5 tablespoons finely grated fresh horseradish or prepared horseradish

Combine all ingredients and mix well. Makes 2½ cups.

Shrimp Remoulade

Color Picture 26

Makes 6 appetizer servings

Make the Remoulade Sauce several hours ahead or, preferably, two to three days before serving. It keeps several days refrigerated and improves with time.

3 cups **Basic Seafood Stock** (page 32) or water
2 bay leaves
½ teaspoon white pepper
½ teaspoon onion powder
½ teaspoon garlic powder
½ teaspoon dry mustard
½ teaspoon ground red pepper (preferably cayenne)
½ teaspoon black pepper
¼ teaspoon dried thyme leaves
¼ teaspoon dried sweet basil leaves
1½ pounds *unpeeled* medium shrimp, without heads
1½ cups **Remoulade Sauce** (recipe follows)
6 large bowl-shaped lettuce leaves
2 cups very thinly shredded lettuce
1½ small tomatoes, cut in 12 wedges
12 black olives
6 large sprigs parsley

Combine the stock or water and the seasonings in a large saucepan. Bring to a boil; reduce heat and simmer 3 minutes. Turn heat to high and add the unpeeled shrimp. Cook uncovered over high heat for 3 minutes. Immediately drain the shrimp and refrigerate. When cool, peel shrimp and then chill well.

In a medium-size bowl, combine the chilled shrimp and Remoulade Sauce. For each serving, place a lettuce leaf on a salad plate and mound about ⅓ cup shredded lettuce in the center; top with 6 to 10 shrimp. Garnish each salad with 2 tomato wedges, 2 black olives and a sprig of parsley.

Remoulade Sauce

2 egg yolks
¼ cup vegetable oil
½ cup finely chopped celery
½ cup finely chopped green onions
¼ cup chopped fresh parsley
¼ cup finely grated fresh horseradish or prepared horseradish
¼ lemon, seeded
1 bay leaf, crumbled
2 tablespoons Creole mustard (preferred) or brown mustard
2 tablespoons catsup
2 tablespoons Worcestershire sauce
1 tablespoon prepared mustard
1 tablespoon white vinegar
1 tablespoon Tabasco sauce
1 tablespoon minced garlic
2 teaspoons sweet paprika
1 teaspoon salt

In a blender or food processor, beat the egg yolks 2 minutes. With the machine running, add the oil in a thin stream. One at a time, blend in the remaining ingredients until well mixed and lemon rind is finely chopped. Chill well. Makes 1½ cups.

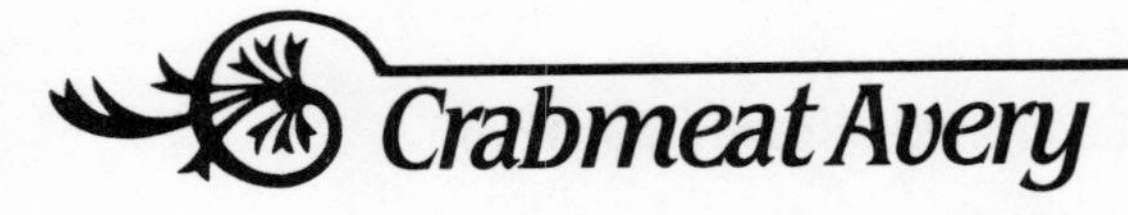

Crabmeat Avery

Makes 8 appetizer servings

2½ tablespoons unsalted butter
⅓ cup finely chopped onions

⅓ cup finely chopped celery
⅓ cup finely chopped green bell peppers
¼ cup finely chopped green onions
½ teaspoon minced garlic
6 tablespoons, *in all*, **Homemade Mayonnaise** (page 268)
4 teaspoons Creole mustard (preferred) or brown mustard
2 teaspoons finely chopped fresh parsley
2 teaspoons Worcestershire sauce
1 teaspoon salt
1 teaspoon ground red pepper (preferably cayenne)
1 teaspoon Tabasco sauce
½ teaspoon white pepper
½ teaspoon black pepper
1 egg
1 pound lump crabmeat (picked over)
½ cup heavy cream
Sweet paprika

Combine the butter, onions, celery, bell peppers, green onions and garlic in a 1-quart saucepan; sauté over high heat until vegetables are tender but still firm, about 5 minutes, stirring occasionally. Remove from heat. Add *2½ tablespoons* of the mayonnaise, the mustard, parsley, Worcestershire, salt, red pepper, Tabasco and the white and black peppers, stirring well. Beat in the egg with a metal whisk. Add crabmeat to vegetable mixture and gently toss, leaving lumps intact as much as possible. Spoon into eight ½-cup ovenproof ramekins. Pour 1 tablespoon cream over the top of each, then spread a thin, even layer of the remaining mayonnaise on top and sprinkle with paprika. Bake at 350° until brown and bubbly, about 15 to 18 minutes. Serve immediately.

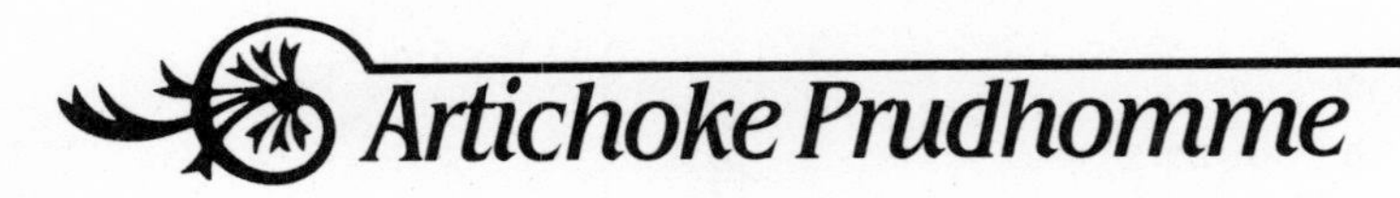

Artichoke Prudhomme

Makes 6 appetizer servings

3 cups cold water
1½ dozen shucked oysters (we use medium-size ones), about ¾ pound
8 quarts water
¼ cup olive oil
3 tablespoons plus 1 teaspoon salt, *in all*
1 tablespoon garlic powder
2 lemons, halved
6 artichokes
¼ pound (1 stick) unsalted butter
¼ cup all-purpose flour
½ cup finely chopped green onions
¾ teaspoon minced garlic
¾ teaspoon white pepper
¾ teaspoon ground red pepper (preferably cayenne)
¼ teaspoon dried thyme leaves
½ cup heavy cream
2 tablespoons finely grated Parmesan cheese (preferably imported)

Add the 3 cups cold water to the oysters; refrigerate at least one hour. Strain and reserve oyster water and oysters in refrigerator until ready to use.

In a large soup pot combine the 8 quarts water, olive oil, *3 tablespoons* of the salt, garlic powder and lemons. Cover and bring to a boil over high heat.

Meanwhile, cut the stems off the artichokes (use a stainless steel knife so the knife and artichokes won't discolor); reserve the stems. Trim artichoke tops down about ½ inch. Add artichokes (top down) and stems to the boiling water; cover pan and boil just until leaves can be pulled off easily, about 25 minutes, stirring occasionally and rotating artichokes once or twice during cooking; drain. Cool slightly, then gently pry open center leaves of artichokes just enough to remove the small purple-tipped leaves and the small adjacent leaves covering the fuzzy choke. With a teaspoon carefully scoop out choke from the center and discard, leaving the artichoke heart intact at the bottom. Chop edible parts from the reserved innermost leaves. Cut off and discard the stringy skin and the ends of the stems; then chop the tender center of the stems. Chopped pulp should come to about ⅔ cup. Clip the pointed tips from the outer leaves of the artichokes with scissors and discard. Set artichokes and chopped pulp aside.

In a large heavy skillet (preferably nonstick) melt the butter over high heat. Whisk in the flour with a metal whisk until smooth. Add the green onions, reserved artichoke pulp, minced garlic, the remaining 1 teaspoon salt, the ground peppers and thyme; sauté for about 2 minutes, stirring frequently. Add the reserved 3 cups oyster water and bring to a boil while whisking frequently with a metal whisk, about 5 minutes; continue cooking 5 minutes more, stirring occasionally. Add the oysters and cook about 3 minutes. Stir in the cream and continue cooking until sauce is creamy and thick, about 8 to 10 minutes, stirring occasionally. Remove from heat.

Place the artichokes upright in an ungreased baking pan just large enough so the 6 artichokes fit in snugly. Open each artichoke slightly if necessary. Spoon about ½ cup sauce into the center of each artichoke, giving each an equal share of oysters; sprinkle 1 teaspoon Parmesan over the sauce. Bake at 400° until cheese starts to brown, about 35 minutes. Remove from oven and serve immediately. To eat, pull outer leaves off artichoke and dip into the sauce in the center.

Stuffed Crabs

Makes 6 appetizer servings

Live crabs are best for this recipe, but if they are not available, use fresh boiled ones and begin the recipe at the point where the crabmeat is removed from the shells. These crabs can be used as part of a seafood platter.

6 medium-size live crabs
Cold salted water
2 quarts **Basic Seafood Stock** (preferred; page 32) or
  water
¼ pound (1 stick) unsalted butter, *in all*
4 tablespoons margarine
½ cup finely chopped onions
½ cup finely chopped celery
½ cup finely chopped green bell peppers
1½ teaspoons minced garlic
1 teaspoon salt
1 teaspoon white pepper
1 teaspoon ground red pepper (preferably cayenne)
½ teaspoon dried thyme leaves
¾ cup very fine dry bread crumbs

Soak the live crabs in cold salted water about 10 minutes. Drain.

Meanwhile, in a 5½-quart saucepan or large Dutch oven, bring the stock to a boil over high heat. Add the live crabs to the pan with metal tongs. Cover pan and return stock to a boil; reduce heat and simmer about 15 minutes, rotating crabs once in the pan. (To test doneness, remove back from one crab; if back lifts up easily and all fat inside is jelled, it's done.) Remove crabs from pan and let cool enough to handle; set aside pan with stock still in it.

Remove back shells from crabs and reserve. Pick out the crabmeat and fat from the bodies and claws and refrigerate meat and fat in separate containers. (You will need about 1½ cups crabmeat and as much fat as possible; the amount of fat yielded will vary depending on the type of crabs you buy.) Break off the lever from the back of each shell (the part you grasp to break open the crab) and discard. Scrape out any residue in the shells and wash inside and outside of the shells well. Drain and set aside for stuffing.

Return stock to high heat and boil until reduced to 3 cups, about 30 minutes. Remove from heat and reserve 1½ cups. (Use the rest in another recipe.)

In a 2-quart saucepan melt 4 *tablespoons* of the butter and the margarine over high heat. Stir in the onions, celery, bell peppers, garlic and fat from the crabs. Cover and cook 4 minutes. Meanwhile, combine the seasonings. After vegetables have cooked 4 minutes, stir in the seasonings and continue cooking for 3 minutes, stirring often. Add the 1½ cups reduced stock; cook 5 minutes without stirring. Stir in the crabmeat; cook 5 minutes, stirring occasionally. Stir in the bread crumbs, then cook 1 minute more, stirring constantly. Remove from heat and add the remaining 4 tablespoons butter, stirring until melted. Makes about 3 cups stuffing.

Stuff each crab shell with about ½ cup stuffing. Place on an ungreased cookie sheet and bake at 450° until crusty brown, about 20 to 25 minutes. Serve immediately.

NOTE: The fairly long cooking time at high heat is correct. This is a typical Cajun recipe; see page 17 in the Introduction.

LUNCH & BRUNCH DISHES

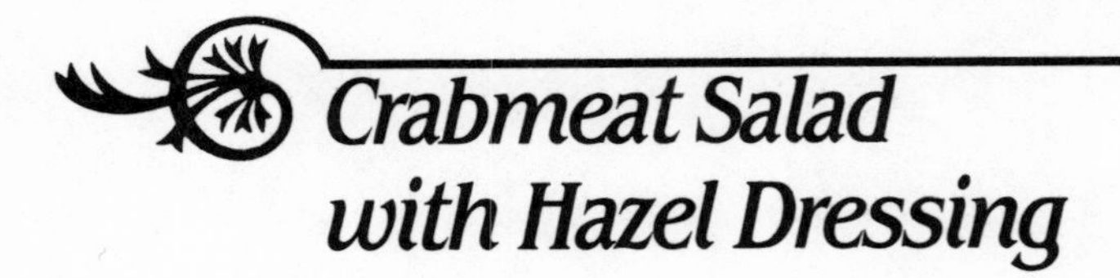

Crabmeat Salad with Hazel Dressing

Color Picture 23

Makes 4 lunch servings

1 pound lump crabmeat (picked over)
1 cup coarsely chopped romaine lettuce
1 cup peeled chopped tomatoes
⅔ cup very finely chopped celery
Hazel Dressing (recipe follows)
4 large lettuce leaves
Freshly ground black pepper to taste

In a medium-size bowl combine the crabmeat, romaine, tomatoes, celery and *1¼ cups* Hazel Dressing, being careful not to break up crabmeat. Serve on a bed of lettuce; sprinkle with freshly ground pepper. Serve the remaining dressing in a bowl at the table.

Hazel Dressing

This may be made several days ahead.

1 egg plus 2 egg yolks
1½ cups vegetable oil
1 cup chopped green onions
½ cup canned tomato sauce
1 tablespoon white vinegar
2 teaspoons sugar
1 teaspoon white pepper
1 teaspoon minced garlic
1 teaspoon Tabasco sauce
¾ teaspoon ground red pepper (preferably cayenne)
½ teaspoon salt

In a food processor or blender, blend the egg and egg yolks for 2 minutes. Leave the machine running and gradually add the oil in a thin stream. Then add the remaining ingredients and blend until thoroughly mixed. Refrigerate until ready to use. Makes about 3 cups.

Fried-Chicken Salad

Makes 4 main-course servings for lunch or brunch

I've given you a tossed salad recipe here, but you may prefer to serve the chicken in your own favorite tossed salad.

Seasoning mix:
1 tablespoon salt
1 teaspoon ground red pepper (preferably cayenne)
¾ teaspoon gumbo filé (filé powder), optional
½ teaspoon white pepper
½ teaspoon onion powder
½ teaspoon garlic powder
½ teaspoon sweet paprika
½ teaspoon black pepper

1 pound boneless chicken, cut into bite-size pieces
3 cups all-purpose flour
2 eggs, beaten
1 cup milk
Vegetable oil for frying
¼ pound (1 stick) unsalted butter
¼ cup minced fresh parsley
2 teaspoons minced garlic
2 quarts iceberg lettuce torn into bite-size pieces
1 cup julienned zucchini (see **Note**)
1 cup chopped celery
1 cup chopped green bell peppers

1 cup chopped red cabbage
1 cup grated carrots
1 cup **Green Onion Salad Dressing** (page 273)
4 romaine or iceberg lettuce leaves
About 8 tomato wedges

NOTE: To julienne the zucchini, cut peelings ⅛ inch thick and cut these into strips ⅛ inch wide and 2 inches long; use only strips that have skin on one surface.

Thoroughly combine the seasoning mix ingredients in a small bowl. Add 2 *teaspoons* of the seasoning mix to the chicken and stir until well coated. Mix the flour with the remaining seasoning mix in a large bowl, mixing well. In a medium-size bowl beat together the eggs and milk until well blended.

In a large skillet or deep fryer, heat ¾ inch oil to 350°. Meanwhile, dredge the chicken in the seasoned flour, coating thoroughly. Then drop the chicken pieces one at a time into the milk mixture and let soak together a couple of minutes. Drain, then dredge chicken again in the flour, separating pieces and coating well. Carefully drop each piece of chicken in the hot oil and fry until golden brown and very crispy, about 1½ to 2½ minutes per side. Drain on paper towels, then place in a single layer in a large pan. Set aside.

In a skillet melt the butter over high heat; cook until bubbles are brown. Immediately stir in the parsley and garlic. Remove from heat and while still frothy drizzle over the chicken; toss with a spoon until coated. Set aside.

Toss together the lettuce pieces, zucchini, celery, bell peppers, red cabbage and carrots in a very large bowl. Stir in the chicken, then stir in the salad dressing. Serve in individual bowls lined with a large lettuce leaf and garnished with 1 or 2 tomato wedges. Allow about 4 cups salad per person.

Grillades and Grits

Makes 8 main-course servings for lunch or brunch

Grillades is one of those dishes like gumbo, in that everyone has his own recipe and uses different meats. The Irish seem to use New Orleans red veal; blacks use baby beef, and the restaurants use New York white veal. My mother, in the country, used pork. The basic brown sauce with tomatoes in it seems to remain the same even though the meat varies.

Seasoning mix:
1 tablespoon salt
1½ teaspoons onion powder
1½ teaspoons garlic powder
1½ teaspoons ground red pepper (preferably cayenne)
1 teaspoon white pepper
1 teaspoon sweet paprika
1 teaspoon black pepper
½ teaspoon dry mustard
½ teaspoon dried thyme leaves
½ teaspoon gumbo filé (filé powder), optional

1 cup chopped onions
1 cup chopped celery
1 cup chopped green bell peppers
1½ teaspoons minced garlic
7 tablespoons vegetable oil
2 pounds baby beef (or veal) chops or shoulder steaks, cut in 8 equal portions
1 cup all-purpose flour, *in all*
4 bay leaves
4 cups **Basic Beef Stock** (page 31)
1 cup canned tomato sauce

Grits:
5 cups **Basic Beef Stock** (page 31)
2 tablespoons minced onions

1 tablespoon sugar, optional
¼ teaspoon dried thyme leaves
¼ teaspoon minced garlic
1 cup hominy grits

Combine the seasoning mix ingredients in a small bowl, mixing well. Combine the onions, celery, bell peppers and garlic in a medium-size bowl and set aside.

In a large heavy skillet heat the oil to about 350°. Meanwhile, sprinkle *2 teaspoons* of the seasoning mix on the meat, seasoning both sides. In a pan (loaf, cake and pie pans work well) thoroughly combine *½ cup* of the flour with *1 teaspoon* of the seasoning mix. Dredge meat lightly in the flour, shaking off excess. Fry the meat in the hot oil until golden brown, about 1 to 3 minutes per side. (If the drippings start to burn, change the oil.) Without draining, transfer the meat to a plate. Leave the oil in the skillet over high heat; gradually add the remaining ½ cup flour to the hot oil and stir constantly with a long-handled metal whisk or wooden spoon until smooth, being careful not to scorch the roux or splash it on your skin. Continue cooking and whisking constantly until roux is medium brown, about 3 minutes. Immediately add the vegetable mixture and stir with a wooden spoon until well blended. Stir in the bay leaves and *2 tablespoons* of the seasoning mix (reserve the remaining mix for the grits). Continue cooking 5 minutes, stirring almost constantly.

✷ See page 26 for more about making roux.

Meanwhile, place 4 cups stock in a 5½-quart saucepan or large Dutch oven. Bring to a boil. Add roux mixture by spoonfuls to the boiling stock, stirring until dissolved between each addition. Add the meat and tomato sauce and bring to a boil over high heat, stirring occasionally. Reduce heat to maintain a simmer; cook until the meat is tender and flavors are married, about 30 to 40 minutes, stirring occasionally and scraping the pan bottom well. Remove from heat and discard the bay leaves.

Meanwhile, heat the serving plates in a 250° oven and make the grits: In a 2-quart saucepan combine 5 cups stock, onions, sugar (if desired), thyme, garlic and the remaining 1 tablespoon seasoning mix. Bring to a boil over high heat. Let boil about 1½ minutes, then stir in the grits. Reduce heat to very low, cover pan, and simmer 15 minutes. Remove cover and stir well, scraping pan bottom; continue cooking uncovered until grits are tender and liquid is absorbed, about 15 to 20 minutes more, stirring occasionally and scraping pan bottom as needed. Serve immediately.

To serve, place ½ cup grits and a portion of meat on each heated serving plate; pour about ½ cup gravy over the meat.

Cajun Bubble and Squeak

Color Picture 27

Makes 8 main-course
or 16 appetizer servings for lunch or brunch

"Bubble and Squeak" is an English national dish made from Sunday dinner leftovers of boiled cabbage, beef and potatoes. We've made ours Cajun style. The eggs can be partially poached several hours in advance. The Potato Patties can be started up to a day ahead.

Potato Patties (recipe follows)

Cream sauce:

4 tablespoons unsalted butter
¾ cup very finely chopped green onions
3 tablespoons all-purpose flour
¾ teaspoon white pepper
½ teaspoon salt
½ teaspoon ground red pepper (preferably cayenne)
¼ teaspoon dried thyme leaves
2 cups **Basic Seafood Stock** (page 32), or 2 cups oyster water (see **Note**)
2 cups very finely chopped tasso (preferred) or other smoked ham (preferably Cure 81)
1 teaspoon minced garlic
2 cups heavy cream

2 dozen small to medium oysters in their liquor, about ¾ pound

1 egg, beaten
½ cup milk

Seasoned flour:
2 cups all-purpose flour
2 teaspoons ground red pepper (preferably cayenne)
1½ teaspoons salt
1 teaspoon sweet paprika
¾ teaspoon garlic powder
¾ teaspoon black pepper
½ teaspoon onion powder
½ teaspoon dried thyme leaves
½ teaspoon dried oregano leaves

Vegetable oil for frying

Sautéed cabbage:
¾ pound (3 sticks) unsalted butter
12 cups coarsely chopped cabbage
3 cups finely chopped onions

Poached eggs:
About 10 cups water
About ¾ cup white vinegar
About 1 tablespoon salt
16 eggs, as fresh as possible

Note: To make oyster water, add 2 cups cold water to the oysters. Refrigerate at least 1 hour. Strain and refrigerate oysters and oyster water until ready to use.

Prepare the Potato Patties up to the frying stage and refrigerate.

Make the cream sauce: Melt the butter in a large skillet over medium heat. Add the green onions, flour, white pepper, salt, red pepper and thyme. Sauté about 1 minute, whisking constantly with a metal whisk. Add the stock (or oyster water), tasso and garlic; cook over high heat about 3 minutes, stirring occasionally. Stir in the cream and continue cooking over high heat until mixture reaches a gentle simmer. Lower heat to maintain a simmer; cook 5 minutes, stirring occasionally. Add the drained oysters; return to a simmer and continue simmering 5 minutes, stirring occasionally. Remove from heat.

Fry the potato patties: In a pan (loaf, cake and pie pans work well) whip the egg and milk with a metal whisk until completely blended. In a separate pan combine the ingredients for the seasoned flour until well mixed. In a large skillet heat ½ inch oil to 350°. Meanwhile, dredge each potato patty in seasoned flour, shaking off excess, then dip in egg mixture until completely wet; just before frying, dredge again in seasoned flour, shaking off excess. Fry the patties in hot oil until golden brown and crisp, about 2 minutes per side. Do not crowd. Drain on paper towels and keep warm in a 200° oven.

Sauté the cabbage: Melt the butter over medium heat in a 4-quart saucepan. Add the cabbage and onions. Sauté over high heat until cabbage is tender but still somewhat crisp, about 6 minutes. Set aside.

Poach the eggs: Combine 2 inches of water with the vinegar and salt in a 4-quart saucepan; bring water to 200° (a near simmer). Meanwhile, crack one egg into a bowl, being careful not to break the yolk. When water has reached 200°, pour in the egg and cook just until white is completely firm, about 2 minutes (adjust heat to maintain 200° water as nearly as possible). Immediately remove with a slotted spoon, draining well to avoid vinegar taste, and place in a large bowl of cold water to stop the cooking process. Poach about 4 eggs at a time. Return water to 200° before adding more eggs. After all 16 eggs are cooked, dip each back in the hot (200°) water on the slotted spoon and let cook 1 minute longer. Drain well and serve immediately. (**Note:** The eggs may each be poached for 2 minutes, as described above, several hours ahead and refrigerated in ice water in a single layer until ready to use. Then poach about 1 minute longer, drain well, and serve immediately.)

LAGNIAPPE

To test the freshness of eggs, break one egg in a bowl, being careful not to break the yolk. If fresh, the yolk will sit noticeably higher than the white, and the white will have lots of body to it.

To serve as a main course, place 2 potato patties on each plate and top each with a poached egg; using a slotted spoon, surround each patty with ½ cup sautéed cabbage, and top the dish with ⅔ cup cream sauce. For an appetizer, use half as much for each serving.

Potato Patties

These may be prepared the day before and refrigerated until ready to fry.

1½ pounds baking potatoes
¼ pound (1 stick) plus 2 tablespoons unsalted butter, *in all*
½ cup evaporated milk
1 cup coarsely chopped cabbage
½ cup finely chopped onions
1½ cups finely chopped cooked roast beef
¼ cup **Basic Chicken** or **Beef Stock** (page 31), or water
¾ teaspoon salt
¾ teaspoon garlic powder
¾ teaspoon ground red pepper (preferably cayenne)
½ teaspoon white pepper
½ teaspoon black pepper

Cover potatoes with water and bring to a boil; reduce heat and simmer covered just until tender, about 30 minutes. Remove from heat and let sit covered 10 minutes. Drain, peel and quarter potatoes while still hot.

In a small pan combine *1 stick* of the butter and the milk; bring to a boil and remove from heat. In a large bowl whip together the potatoes and butter mixture with a metal whisk or electric mixer until smooth. Set aside.

In a large skillet, melt the remaining 2 tablespoons butter over medium heat. Add the cabbage and onions; sauté until vegetables are wilted, about 4 minutes, stirring occasionally. Add the roast beef and stock and continue cooking 5 minutes, stirring occasionally. Add this mixture to the whipped potatoes, mixing thoroughly. Then add the salt, garlic powder and the ground peppers; mix well. Drop ¼-cup portions of the mixture on a cookie sheet and refrigerate until firm, about 25 minutes; then shape each portion into a 3-inch patty about ½ inch thick. Refrigerate until ready to cook. Makes 16 patties.

Eggs Basin Street

Makes 8 main-course
or 16 appetizer servings for brunch

Make the Red Beans and the Andouille Sauce the day before and reheat them just before serving. You may also partially poach the eggs several hours ahead (see directions page 301).

Red Beans (recipe follows)
Andouille Smoked Sausage Sauce (page 250)

Rice patties:
2 eggs
1 tablespoon sugar
1 teaspoon baking powder
½ teaspoon salt
¼ teaspoon white pepper
⅛ teaspoon ground cinnamon
⅛ teaspoon ground nutmeg
½ cup all-purpose flour
¼ cup milk
½ teaspoon vanilla extract
2 cups hot **Basic Cooked Rice** (page 224)
Vegetable oil for frying

Béarnaise Sauce (recipe follows)

Poached eggs (page 301):
About 10 cups water
About ¾ cup white vinegar
About 1 tablespoon salt
16 eggs, as fresh as possible

Make the Red Beans and the Andouille Smoked Sausage Sauce and set aside. (Refrigerate if making a day ahead.)

Make the rice patties: In a large mixing bowl, beat the eggs with a metal whisk until very frothy, about 1 minute. Mix in the sugar, baking powder, salt, white pepper, cinnamon and nutmeg until well blended. Whisk in the flour, beating until smooth. Then stir in the milk and vanilla until smooth. With a spoon fold in the cooked rice.

In a large skillet heat ¼ inch oil to about 325°. Slip rounded tablespoons of the batter into the hot oil, patting them into a relatively flat shape to cook. Fry until golden brown and cooked in the middle, about 1 to 2 minutes per side. Do not crowd. Drain on paper towels. Keep the patties warm in a 200° oven while at the same time heating the serving plates. Makes about 18 patties. (We've allowed for a couple of extras for testing and/or munching.)

Poach the eggs. Make the Béarnaise Sauce, then reheat the beans with about ½ cup water. Reheat the Andouille Smoked Sausage Sauce, reducing it to about 2½ cups.

To serve as a main course, place 2 rice patties on each heated serving plate, leaving a space in the center. Spoon ¼ cup red beans (without meat) on each rice patty, then top with 2 tablespoons Andouille Smoked Sausage Sauce. Add 1 poached egg on top and then spoon on about 1½ tablespoons Béarnaise Sauce. Spoon 2 or 3 chunks of meat (from the beans) in the center of the plate. For an appetizer, serve half these amounts.

Red Beans

½ pound dry red kidney beans
Water to cover the beans
About 10 cups water, *in all*

3 pounds small ham hocks
1¼ cups finely chopped celery
1 cup finely chopped onions
1 cup finely chopped green bell peppers
3 bay leaves
1½ teaspoons Tabasco sauce
1 teaspoon white pepper
1 teaspoon dried thyme leaves
¾ teaspoon garlic powder
¾ teaspoon dried oregano leaves
½ teaspoon ground red pepper (preferably cayenne)
¼ teaspoon black pepper

Cover the beans with water 2 inches above the beans; soak overnight. Drain.

Place *8 cups* of the water and remaining ingredients in a 5½-quart saucepan or large Dutch oven; stir well. Cover and bring to a boil over high heat. Remove cover, reduce heat, and simmer 1 hour, stirring occasionally. Raise heat and boil until meat falls off the bones, about 15 to 20 minutes, stirring occasionally. Remove the meat and bones from the pan; set meat aside and discard bones.

Add the drained beans and remaining 2 cups water to the pot. (You may not need to add this extra water; it depends on how much evaporation has taken place. Use your own best judgment.) Bring mixture to a boil; reduce heat to maintain a simmer, and cook until beans are tender and start breaking up, about 1 hour, stirring occasionally and scraping pan bottom fairly often. (If beans start to scorch, do not stir. Immediately remove from heat and change pots without scraping up any scorched beans into the mixture.) Add the ham and cook and stir 10 minutes more. Discard bay leaves and break up any large meat chunks. Cool and refrigerate until ready to use. Makes about 7 cups.

Béarnaise Sauce

¾ pound (3 sticks) unsalted butter
4 tablespoons margarine
3 tablespoons plus 2 teaspoons white wine, *in all*
1 teaspoon dried tarragon leaves
3 egg yolks
2 teaspoons lemon juice
¾ teaspoon Tabasco sauce
¾ teaspoon Worcestershire sauce

Melt the butter and margarine in a 1-quart saucepan over low heat. Raise heat and bring to a rapid boil. Remove from heat and cool 5 minutes. Skim froth from the top and discard. Pour into a large glass measuring cup and set aside.

In a separate 1-quart saucepan combine *3 tablespoons* of the wine and the tarragon. Cook over high heat until most of the liquid has evaporated, about 2 minutes, stirring occasionally. Let cool 5 minutes.

In a medium-size stainless steel mixing bowl or the top of a double boiler, combine the remaining 2 teaspoons wine, the cooled tarragon mixture and all the remaining ingredients. Mix together with a metal whisk until frothy, about 1 minute.

Place bowl over a pan of slowly simmering (not boiling) water. (Bowl must never touch the water.) Vigorously whisk the egg mixture, picking up the bowl frequently to let the steam escape; whip until the egg mixture is very light and creamy and has a sheen, about 5 to 7 minutes. (This amount of beating is important so that the cooked eggs will better be able to hold the butter.) Remove bowl from the pan of hot water. Gradually ladle about ¼ cup of the butter mixture (use the top butterfat, not the butter solids on the bottom) into the egg mixture while vigorously whipping the sauce; make sure the butter you add is well mixed into the sauce before adding more. Continue gradually adding the surface butterfat until you've added about 1 cup.

So that you can get to the butter solids, ladle out and reserve about ½ cup surface butterfat in a separate container. (The butter solids add flavor and also thin the sauce.) Gradually ladle all but ⅓ cup of the bottom solids into the sauce, whisking well. (Use any remaining bottom solids in another dish.) Then gradually whisk in enough of the reserved top butterfat to produce a fairly thick sauce. (The butterfat thickens the sauce, so you may not need to use it all.) Keep the sauce in a warm place until ready to serve. Makes about 1½ cups.

Eggs Paulette

Color Picture 25

Makes 6 main-course or 12 appetizer servings for lunch or brunch

The artichokes can be prepared a day ahead, and the eggs can be partially poached several hours in advance (see directions page 301).

About 8 quarts water
¼ cup olive oil
3 tablespoons salt
1 tablespoon garlic powder
2 lemons, halved
6 medium artichokes (see **Note**)
Artichoke Hollandaise Sauce (recipe follows)
Czarina Sauce (recipe follows)

Poached eggs (page 301):
About 10 cups water
About ¾ cup white vinegar
About 1 tablespoon salt
12 eggs, as fresh as possible

Brabant Potatoes (page 233), hashed brown potatoes or French fries, optional

Note: The artichoke trimmings are used to make the Artichoke Hollandaise. If you prefer, cook 2 extra artichokes and use the hearts in the hollandaise.

In a large soup pot combine the water, olive oil, salt, garlic powder and lemons. Cover and bring to a boil over high heat.

Meanwhile, cut the stems off the artichokes with a stainless-steel knife (so the artichokes and knife won't discolor). Remove any small leaves at the base to make the artichokes more attractive. Reserve stems (unless you're cooking extra artichokes for the hollandaise). Cut artichoke tops down about ½ inch.

Add the artichokes (top down) and stems to the boiling water; cover pan and boil just until leaves can easily be pulled off, about 25 minutes, stirring occasionally to rotate them in the pot. Drain and cool slightly.

Cut each artichoke in half lengthwise. With your fingers, remove the small purple-tipped and small adjacent leaves in the center; trim and reserve edible parts (unless you've cooked extra for the hollandaise). With a teaspoon carefully remove and discard the fuzzy choke, leaving the heart intact. Each artichoke half should look like a shallow bowl.

Cut off the stringy skin and the ends of the stems and chop the tender center of the stem. If necessary, remove a layer of the outer leaves from the halved artichokes and scrape enough meat from the detached leaves so that trimmings yield about ⅔ cup. (If you cooked 2 extra artichokes for the hollandaise, remove the hearts and chop; discard leaves.) If preparing in advance, wrap artichokes and pulp well and refrigerate; bring to room temperature before using.

Clip the pointed tips from the outer leaves with scissors and discard. Set artichoke halves aside.

Make the Artichoke Hollandaise and set aside in a warm place; then make the Czarina Sauce.

Heat the serving plates in a 250° oven. Meanwhile poach the eggs; see page 301.

To serve as a main course, place 2 artichoke halves on each heated serving plate, cut side up. Spoon about ¼ cup Czarina Sauce into each one, then place a poached egg on top and spoon on about ¼ cup hollandaise. If desired, serve a portion of potatoes between the artichoke halves. For an appetizer serve one artichoke half per person.

Artichoke Hollandaise Sauce

⅔ cup reserved cooked and peeled artichoke trimmings, or
 2 whole artichoke hearts, chopped
2 tablespoons very finely chopped onions
¾ pound (3 sticks) plus 2 tablespoons unsalted butter, *in all*
⅛ teaspoon salt
3 tablespoons water
4 tablespoons margarine
3 egg yolks
2 teaspoons white wine
1 teaspoon lemon juice
1 teaspoon Tabasco sauce
½ teaspoon Worcestershire sauce

Place the reserved artichoke trimmings (or chopped hearts) in a 1-quart saucepan with the onions and 2 *tablespoons* of the butter. Sauté over medium heat for 5 minutes, stirring almost constantly and scraping the pan bottom well. Add the salt and continue cooking until browned, about 3 minutes more, stirring constantly, scraping the pan bottom and breaking up the artichoke pieces (add the water to pan when mixture starts sticking excessively toward the end of the cooking time). Remove from heat. Place in a blender (preferably, since there's not much bulk) or food processor and purée until very smooth, about 1 minute. Let cool.

Melt the remaining ¾ pound butter and the margarine in a 1-quart saucepan over low heat. Raise heat and bring to a rapid boil. Remove from heat and cool 5 minutes. Skim foam from the top and discard. Pour into a large glass measuring cup and set aside.

Meanwhile, in a medium-size stainless-steel mixing bowl or in the top of a double boiler, combine the puréed artichoke and all the remaining ingredients; mix together with a metal whisk until blended. Place bowl over a pan of slowly simmering (not boiling) water. (Bowl must never touch the water.) Vigorously whisk the egg mixture, picking up the bowl frequently to let the steam escape; whip until the mixture is very light, creamy and has a sheen, about 6 to 8 minutes. (This amount of beating is important so that the cooked eggs will better be able to hold the butter.) Remove bowl from pan of hot water. Gradually pour the butter mixture in a very thin stream into the egg mixture while whipping the sauce; make sure the butter you add is well mixed into the sauce before adding more. Set aside in a warm place until ready to serve. Makes about 2 cups.

Czarina Sauce

½ pound (2 sticks) unsalted butter, *in all*
1 cup julienned carrots (see **Note**)
1 cup julienned onions (see **Note**)
1 cup julienned zucchini (see **Note**)
1 cup julienned yellow squash (see **Note**)
1 pound peeled crawfish tails or medium shrimp
1 tablespoon lemon juice
1 cup heavy cream
½ cup finely grated Parmesan cheese (preferably imported)

Note: To julienne squashes, cut peelings ⅛ inch thick and cut these into strips ⅛ inch wide and 2 inches long; use only strips that have skin on one surface. Cut carrots and onions into similar strips.

In a large skillet (preferably nonstick) melt *1 stick* of the butter over medium heat. Add the carrots and sauté about 1 minute, stirring occasionally. Add the onions and cook and stir 1 minute. Add the zucchini and yellow squash; turn heat to high and cook until vegetables are noticeably brighter, about 4 to 5 minutes, stirring occasionally. Add the crawfish or shrimp, the lemon juice and the remaining 1 stick butter; cook until butter is about half melted, stirring occasionally. Add the cream; cook until butter is melted and sauce comes to a boil, about 3 minutes, stirring frequently. Add the Parmesan and continue cooking until cheese is melted and sauce has thickened a little, about 3 minutes. If oil starts separating out of sauce, add a little more cream (preferred), stock or water, and stir until blended. Remove from heat. Makes about 4 cups.

SWEETS

New Orleans Bread Pudding with Lemon Sauce and Chantilly Cream

Makes 8 servings

During the preparation of this dish, the milk-and-egg mixture is too sweet and all the elements are very strong because they will be absorbed by bland bread. After baking, the result is a magnificent pudding.

3 large eggs
1¼ cups sugar
1½ teaspoons vanilla extract
1¼ teaspoons ground nutmeg
1¼ teaspoons ground cinnamon
¼ cup unsalted butter, melted
2 cups milk
½ cup raisins
½ cup coarsely chopped pecans, dry roasted
5 cups very stale French or Italian bread cubes, with crusts on
Lemon Sauce (recipe follows)
Chantilly Cream (page 335)

In a large bowl of an electric mixer, beat the eggs on high speed until extremely frothy and bubbles are the size of pinheads, about 3 minutes (or with a metal whisk for about 6 minutes). Add the sugar, vanilla, nutmeg, cinnamon and butter and beat on high until well blended. Beat in the milk, then stir in the raisins and pecans.

Place the bread cubes in a greased loaf pan. Pour the egg mixture over them and toss until the bread is soaked. Let sit until you see only a narrow bead of liquid around the pan's edges, about 45 minutes, patting the bread down into the liquid occasionally. Place in a preheated 350° oven. Immediately lower the heat to 300° and bake 40 minutes. Increase oven temperature to 425° and bake until pudding is well browned and puffy, about 15 to 20 minutes more.

To serve, put 1½ tablespoons warm lemon sauce in each dessert dish, then spoon in ½ cup hot bread pudding and top with ¼ cup Chantilly Cream.

Lemon Sauce

1 lemon, halved
½ cup water
¼ cup sugar
2 teaspoons cornstarch dissolved in ¼ cup water
1 teaspoon vanilla extract

Squeeze 2 *tablespoons* juice from the lemon halves and place juice in a 1-quart saucepan; add the lemon halves, water and sugar and bring to a boil. Stir in the dissolved cornstarch and vanilla. Cook 1 minute over high heat, stirring constantly. Strain, squeezing the sauce from the lemon rinds. Makes about ¾ cup. Serve warm.

Rice Pudding

Makes 14 servings

2½ cups milk
2 cups heavy cream, *in all*
1½ cups uncooked rice (preferably converted)
¾ cup sugar, *in all*
1 teaspoon ground nutmeg, *in all*
1 cup raisins
4 egg whites
4 egg yolks, well beaten
1 tablespoon plus 2 teaspoons vanilla extract
3½ cups **Chantilly Cream** (page 335)

In the top of a double boiler over high heat, combine the milk, *1 cup* of the cream, the rice, *½ cup* of the sugar and *½ teaspoon* of the nutmeg; cover and cook 25 minutes. Stir in the raisins; cover and cook 30 minutes more. Remove from heat (leave covered) and set aside.

Beat the egg whites in an electric mixer on medium speed until frothy. Add the remaining ¼ cup sugar and continue beating just until stiff moist peaks form, about 3 minutes. Set aside.

Place the egg yolks in a small bowl. Gradually add about 1 cup of the rice mixture to the yolks, mixing quickly so egg yolks don't cook. Then stir this mixture into the remaining rice mixture, blending thoroughly. Stir in the remaining 1 cup cream, the vanilla and the remaining ½ teaspoon nutmeg. Pour into an ungreased 13x9-inch baking pan. Gently fold in the egg-white mixture. Bake at 250° until meringue cooks and rice is tender but still firm, about 30 minutes. Serve hot or lukewarm. For each serving allow ½ cup of pudding topped with ¼ cup Chantilly Cream.

Calas
(Rice Cakes)

Makes 4 servings or about 1 dozen

1 egg
2½ tablespoons sugar
1½ teaspoons baking powder
¼ teaspoon salt
1 tablespoon vanilla extract
½ cup all-purpose flour
Cooked Rice (recipe follows)
Vegetable oil for deep frying
Sifted powdered sugar

In a medium-size bowl beat the egg vigorously with a metal whisk until frothy and bubbles are the size of pinheads, about 1 to 2 minutes. Add the sugar, baking powder (break up any lumps) and salt and whisk until well blended. Whisk in the vanilla, then the flour. With a spoon fold in the rice. Cover bowl with a tea towel and let stand 20 minutes at room temperature.

In a deep skillet or deep fryer, heat the oil to 350°. Drop batter by rounded tablespoonfuls into the hot oil, slipping it into the oil so it maintains a relatively flat shape. Fry, turning at least once, until both sides are golden brown and middles are cooked, about 3 to 4 minutes. Do not crowd. Drain on paper towels. Keep calas warm in a 275° oven while frying the rest.

Sprinkle with powdered sugar and serve immediately.

Cooked Rice for Rice Cakes

½ cup **Basic Chicken** or **Beef Stock** (page 31)
Scant ½ cup uncooked rice (preferably converted)
½ tablespoon finely chopped onions
½ tablespoon finely chopped celery
½ tablespoon finely chopped green bell peppers

Combine all ingredients in a 1-quart saucepan. Cover and bring to a rapid boil. Simmer over very low heat for 8 minutes. Turn off the heat and let sit, covered, for 20 minutes. Remove cover and cool 5 to 10 minutes. Makes 1 cup.

Strawberry Pie

Color picture 29

Makes two 9-inch pies

Louisiana strawberries are usually quite sweet. If your strawberries are tart, you will probably want to add more sugar.

1½ cups all-purpose flour
6 tablespoons margarine, softened
½ teaspoon salt
½ cup cold milk
6 pounds strawberries, *in all*, rinsed and stems removed

1 cup sugar
½ cup water
2 envelopes unflavored gelatin

In a large bowl combine the flour with the margarine and salt, cutting the margarine into the mixture until it's reduced to small lumps. Refrigerate 20 minutes. Remove from refrigerator and add the milk, stirring until well blended, then continue mixing 1 minute more; do *not* overmix. Divide dough into 2 equal portions.

On a well-floured surface, roll each portion of dough ⅛ to ¼ inch thick. Place a 9-inch pie pan face down over each piece and cut out the dough, leaving about a 1½-inch border. Fold each piece of dough into quarters and place each in an ungreased 9-inch pan with the point centered. Unfold dough and line the pan bottom and sides, draping a little over the rim; gently press dough into place. Trim the edges. Cover the dough with waxed paper and carefully place pie weights (or dried beans) in the bottom and up the sides. Bake at 400° until edges are golden brown, about 15 minutes. Remove pie weights and waxed paper and cook until crust bottoms are lightly browned, about 11 to 13 minutes more, rotating the pans once during cooking so crusts will brown evenly. (Baking time may vary, from 10 to 15 minutes, depending on what you used to weigh down the dough.)

Place *1½ quarts* of the strawberries (use the smallest and least attractive ones) and the sugar in a food processor or blender; process until smooth, about 10 to 20 seconds. Transfer mixture to a 2-quart saucepan. Add the water. Bring to a boil over high heat and boil about 3 minutes, stirring occasionally. Remove from heat and pour into a large bowl. Add the gelatin and beat with a metal whisk until gelatin is dissolved. Set aside to cool.

Clip any green tips from the remaining strawberries. Arrange the strawberries in the cooked pie crusts, stem ends down and in circles with the largest berries in the center. Then use smaller berries and for the outer circle cut berries in half lengthwise and arrange cut side down with tips pointing outward. Refrigerate 30 minutes. Ladle half the strawberry sauce over the top of each pie, coating all the berries well. Refrigerate at least 2 hours (until sauce is firm) before serving. If you wish you may serve the pie with **Chantilly Cream** (page 335).

Fig Sweet-Dough Pie

Color Picture 28

Makes one 8-inch pie

¼ pound (1 stick) plus 1 tablespoon unsalted butter, *in all*
1 tablespoon margarine
1½ cups all-purpose flour
2 teaspoons baking powder
½ teaspoon salt
1 egg plus 1 egg yolk
½ cup plus 2 tablespoons water, *in all*
2 cups sugar, *in all*
2 (17-ounce) jars whole figs in heavy syrup
½ large unpeeled orange, very thinly sliced and seeded
½ unpeeled lemon, very thinly sliced and seeded
7 tablespoons cornstarch

In a 1-quart saucepan melt *5 tablespoons* of the butter with the margarine and set aside.

In a medium-size bowl sift together the flour, baking powder and salt.

In another medium-size bowl beat the egg, egg yolk and *2 tablespoons* of the water vigorously with a metal whisk until frothy, about 30 seconds. Whisk in *3 tablespoons* of the sugar until dissolved. Very gradually add the hot butter mixture to the egg mixture in a thin stream, whisking constantly. Gradually stir all but about ¼ cup of the flour mixture into the egg mixture, stirring until the flour is mixed in well; continue mixing 2 minutes more. Place the dough on a surface floured with the remaining ¼ cup flour mixture and knead 1 minute, working in all the flour. Let dough rest on board.

Meanwhile, drain as much syrup as possible from the figs into a 2-quart saucepan. Add the orange and lemon slices and bring to a boil over medium-high heat. Dissolve the cornstarch in the remaining ½ cup water and stir into the boiling fig syrup mixture; return to a boil and stir in the remaining 1¼ cups sugar. Cook about 1 minute more, stirring frequently. Remove from heat and add *half* the drained figs; transfer mixture to a food processor and process a few seconds until citrus skins are minced. Return purée to the saucepan. Add the remaining 4 tablespoons butter and whisk until melted. Add the remaining figs and bring to a boil, stirring occasionally and keeping figs intact as much as possible. Remove from heat and let cool slightly, then refrigerate until lukewarm, about 30 minutes.

Meanwhile, cut dough in two so that one portion is slightly larger. Form the larger portion of dough into a ball and place on a lightly floured surface and roll it out about 4 times (once or twice in each direction). Form dough into a ball again, reflour board lightly, and repeat rolling-out procedure. Re-form dough into a ball, flour board once more, and roll out dough about ⅛-inch thick. Place an 8-inch round *cake* pan (1½ inches deep) on top and cut the dough out, leaving a 1½-inch border. Lightly flour top of dough and fold in quarters. Carefully place in the ungreased cake pan, with the corner of the folded dough centered. Unfold and line the bottom and sides with the dough, pressing gently into place; trim edges. Use scraps to patch any tears in the dough. Refrigerate prepared pie shell and other half of dough until ready to use.

Pour cooled fig mixture into the prepared pie shell, filling the shell up to about ¼ inch from the top; arrange figs evenly within the filling. (Leftover filling is great to eat while the pie is baking; this was my lagniappe from my mother for helping her make the pie. It's also good frozen like sherbert.)

On a floured surface roll out the other piece of dough about ⅛ inch thick. Cut 5 strips (about ¾ inch wide) and place across the pie in one direction; cut 4 to 6 more strips and crisscross on top of the other strips. (I leave these strips roughly cut and sized because that's the way we did it at home when I was a boy.)

Bake at 300° for 45 minutes. Then increase temperature to 350° and bake until crust is dark golden brown, about 55 minutes more. Cool at room temperature until filling is firm, about 2 hours.

Sweet-Potato Pecan Pie

Color picture 30

Makes one 8-inch pie

Dough:

3 tablespoons unsalted butter, softened
2 tablespoons sugar
¼ teaspoon salt
½ of a whole egg, vigorously beaten until frothy (reserve the other half for the sweet-potato filling)
2 tablespoons cold milk
1 cup all-purpose flour

Sweet-Potato Filling:

2 to 3 sweet potatoes (or enough to yield 1 cup cooked pulp), baked
¼ cup, packed, light brown sugar
2 tablespoons sugar
½ egg, vigorously beaten until frothy (reserved above)
1 tablespoon heavy cream
1 tablespoon unsalted butter, softened
1 tablespoon vanilla extract
¼ teaspoon salt
¼ teaspoon ground cinnamon
⅛ teaspoon ground allspice
⅛ teaspoon ground nutmeg

Pecan Pie Syrup:

¾ cup sugar
¾ cup dark corn syrup
2 small eggs
1½ tablespoons unsalted butter, melted
2 teaspoons vanilla extract
Pinch of salt
Pinch of ground cinnamon
¾ cup pecan pieces or halves

Chantilly Cream (page 335)

For the dough: Place the softened butter, sugar and salt in the bowl of an electric mixer; beat on high speed until the mixture is creamy. Add the ½ egg and beat 30 seconds. Add the milk and beat on high speed 2 minutes. Add the flour and beat on medium speed 5 seconds, then on high speed just until blended, about 5 seconds more (overmixing will produce a tough dough). Remove the dough from the bowl and shape into a 5-inch patty about ½ inch thick. Lightly dust the patty with flour and wrap in plastic wrap; refrigerate at least 1 hour, preferably overnight. (The dough will last up to one week refrigerated.)

On a lightly floured surface roll out dough to a thickness of ⅛ to ¼ inch. Very lightly flour the top of the dough and fold it into quarters. Carefully place dough in a greased and floured 8-inch round *cake* pan (1½ inches deep) so that the corner of the folded dough is centered in the pan. Unfold the dough and arrange it to fit the sides and bottom of pan; press firmly in place. Trim edges. Refrigerate 15 minutes.

For the sweet-potato filling: Combine all the ingredients in a mixing bowl. Beat on medium speed of electric mixer until the batter is smooth, about 2 to 3 minutes. Do not overbeat. Set aside.

For the pecan pie syrup: Combine all the ingredients except the pecans in a mixing bowl. Mix thoroughly on slow speed of electric mixer until the syrup is opaque, about 1 minute; stir in pecans and set aside.

To assemble: Spoon the sweet-potato filling evenly into the dough-lined cake pan. Pour the pecan syrup on top. Bake in a 325° oven until a knife inserted in the center comes out clean, about 1¾ hours. (**NOTE**: The pecans will rise to the top of the pie during baking.)

Cool and serve with Chantilly Cream. Store pie at room temperature for the first 24 hours, then (in the unlikely event there is any left) refrigerate.

23. *Crabmeat Salad with Hazel Dressing*

***24.** Rabbit Tenderloin with Mustard Sauce*

25. *Eggs Paulette*

***26.** Shrimp Remoulade*

***27.** Cajun Bubble and Squeak*

28. *Fig Sweet-Dough Pie*

29. *Strawberry Pie*

30. Following page:
Sweet-Potato Pecan Pie

Orange Crêpes with Honey Butter Sauce

Makes 8 servings

You can make the crêpe batter ahead of time and refrigerate it. Allow it to return to room temperature before using.

2 eggs
2 tablespoons unsalted butter, melted
1 tablespoon plus 1½ teaspoons grated orange rind
2 tablespoons plus 1 teaspoon orange juice, *in all*
1 tablespoon sugar
¼ teaspoon ground nutmeg
Salt
¾ cup all-purpose flour
1 cup milk
Vegetable oil for the crêpe pan
⅜ pound (1½ sticks) plus 2 tablespoons unsalted butter, *in all*
⅓ cup honey
½ cup Grand Marnier, *in all*

In a large bowl combine the eggs, melted butter, orange rind, *1 tablespoon* of the orange juice, sugar, nutmeg and a pinch of salt; beat with a metal whisk until very frothy, about 1 minute. Add the flour and whisk just until mixed and no flour lumps remain, about 1 minute. Add the milk and whisk just until blended, about 30 seconds; do not overbeat.

Very lightly oil an 8-inch slope-sided crêpe pan, then wipe it with a towel until the pan has only enough oil on it to be shiny. Heat the pan over medium heat about 2 minutes or until a drop of batter sizzles as soon as it's dropped in the pan. Then pick up the pan and pour in 2 tablespoons batter, quickly tilting the pan so the batter coats the bottom and slightly up the sides; make the crêpe as thin as possible. Cook until edges and bottom are golden brown, about 30 seconds to 1 minute, browning only one side. Remove crêpe from pan and place on a plate to cool, browned side up. Heat the pan a few seconds before cooking the next crêpe. Repeat with the remaining batter (re-oil the pan as needed). Cover crêpes with a damp cloth until serving time. They should be used within 2 hours. (You will have enough batter for 16 crêpes plus one to practice on.)

Heat the dessert plates in a 250° oven.

In a 1-quart saucepan heat *1½ sticks* of the butter over low heat until about half melted. Remove from heat. Add the honey, a pinch of salt and the remaining 4 teaspoons orange juice and beat with a metal whisk until smooth, about 1 minute. Then cook over low heat 1 minute, whisking constantly. Remove this honey butter topping from heat and set aside.

In a large skillet (preferably nonstick) melt *1 tablespoon* of the remaining butter over low heat. Place 8 of the crêpes, folded in quarters with brown side out, in the pan in a single layer. Turn heat to high and cook about 1 minute. Remove from heat.

In a 2-quart saucepan, heat *¼ cup* of the Grand Marnier over medium heat just until warm, about 10 seconds. Then carefully ignite the liquor by touching a lighted match to it (be *very* careful, as it will flare up; it's best to use a long match). Remove from heat and let flame burn about 30 seconds, then immediately pour it over the 8 hot crêpes. Remove crêpes from pan and place 2 crêpes on each heated dessert plate. Melt the remaining 1 tablespoon butter in skillet and repeat procedure for the remaining 8 crêpes. Serve immediately.

To serve, spoon 1 to 2 tablespoons honey butter topping over each pair of crêpes.

Puffy Pecan Meringue Crêpes

Makes 6 servings

The crêpe batter may be made ahead of time and refrigerated. Let it return to room temperature before using.

½ cup milk
1 egg

2 teaspoons vegetable oil
1½ teaspoons granulated sugar
⅛ teaspoon ground nutmeg
Pinch of salt
6 tablespoons sifted all-purpose flour
⅓ cup light corn syrup
⅓ cup dark corn syrup
3 tablespoons unsalted butter, melted and cooled
1 egg yolk
½ teaspoon vanilla extract
1 cup chopped pecans, dry roasted until dark in color
¼ cup heavy cream
3 medium to large egg whites (about ⅓ cup)
½ cup powdered sugar
1 tablespoon light rum

In a small bowl combine the milk, egg, oil, granulated sugar, nutmeg and salt; mix well with a metal whisk. Add the flour and whisk just until blended and no lumps of flour remain; do not overbeat.

Very lightly oil an 8-inch slope-sided crêpe pan, then wipe it with a towel until the pan has only enough oil on it to be shiny. Heat the pan over medium heat about 2 minutes or until a drop of batter sizzles as soon as it's dropped in the pan. Then pick up the pan and pour in 2 tablespoons batter, quickly tilting the pan so the batter coats the bottom and slightly up the sides; make the crêpe as thin as possible. Cook until edges and bottom are golden brown, about 30 seconds to 1 minute; brown only one side of the crêpe. Remove crêpe from pan and place on a plate to cool, browned side up. Heat the pan about 15 seconds before cooking the next crêpe. Repeat with remaining batter (re-oil the pan as needed). Cover crêpes with a damp cloth until ready to serve. They should be used within 2 hours. (You will have enough batter for 6 crêpes plus 2 practice crêpes.)

In a medium-size bowl combine the corn syrups, butter, egg yolk and vanilla, stirring until well blended. Add the pecans and cream, mixing well. Set this sauce aside.

Place the egg whites in a small mixing bowl and beat with an electric mixer until frothy. Add the powdered sugar and beat until fairly stiff peaks form, 1 to 2 minutes. Add the rum and continue mixing until smooth and stiff peaks form again, about 1 minute more.

Fold ¾ cup of this meringue mixture into the reserved pecan sauce, blending well.

Place on open crêpe, brown side down, on each of 6 ovenproof dessert plates. Spread about 2 tablespoons pecan sauce down the middle third of each (make sure to get some of the pecans in), then top sauce with ¼ cup of the meringue, spreading it evenly. Roll crêpe in thirds, turning it over so seam side is down. (Wipe plate well around crêpe to keep any bits of spilled sauce or meringue from burning when baked.) Bake at 475° until meringue puffs up and any exposed part browns, about 5 minutes. Remove from oven and serve immediately, spooning about ¼ cup additional sauce around the crêpe with a little of it on top.

Pecan Pralines

Makes about 3 dozen

The trickiest part about making pralines is judging the precise moment when they are done (see **Note***) and then spooning them out quickly so they will harden with just the right texture.*

Note: To judge doneness, use one or more of the following guides.
1. Candy thermometer will read 240°.
2. When done, the batter will begin forming distinct threads on the sides or bottom of the pan.
3. Near the end of the cooking time, make a test praline every few seconds. The early-test pralines will be somewhat runny, very shiny and somewhat translucent. The ideal praline will have progressed past that stage—it will not be runny and will be less shiny; when cooled it will be opaque, lusterless and crumbly instead of chewy.
4. Near the end of the cooking time, drizzle spoonfuls of the mixture across the surface of the mixture. When ready, the mixture will form a neat thread across the surface.

⅜ pound (1½ sticks) unsalted butter
1 cup sugar
1 cup, packed, light brown sugar
½ cup heavy cream
1 cup milk
1 cup chopped pecans
2 cups pecan halves
2 tablespoons vanilla extract

Assemble all ingredients and utensils before starting to cook. You will need a large heavy-bottomed aluminum pot or skillet with deep sides, a long-handled metal whisk or spoon, 2 large spoons (or an ice cream scoop with a manual release) and a lightly buttered cookie sheet.

Be careful not to get any of the mixture on your skin, as it sticks and can cause serious burns.

Melt the butter in the pot over high heat. As soon as it's melted, add the sugars and cream. Cook 1 minute, whisking constantly. Add the milk and chopped pecans. Cook 4 minutes more, whisking constantly. Reduce heat to medium and continue cooking and whisking 5 minutes. Add the pecan halves and vanilla and continue whisking and cooking until done, about 15 to 20 minutes longer (see **NOTE** above on tests for doneness). If the mixture starts to smoke toward the end of cooking, lower the heat.

Remove pan from heat. Quickly and carefully drop the batter onto the cookie sheet by heaping spoonfuls, using the second spoon to scoop the batter off the first (or use ice cream scoop). Each praline should form a 2-inch patty about ½ inch thick. Cool and store in an airtight container, or wrap each praline in plastic wrap or foil.

LAGNIAPPE

To clean the pot and utensils, boil water in the pot with the utensils in it. This will melt the batter off.

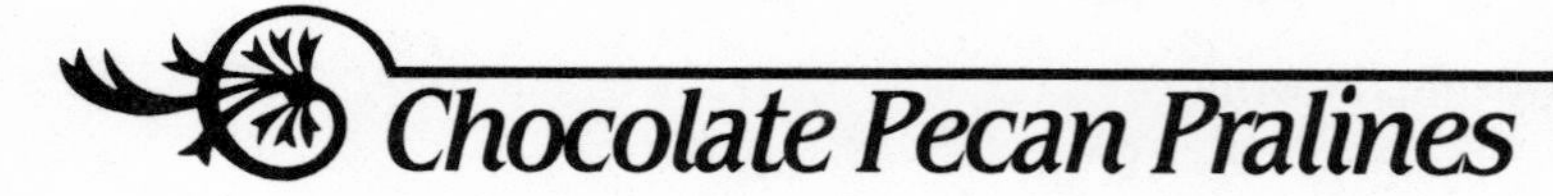

Chocolate Pecan Pralines

Makes about 2 dozen

To judge when the syrup has finished cooking, use the same guidelines as for Pecan Pralines (preceding recipe).

⅜ pound (1½ sticks) unsalted butter
1 cup sugar
1 cup, packed, light brown sugar
1 cup milk
½ cup heavy cream
1 cup coarsely chopped pecans
2 cups whole pecan halves
2 tablespoons vanilla extract
1½ cups semisweet chocolate chips, chilled

Assemble all the ingredients and utensils before starting to cook. (Measure out the chocolate chips and keep them refrigerated until just before needed.) You will need a large, heavy-bottomed aluminum pot or skillet with deep sides, a long-handled metal whisk or spoon, 2 large spoons (or an ice cream scoop with a manual release) and a very lightly greased cookie sheet.

Melt the butter in the pot over high heat; add the sugars, milk, cream and chopped pecans. Cook 5 minutes, whisking constantly. Reduce heat to medium, and continue cooking and whisking 10 minutes. Add the pecan halves and continue whisking and cooking until done, about 8 to 10 minutes. (If the mixture smokes excessively toward end of cooking time, lower the heat.) Stir in vanilla. Then immediately drop about ¼ cup of chocolate chips onto about one-sixth of the batter. Stir quickly and just enough to cover some of the chips with batter but not enough to allow the chips to melt. Quickly drop the chocolate mixture onto the cookie sheet by heaping spoonfuls, using the second spoon to push the batter off the first (or use ice cream scoop); each praline should be about 2 inches in diameter and ½ inch thick. Repeat with remaining mixture, stirring briefly before adding more chocolate chips. The cooled pralines should be light brown, opaque, somewhat chunky and crumbly.

Cool pralines and store at room temperature in an airtight container or wrapped individually in plastic wrap or foil.

LAGNIAPPE

To clean the pot and utensils, boil water in the pot with the utensils in it. This will melt the batter off.

Sesame Seed Pralines

Makes about 2 dozen

¾ pound (3 sticks) unsalted butter
1 cup sugar
1 cup, packed, light brown sugar
1 cup milk
½ cup heavy cream
1 cup sesame seeds, toasted
2 tablespoons vanilla extract
1 tablespoon water

Assemble all the ingredients and utensils before starting to cook. You will need a large, heavy-bottomed aluminum pot or skillet with deep sides, a long-handled metal whisk or spoon, 2 large spoons (or an ice cream scoop with a manual release), and a very lightly greased cookie sheet.

Melt the butter in the pot over high heat. Add the sugars, milk and cream; bring to a boil, whisking constantly. Reduce heat to medium. Cook and stir until syrup is the consistency of runny caramel and a rich tan color (or 260° on a candy thermometer), about 15 to 20 minutes. Immediately add the sesame seeds, vanilla and water. Cook and stir just until the mixture foams up in the pan when you stop stirring, about 1 to 2 minutes. Quickly drop the mixture by heaping spoonfuls onto the greased cookie sheet, using the second spoon to push the batter from the first (or use ice cream scoop); each praline should be about 2 inches in diameter and ½ inch thick. Cooled pralines should be opaque and crumbly rather than chewy.

After cooling, store pralines in an airtight container or wrap individually in plastic wrap or foil.

LAGNIAPPE

To clean the pot and utensils, boil water in the pot with the utensils in it. This will melt the batter off.

Chocolate Cake with Mocha Icing

Makes one 3-layer cake

2⅔ cups sifted cake flour
1½ teaspoons baking soda
½ teaspoon salt
1 cup, packed, dark brown sugar
⅜ pound (1½ sticks) unsalted butter, softened
3 eggs
¾ cup light corn syrup
1 tablespoon vanilla extract
4 ounces unsweetened chocolate, melted and cooled to lukewarm (110° on a candy thermometer)
1½ cups buttermilk
Glaze (recipe follows)
Mocha Icing (recipe follows)

Sift the flour, baking soda and salt together in a medium-size bowl and set aside.

Place the brown sugar in a large bowl of an electric mixer; beat on high speed about 10 seconds to break up sugar. Add the butter and beat until the mixture is the consistency of wet sand, about 1 minute. Beat in the eggs one at a time until well blended, about 10 seconds each time. Add the corn syrup and vanilla and beat until smooth, about 5 seconds. Beat in the cooled chocolate until well blended and smooth, about 3 to 5 minutes, scraping bowl sides well. Add flour mixture and buttermilk alternately to chocolate mixture, beginning and ending with flour and beating after each addition just until smooth. Pour equal amounts of the batter into three 8-inch round greased and lightly floured cake pans (1½ inches deep). Bake at 350° until centers spring back when lightly pressed, about 35 to 40 minutes. Remove cake layers from pans to a wire rack and glaze while still hot. Cool thoroughly. Spread generously with icing between layers and on top and sides.

Glaze

1 cup water
½ cup sugar
1 teaspoon vanilla extract

In a small saucepan combine the water and sugar; bring to a boil. Remove from heat and stir in the vanilla. With a pastry brush, brush hot glaze over the surface and a little on the sides of each cake layer, using all the glaze. Makes about 1 cup glaze.

Mocha Icing

¾ pound (3 sticks) unsalted butter, at room temperature
4½ cups powdered sugar (1½ pounds)
⅓ to ½ cup heavy cream
3 tablespoons instant coffee powder or crystals
2 teaspoons unsweetened cocoa powder
2 teaspoons vanilla extract
¼ teaspoon salt

Cream the butter in a large bowl of an electric mixer on high speed until very creamy, about 2 minutes. Gradually add the sugar and beat until smooth, about 3 minutes.

In a separate bowl, combine *⅓ cup* of the cream and the remaining ingredients, stirring until thoroughly dissolved. Add cream mixture to the butter mixture. Beat until well blended and sugar is completely dissolved, about 5 minutes, scraping bowl well. Thin with a little more cream if desired. Makes enough frosting for one 3-layer cake.

Spiced Pecan Cake with Pecan Frosting

Makes one 3-layer cake

2 cups coarsely chopped pecans
¼ cup, packed, light brown sugar
2 tablespoons ground cinnamon
1 teaspoon ground nutmeg
4 tablespoons unsalted butter, softened
2 tablespoons plus 2 teaspoons vanilla extract, *in all*
⅜ pound (1½ sticks) unsalted butter

2 cups sugar, *in all*
3 cups sifted all-purpose flour
2 tablespoons baking powder
1 cup plus 2 tablespoons milk
3 egg whites
Glaze (recipe follows)
Frosting (recipe follows)

Place the pecans in a large ungreased roasting pan and roast at 425° for 10 minutes, stirring occasionally. Meanwhile, in a medium-size bowl combine the brown sugar, cinnamon and nutmeg. Then mix in the 4 tablespoons butter. Add the roasted pecans to the butter mixture and coat them thoroughly. Return mixture to pan and roast for 10 minutes more, stirring once or twice. Stir in 2 *tablespoons* of the vanilla and roast 5 minutes more. Remove from oven and set aside.

In a large bowl of an electric mixer, cream the 1½ sticks butter and 1½ *cups* of the sugar on high speed until *very* light and fluffy, about 6 to 8 minutes.

In a separate bowl sift together the flour and baking powder. In a third bowl combine the milk and the remaining 2 teaspoons vanilla. Add the flour mixture and milk mixture alternately to the butter mixture, beating on high speed until well blended and scraping the bowl sides between additions. Stir in the pecans.

In a separate bowl whip the egg whites on high speed until frothy, about 30 seconds. Add the remaining ½ cup sugar and continue beating until mixture is stiff and holds peaks, about 2 minutes. Gently fold egg-white mixture into the batter, a third at a time.

Spoon batter into 3 greased and lightly floured 8-inch round cake pans (1½ inches deep). Spread batter so it is slightly lower in the center (since it peaks in the center during cooking). Bake at 350° until a toothpick inserted near the center comes out clean, about 40 minutes. Let cool 10 minutes, then carefully remove from pans and place on a wire rack; cool thoroughly. Glaze, then spread generously with icing between layers and on top and sides.

Glaze

1 cup water
½ cup sugar
1 teaspoon vanilla extract

Combine the water and sugar in a small saucepan; bring to a boil. Remove from heat and stir in the vanilla. Immediately brush glaze over the top of each cake layer with a pastry brush, a little at a time, using all the glaze.

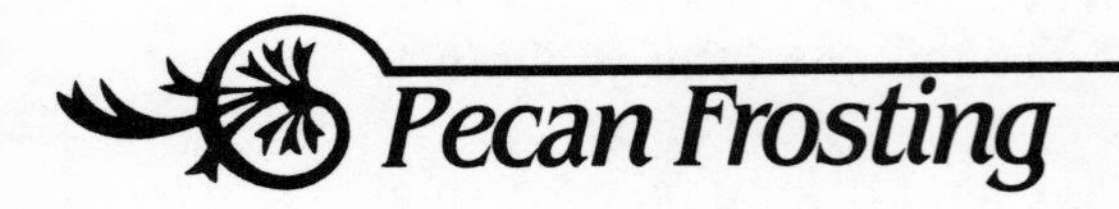

Pecan Frosting

1½ cups granulated sugar
¾ cup water
8 egg yolks
¾ pound (3 sticks) margarine, softened (see **Note**)
2½ cups powdered sugar
4½ teaspoons vanilla extract
2½ cups coarsely chopped pecans, dry roasted until dark
 in color, then cooled

Note: It's best to use margarine rather than butter in this frosting because butter tends to melt out of the frosting as the cake sits awhile.

Combine the granulated sugar and water in a 1-quart saucepan. Cook over medium heat to soft-thread stage (230° on a candy thermometer), about 15 minutes; do *not* stir.

In a large bowl of an electric mixer beat the egg yolks on high speed just slightly, about 5 seconds. Gradually add the hot sugar-water mixture and beat until thoroughly cooled, thick, shiny and very pale, about 10 minutes. (Start at low speed so it won't splash and then go to high speed.) If crystallized sugar builds up around the sides of the bowl, don't scrape it into mixture; it will make the frosting lumpy, and you will have plenty of frosting without it. Gradually add the margarine and mix on medium speed until completely blended and very smooth, about 5 minutes. Blend in the powdered sugar and vanilla on low speed until smooth; then add the pecans and beat on high speed until thoroughly mixed and very thick. If frosting is too thick, thin with a little cream (preferred), milk or water.

Chocolate Mousse

Makes 6 servings

4 ounces unsweetened chocolate
4 egg whites
1 cup heavy cream
¾ cup powdered sugar

Melt the chocolate in the top of a double boiler over low heat; let cool to 110° on a candy thermometer.

Meanwhile, in a medium-size bowl of an electric mixer, beat the egg whites until stiff peaks form, about 1 minute.

In a separate bowl beat the cream until frothy, about 1 minute. Add the sugar and continue beating until soft peaks form; do not overbeat. Gently fold the cream mixture into the egg whites, then add the cooled chocolate (heat to 110° if it has cooled below that temperature), and quickly fold it in until well blended. Spoon into a serving bowl or individual ramekins. Refrigerate at least 2 hours before serving.

Serve as is or topped with **Chantilly Cream** (page 335).

Fig Sherbet

Makes about 1 gallon

The fig-sauce base can be made a day ahead.

2 quarts water
3 cups sugar
2 teaspoons lemon juice
2 teaspoons very finely grated orange rind
1 (20-ounce) jar fig preserves (1⅔ cups)
5 egg whites

In a 4-quart saucepan bring the water to a boil. Add the sugar, lemon juice and orange rind, stirring until the sugar is dissolved. Return mixture to a boil. Stir in the preserves. Cover and return to a boil. Reduce heat to a simmer and continue cooking about 5 minutes. Remove from heat. Cool slightly and refrigerate until well chilled, about 6 hours or overnight. Freeze in an ice cream machine according to machine directions until thick and almost frozen, about 20 minutes.

Meanwhile, beat the egg whites in an electric mixer until soft peaks form, about 1 to 2 minutes. When the sherbet is almost frozen, add the egg whites and continue freezing in the ice cream machine until hard, about 20 minutes.

Pecan Ice Cream Sundae Sauce

Makes 10 servings or 3½ cups

2 cups pecan halves, dry roasted
1 cup light corn syrup

1 cup dark corn syrup
½ pound (2 sticks) unsalted butter
¼ teaspoon imitation butterscotch flavoring
Ice cream

In a large skillet combine the pecan halves and corn syrups. Over high heat, stir constantly until mixture reaches a boil. Remove from heat. Add the butter and stir until melted, then stir in the butterscotch flavoring.

For each serving, spoon some of the pecans and about ¼ cup syrup (warm or at room temperature) over 2 scoops of your favorite ice cream.

Chantilly Cream

Makes about 2 cups

⅔ cup heavy cream
1 teaspoon vanilla extract
1 teaspoon brandy
1 teaspoon Grand Marnier
¼ cup sugar
2 tablespoons dairy sour cream

Refrigerate a medium-size bowl and beaters until very cold. Combine cream, vanilla, brandy and Grand Marnier in the bowl and beat with electric mixer on medium speed 1 minute. Add the sugar and sour cream and beat on medium just until soft peaks form, about 3 minutes. *Do not overbeat*. (Overbeating will make the cream grainy, which is the first step leading to butter. Once grainy you can't return it to its former consistency, but if this ever happens, enjoy it on toast!)

Brown Sugar Cookies

Makes about 3 dozen cookies

1¼ cups, packed, light brown sugar
¼ cup water
3 tablespoons honey
1 egg
2⅓ cups all-purpose flour
1 cup coarsely ground pecans
2½ tablespoons ground cinnamon
1 tablespoon baking soda
1 tablespoon ground allspice

In a large mixer bowl combine the brown sugar, water, honey and egg. Beat on high speed of an electric mixer until mixed, about 10 seconds, scraping bowl well.

In a separate bowl combine the flour, pecans, cinnamon, baking soda and allspice, mixing well. Add to wet ingredients and stir until mixed thoroughly.

Drop batter by teaspoonfuls onto a greased cookie sheet, about 1½ inches apart. Bake at 375° until lightly browned on edges, about 12 minutes. Remove from pan immediately with a spatula and cool on a wire rack (the cookies will be quite soft until cooled). Store in an airtight container. (If you live in a humid climate, store uncovered.) These are best when allowed to sit a few hours.

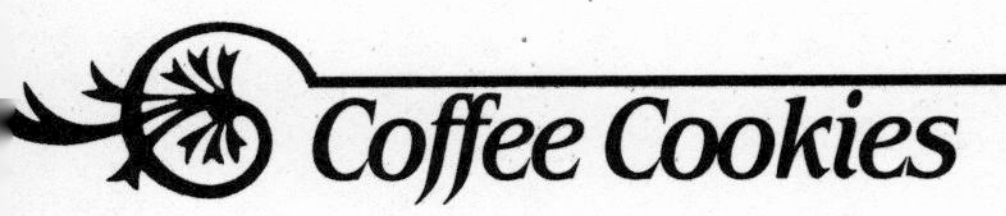

Coffee Cookies

Makes 3 to 4 dozen cookies

These are best if allowed to sit for a few hours (if you can resist).

½ pound (2 sticks) unsalted butter, slightly softened
1¼ cups sugar
½ cup instant coffee powder, or 6 tablespoons plus 1 teaspoon instant coffee-and-chicory powder (see **Note**)
2 tablespoons plus 1½ teaspoons vanilla extract
3 egg yolks
2½ cups plus 3 tablespoons cake flour

Note: Available in many southern grocery stores and in some gourmet coffee and spice shops.

Cream the butter with an electric mixer on high speed until smooth, about 1 minute. Add the sugar and beat on high speed until thoroughly blended, about 1 minute. Set aside.

In a small bowl mix the coffee, vanilla and egg yolks until the coffee is dissolved. Add coffee mixture to the butter mixture and beat on high speed until well blended and an even color, scraping the bowl. Add the flour and mix on high speed until well blended, about 1 to 2 minutes. Drop batter by teaspoonfuls onto a greased cookie sheet, leaving about 1½ to 2 inches between cookies. Bake at 350° until cookies are very lightly browned on the edges, about 16 to 18 minutes. Cool until cookies start to harden, about 3 to 5 minutes, then remove from pan with a spatula and finish cooling on a wire rack. Store in an airtight container. (If you live in a humid climate, store uncovered.)

Lori Taylor's Chocolate Chippers

The most deliciously expensive cookie in the world

Makes about 4 dozen cookies

¼ pound (1 stick) unsalted butter, softened
¾ cup, packed, light brown sugar
1 egg
2 tablespoons vanilla extract
¾ cup coarsely chopped dates
1 cup all-purpose flour
½ teaspoon baking soda
½ teaspoon salt
¼ teaspoon baking powder
½ cup grated coconut
½ cup granola
¾ cup coarsely chopped walnuts
1¾ cups semisweet chocolate chips

In the large bowl of an electric mixer cream the butter and brown sugar until smooth. Add the egg and vanilla and beat well. Stir in the dates and let the mixture sit 5 minutes to soften the dates. Then beat at high speed for 3 minutes or until very light brown and creamy. Combine the flour, baking soda, salt and baking powder in a small bowl, breaking up any lumps; stir into creamed mixture, mixing well. Stir in the coconut, granola, walnuts and chocolate chips. Drop the batter by tablespoonfuls onto a lightly greased cookie sheet about 1½ inches apart.

Bake in a 350° oven until lightly browned, about 10 to 15 minutes. With a spatula, immediately remove cookies from cookie sheet and cool on a wire rack. Store in an airtight container.

INDEX

H

I

O

P

Q

R

S

T